Recovering Political Philosophy

Postmodernism's challenge to the possibility of a rational foundation for and guidance of our political lives has provoked a searching re-examination of the works of past political philosophers. The re-examination seeks to recover the ancient or classical grounding for civic reason and to clarify the strengths and weaknesses of modern philosophic rationalism. This series responds to this ferment by making available outstanding new scholarship in the history of political philosophy, scholarship that is inspired by the rediscovery of the diverse rhetorical strategies employed by political philosophers. The series features interpretive studies attentive to historical context and language, and to the ways in which censorship and didactic concern impelled prudent thinkers, in widely diverse cultural conditions, to employ manifold strategies of writing, strategies that allowed them to aim at different audiences with various degrees of openness to unconventional thinking. Recovering Political Philosophy emphasizes the close reading of ancient, medieval, early modern and late modern works that illuminate the human condition by attempting to answer its deepest, enduring questions, and that have (in the modern periods) laid the foundations for contemporary political, social, and economic life. The editors encourage manuscripts from both established and emerging scholars who focus on the careful study of texts, either through analysis of a single work or through thematic study of a problem or question in a number of works.

More information about this series at
http://www.palgrave.com/gp/series/14517

Emily Katherine Ferkaluk

Tocqueville's Moderate Penal Reform

Emily Katherine Ferkaluk
Cedarville University
Cedarville, OH, USA

Recovering Political Philosophy
ISBN 978-3-030-09269-6 ISBN 978-3-319-75577-9 (eBook)
https://doi.org/10.1007/978-3-319-75577-9

Softcover re-print of the Hardcover 1st edition 2018

Cover illustration: Stefano Bianchetti / Alamy Stock Photo

Printed on acid-free paper

This Palgrave Macmillan imprint is published by the registered company
Springer International Publishing AG part of Springer Nature
The registered company address is: Gewerbestrasse 11, 6330 Cham, Switzerland

"This is a long over-due analysis of Tocqueville's real first book. Sociologists, criminologists, political theorists, or anyone thinking about criminality and moderation will find this to be an enlightening book."

—Richard Avramenko, *Department of Political Science, University of Wisconsin*

"This book persuaded me beyond any doubt that *On the Penitentiary System* is a book of real theoretical and practical significance. One comes away with a fuller and deeper appreciation of Tocqueville's thought as a whole. The book also provides welcome guidance for thinking soberly about prison reform in this or any other context."

—Daniel Mahoney, *Professor of Political Science, Assumption College*

To my family.

Series Editor Preface

Palgrave's *Recovering Political Philosophy* series was founded with an eye to postmodernism's challenge to the possibility of a rational foundation for and guidance of our political lives. This invigorating challenge has provoked a searching re-examination of classic texts, not only of political philosophers, but of poets, artists, theologians, scientists, and other thinkers who may not be regarded conventionally as political theorists. The series publishes studies that endeavor to take up this re-examination and thereby help to recover the classical grounding for civic reason, as well as studies that clarify the strengths and the weaknesses of modern philosophic rationalism. The interpretative studies in the series are particularly attentive to historical context and language, and to the ways in which both censorial persecution and didactic concerns have impelled prudent thinkers, in widely diverse cultural conditions, to employ manifold strategies of writing—strategies that allowed them to aim at different audiences with various degrees of openness to unconventional thinking. The series offers close readings of ancient, medieval, early modern, and late modern works that illuminate the human condition by attempting to answer its deepest, enduring questions, and that have (in the modern periods) laid the foundations for contemporary political, social, and economic life.

In *Tocqueville's Moderate Penal Reform* we offer a companion volume to Emily Ferkaluk's recent translation of Tocqueville's and Beaumont's *On the Penitentiary System in the United States and Its Application to France* (also published in this series). Ferkaluk shows that Tocqueville and Beaumont responded to two important questions in their first work. The first is that what type of penal discipline best represents a *moderate* view of individual reformation? Incarceration, they argued, should seek to perfect or restrain prisoners by articulating a specific relationship between body, mind, and soul as a moderating limit to penal discipline. Here they found the American penitentiary system to disclose three helpful sets of contraries: theory and experience, solitude and labor, and corporal punishment and religion. The second question they addressed is that what type of penal institution would *best remedy* the problem of growing recidivism in France? Here Ferkaluk shows how Tocqueville and Beaumont sought to temper French fears of recidivism by rejecting the easy but risky solution modeled after Britain's penal colonies, such as Australia. They instead advocated American penal institutions as properly balancing centralized and decentralized administrative power. In both arguments, they taught the French public how to be moderate in penal reform—to obtain justice for the criminal and to avoid a reputation for injustice garnered by imperial actions.

Ferkaluk also clarifies Tocqueville's and Beaumont's significant disagreements with Francis Lieber, the first American translator of their book. She then analyzes Tocqueville's and Beaumont's sustained efforts in penal reform—after the 1832 publication of their work—in French debates. This permits her the better to analyze two major changes to the revised editions of *On the Penitentiary System*: the substantive introduction added to the second edition and Tocqueville's speech to the Chamber of Deputies in 1843, which was added to the third edition. She concludes that Tocqueville's moderate penal reform enables readers to navigate the relationship between crime and social mores, to address multiple causes of crime, and to understand the proper objects of the contemporary penal system with moderation.

Baylor University
Waco, TX, USA
University of Texas at Austin
Austin, TX, USA

Timothy W. Burns

Thomas L. Pangle

Acknowledgments

This book reflects the deep generosity of many persons. I am especially grateful to Richard Dougherty, whose discussions of Tocqueville as a political thinker inspired this project and whose critical review of early drafts was indispensable to its success. I am also grateful to Tiffany Miller, Gerard Wegemer, Joshua Parens, and Alexander Duff for their helpful and thoughtful comments on various drafts of the project. Thank-you to Stephen Maddux, whose review of my translation of the French text deepened my understanding and engagement with Tocqueville's political thought. Zane Merkle assisted in formatting the final manuscript, for which I am thankful. Thank-you also to the staff at the Yale Beinecke Rare Book and Manuscript Library, who spent many days assisting me with research in the Yale Tocqueville Manuscripts; and to the Johns Hopkins Sheridan Library for their help with the Francis Lieber papers. Thank-you to Mark Caleb Smith, who first gave me my love for Tocqueville's political thought. Many thanks go to the series editors Timothy Burns and Thomas Pangle, Michelle Chen, the anonymous reviewers, and the rest of the editorial team at Palgrave, who supported and refined the project. I am thankful also for Bruce and Nan Ransom, and to the Braniff Graduate School at the University of Dallas, who each generously funded the project at different times. Finally, I am grateful to my mother and father for first teaching me the joy of learning; to Hanna, for her support and friendship; and especially to David, who has been a constant source of love and encouragement. I take full responsibility for any remaining errors in this work. *Soli Deo Gloria.*

Contents

CHAPTER 1

An Introduction to Tocqueville's First Work

The following chapters seek to interpret the meaning of Alexis de Tocqueville's and Gustave de Beaumont's *On the Penitentiary System in the United States and Its Application to France* to show the place the work holds in Tocqueville's corpus and political thought.[1] The fundamental questions that the book seeks to answer are whether we should study *On the Penitentiary System* and, if so, why. The work resulted in part from my translation of the first edition; this endeavor uncovered the theoretical merits of the work and sparked curiosity regarding the general lack of discussion of *On the Penitentiary System* among English-speaking scholars. Although the penal report was ostensibly the purpose of Tocqueville's and Beaumont's famous journey to America, to date there have been only a handful of articles and book chapters that primarily explain some of the textual themes or purposes of *On the Penitentiary System*.[2] Many scholars have argued that the authors' interest in penal reform was a pretext, intended to boost their political careers and reputations more than anything else.[3] Still, this argument does not account for Tocqueville's continued work in reforming the French penal system throughout his political career, nor does it explain why Tocqueville and Beaumont chose to study penitentiaries (as opposed to any other social or political problem) in the first place.

Indeed, Tocqueville and Beaumont asked similar questions—should we study penitentiary systems, and why—when approaching the task of

E. K. Ferkaluk, *Tocqueville's Moderate Penal Reform*,
Recovering Political Philosophy,
https://doi.org/10.1007/978-3-319-75577-9_1

researching and writing *On the Penitentiary System* in 1832–1833. At the time, France faced a growing need to reform their prison system. When Tocqueville and Beaumont wrote their first edition, France had just begun to shift from using prisons as temporary holding places for criminals on their way to punishment (often death, mutilation, galley labor, or exile), to using imprisonment as the punishment itself.[4] France's penal system was divided into a national criminal justice system and departmental prisons. Within the national system, penal institutions included central prisons (those that housed prisoners serving sentences for longer than a year) and agricultural colonies. At the department level, there were *maisons de justice*, *maisons d'arret*, cantonal prisons, and police jails (O'Brien 1982, p. 3). Because these departmental prisons housed any person associated with a crime, witnesses and accused included, they were overcrowded and contributed to increasing recidivism. Most importantly, the use of *bagnes*, sites of forced labor on naval stockyards which relied heavily on corporal punishment, became the focus of needed reform (Forster 1991, pp. 137–8).

In the text of *On the Penitentiary System*, we see two specific penal questions stemming from the general problem of recidivism in the French criminal justice system. First, there is a need to compare and contrast the relative merits of three alternative policy solutions to the problem of recidivism: domestic agricultural colonies, penitentiaries, and foreign penal colonies. As will be shown, in choosing to promote penitentiaries as the primary means of penal reform, the authors seek to temper the risks that penal colonies pose in light of France's geopolitical rivalry with Britain.[5] Second, *On the Penitentiary System* contains a comparison of two penal disciplinary methods: The Auburn (New York) system of mandatory silent labor in common workrooms, and the Philadelphia (Pennsylvania) system of absolute solitary confinement. Both systems operated on the assumption that human nature can undergo significant moral reformation as the result of environment and education.[6] Tocqueville and Beaumont evaluate these two penal disciplinary methods against a standard of human nature to determine their potential for moral reformation of the criminal. *On the Penitentiary System* is therefore the product of Tocqueville's and Beaumont's official investigation on behalf of the French government, designed to elucidate whether a penitentiary system was the best penal remedy for rising criminal recidivism in France and, if so, which one of two primary American prison discipline systems (Philadelphia or Auburn) could be implemented to successfully reform French prisons and prisoners.

What unites Tocqueville's thinking on penitentiaries as the best possible solution to recidivism, his approach to colonial imperialism (penal colonization in particular), and his arguments on the potential moral reformation of criminals is his underlying concern to pursue moderation between institutional and theoretical extremes. Tocqueville holds a moderate view of the potential and limits of human nature, especially when evaluating methods to reform criminals. Further, *On the Penitentiary System* acts as a tool of moderation between three penal alternatives available to France in the nineteenth century. In both thinking moderately and advocating for moderate political action, Tocqueville's *On the Penitentiary System* renews an emphasis on the importance of civic engagement and the balance between philosophy and praxis. *On the Penitentiary System* teaches us that liberalism works best when its statesmen work moderately. Hence, Tocqueville's study on crime and punishment yields fruitful answers to questions regarding political nuances in nineteenth-century French penal reform and Tocqueville as a political thinker and actor.

Is the Report Practical or Philosophical?

At first glance, *On the Penitentiary System* appears to be merely a systematic report on the practical application of the American penitentiary system to the French criminal justice structure, rather than an exercise in political or intellectual moderation.[7] The details of the report resulted from a nine-month study of American penitentiaries. Tocqueville and Beaumont arrived in New York on May 10, 1831, and began their return journey to France on February 20, 1832. During that time, they spent 10 days at both Sing Sing and Auburn (New York penitentiaries), 8 days at the New York House of Refuge, and 12 days at the Cherry Hill Penitentiary (in Philadelphia).[8] Although the pair only stayed a short time in the United States, they were aided by many distinguished American citizens who gave them access to explore the penitentiaries and provided documents for them to take back to France.[9] Throughout the report, Tocqueville and Beaumont provide a seemingly balanced, impartial record of facts and a multitude of statistics.[10] Indeed, the original study published in 1833 begins with a list of six volumes of primary sources, which Tocqueville and Beaumont deposited at the Ministry of Commerce and Public Works to accompany their official report. A large portion of the text is devoted to the comparative question of how to equate data and systems between two countries. Additionally, much of the text is devoted to explaining the differences between two main penitentiary systems in America, the Auburn and Pennsylvania systems, without necessarily endorsing one over the other. The overall tone appears to be one of detached analysis.[11]

Furthermore, the organizational structure of *On the Penitentiary System* lends doubt as to whether it contains a cohesive penal philosophy. The first edition is bifurcated into a main text and an extended set of appendices. The main text is divided into three parts. The first part contains a brief history of penitentiary reform in America and detailed accounts of the fundamental principles, administration, disciplinary means, prisoner reformation, and financial administration of the different American penitentiary systems. Part two analyzes the French penal system and addresses the question of whether the American penitentiary model can be successfully executed in France. Part three adds a study of the house of refuge as an ancillary institution to the American penitentiary system. In sum, the main text of the first French publication includes roughly 226 pages (including a four-page preface by the authors) of analysis on penal law and systems.[12]

Nineteen appendices follow the main text.[13] Constituting about 212 pages, the appendices form, as George Wilson Pierson says, "a small encyclopedia of information and surprises" (1938, p. 705). They contain, in their original order, a study on penal colonies, alphabetical notes to the main text, studies on agricultural colonies, public instruction, pauperism, imprisonment for debt, imprisonment of witnesses, and temperance societies. Additionally, Tocqueville's personal interviews with the inmates of the Philadelphia penitentiary, a recorded conversation with Mr. Elam Lynds, extracts from a letter from Judge Martin Welles of Wethersfield, regulations of both the Wethersfield prison and the House of Refuge in Boston, a letter from Mr. Gerrish Barrett, a conversation with the superintendent of the Philadelphia House of Refuge, three appendices full of statistical notes, a comparison between France and America on factors such as race and gender in prison populations, and some "financial observations" are included in assorted appendices.[14] In their combined length, the appendices constitute half of the completed work; in their scope and content, the appendices appear to depart from the penological object of the work as a whole. Thus, the text of *On the Penitentiary System* seems, at first glance, too fragmented and pragmatic to present a cohesive penal philosophy.

The organization and technical nature of *On the Penitentiary System* have, perhaps, been two of the causes for the relative dearth of scholarship in the English-speaking world on the themes of the text. Much of the secondary scholarship which does exist focuses on the theme of despotism, particularly the tyranny of nineteenth-century prisons over prisoners. Most recently, Richard Avramenko and Robert Gingerich argue that *On the Penitentiary System* "provides an imaginative lens" through which to view the potential despotic future of unlimited democratic equality; in other words, the text acts as a dystopia which reveals the potential in democracy for stripping away religious liberty, subjecting individuals to the tyranny of public opinion, and depriving individuals of association (2014, pp. 58–59).[15] Avramenko and Gingerich build upon Roger Boesche's earlier argument that Tocqueville discovered a model of despotism in his study of American penitentiaries. However, Boesche characterizes democratic despotism displayed through the penitentiary as rooted in isolation, equality, preoccupation with private goods, and the presumed ability to reform a person from within (1980, pp. 550–563). Seymour Drescher suggests that Tocqueville and Beaumont embraced the punitive severity of isolation in penitentiary systems "as the opposite side of the coin of a free society" (1968, pp. 138–139). Sheldon Wolin similarly argues that "*The Penitentiary System* flirts with a new and antidemocratic theory of despotism that serves, paradoxically, as the precursor of the conception of democratic despotism which *Democracy* will coil against but not before exposing a distinctively modern or liberal temptation" (2001, p. 384; see also Brogan 2006).[16]

Although these essays properly begin to interpret the philosophical and political themes of the work, the discussion of despotism within American penitentiaries often obscures a vision of Tocqueville's tempering and moderate evaluation of penal disciplines which emerges from a close reading of the original text. Many of the evaluations utilize either a Foucauldian understanding of the relationship between penal institutions and the body, the fuller and later expression of ideas within *Democracy in America*, or the historical penal debates in France during the early to mid-nineteenth century, as lenses through which to understand the themes of *On the Penitentiary System*. On the other hand, in reading the text from an "innocent" point of view, avoiding as much as possible external theoretical and historical contexts which time has given us, we are struck with Tocqueville's and Beaumont's thoughtful balancing of competing purposes, systems, and persons in both American and French penal reform. Tocqueville's treatment of despotism within *On the Penitentiary System* should be understood more broadly as part of this effort in moderation.

Hence, this book poses new questions to *On the Penitentiary System* and expands upon the abovementioned research in order to reach a deeper understanding of its major themes and purpose. While the following text is not by any means an exhaustive analysis, it is the hope of its author that the work inspires a renewed and robust conversation on the place *On the Penitentiary System* holds in Tocqueville's corpus and in our understanding of penal methods, both historic and current.

Definitional Understandings of Key Terms and Ideas

As will be shown, *On the Penitentiary System* displays moderation as both a political and intellectual virtue which depends on the proper use of the imagination. Tocqueville's exercise of moderation has been well documented, but not yet understood in relation to his work in shaping French public policy on penal reform.[17] Moderation as an intellectual virtue demands self-restraint, which in turn requires self-knowledge of one's own tendencies toward extremes. In the case of penal reform, such extremes stem from a misdirected imagination. Tocqueville suggests that moderation is needed to avoid overreach of the penal reformer's, public's, and prisoner's imaginations regarding what is possible within a liberal democratic criminal justice system.[18] To succeed at penal reform, reformers must temper their political imagination with experience, engage the general public's imagination to conceive of their own civic responsibility for implementing the criminal justice system, and seek to moderately guide the prisoner's imagination toward desirable social ends.[19] In all three cases, moderation produces and depends upon a well-used imagination. Through the text of *On the Penitentiary System*, Tocqueville seeks to give self-knowledge of France's capacities for penal reform that will provide self-control to the French when choosing the best penal discipline.

As a political virtue, moderation represents a general approach to policymaking that seeks the most prudent course of action which will best preserve the justice of a nation in light of particular political and social circumstances.[20] In liberal democracies, the statesman especially seeks to understand the types of institutional and constitutional arrangements that are necessary to justly preserve individual liberty.[21] Tocqueville's evaluation of which penal institution the French public should choose represents his own exercise of political moderation.[22] By examining which penal institutions best preserve the liberty of both prisoner and society, Tocqueville seeks to attain justice for the criminal and preserve France's reputation for justice as a burgeoning liberal democracy.

The intellectual and political virtue of moderation as displayed in the penal case study of *On the Penitentiary System* helps us to better understand Tocqueville's liberalism. Many scholars consider Tocqueville to be a peculiar type of liberal; most notably, Tocqueville seems comparatively reserved in promoting liberal principles such as individual freedom or the sacredness of property rights. According to some, Tocqueville's praise for aspects of aristocracy implies a disagreement with certain liberal democratic principles.[23] On the other hand, others argue that Tocqueville participated in a broad liberal tradition which supported "a commitment to certain individual rights (specifically equality before the law, freedom of the press, and religious freedom), opposition to the policies of the mercantilist state, opposition to monarchical power if not monarchical government, and a certain expansiveness of social sympathies" (Welch 1984, p. 4).[24] Tocqueville might also be understood as a Republican liberal who emphasizes freedom as the absence of dominion.[25] Still, the classical liberal tradition was changing during Tocqueville's lifetime, especially as it faced challenges of democratization, which complicates our view of Tocqueville as a liberal.[26]

All agree that Tocqueville's liberalism differed from the tradition established by Locke and Mill. Tocqueville rejected idealist or romanticist notions of the political world. Instead, Tocqueville's liberalism emphasizes practical political values such as self-knowledge, prudence, and moderation. This work seeks to further define and expand our notions of Tocqueville's liberalism, particularly in relation to his ideas of the moderated use of the imagination in liberal democratic political orders as they grapple with the problem of crime. In other words, we are seeking to view Tocqueville's moderate liberalism in action as applied to a specific policy question.

Assumptions

The argument of the book depends on some assumptions that must be acknowledged. As indicated, one goal of the book is to understand the themes of *On the Penitentiary System* in relation to, and as reflective of, Tocqueville's political philosophy. This goal depends on the assumption that *On the Penitentiary System* contains Tocqueville's thoughts. Yet it is commonly understood that Beaumont wrote the majority of the text for

On the Penitentiary System.[27] Thorsten Sellin and George Wilson Pierson argue that Tocqueville's only contributions to the report were the statistical appendices and some notes.[28] Harry Elmer Barnes similarly asserts that Beaumont wrote the report and Tocqueville merely assisted in conducting the personal interviews and investigations during the trip to America, on the basis that Tocqueville's notebooks "contain relatively little about prisons."[29] The argument that Beaumont wrote the majority of the report is partially based on a letter written by Tocqueville to Beaumont from Paris on April 4, 1832, in which Tocqueville complains of his difficulty in drafting the report on prisons.[30] Nevertheless, the letter does not ask Beaumont to take over the writing alone, nor has any other communication regarding the distribution of the work for writing the report been found. Further evidence that Tocqueville had a minimal role in drafting the report can be found in a letter to Mignet from June 26, 1841, where Tocqueville writes: "The first work that we have published in common [...] has for its unique writer M. de Beaumont. I furnished only my observations and some notes..."[31] If Tocqueville had played a larger role in drafting the report, he was unwilling to admit that contribution privately.

Still, Avramenko and Gingerich make a compelling case as to why *On the Penitentiary System* should be considered as Tocqueville's first book, including the fact that "Chapter II and other sections bear witness to the crisp, declarative style of Tocqueville," "the work is replete with observations and analysis gleaned from Tocqueville's journals and letters," and "Tocqueville and Beaumont refused to publish anything until they had thoroughly deliberated upon the ideas involved and achieved unanimity on the text" (2014, p. 9).[32] Indeed, many stylistic phrases and ideas are exactly replicated from *On the Penitentiary System* in *Democracy in America*, allowing for a direct correlation and comparison between the works but also lending support in favor of Tocqueville's co-authorship of *On the Penitentiary System.*[33]

Further knowledge of which portions were written by the different authors has been gleaned from notes on the manuscripts in the Yale Beinecke Tocqueville Collection. According to Pierson's work identifying the handwriting of the manuscripts in the collection, Tocqueville wrote the appendices dealing with Agricultural Colonies, Pauperism in America, Imprisonment for Debt, Imprisonment of Witnesses, and the Statistical Notes (No. 16 and No. 17). Alternatively, the manuscripts in Beaumont's handwriting within the Yale collection include "Part I, Chapter I: History of the Penitentiary System," "Part I, Chapter III, Section III: Disciplinary

Means" and "Part III: On Houses of Refuge." Other portions of the text in manuscript form are not included in the collection, leaving it an open question as to the specific author of the remaining sections.[34]

Regardless of the exact contributions Beaumont and Tocqueville made to the actual writing of the manuscript, it is certain that both agreed on the meaning and intended purpose of *On the Penitentiary System*.[35] In his seminal work *Tocqueville and Beaumont on Social Reform*, Drescher provides a helpful appendix in which he explains the depth of intimacy and shared opinions between Tocqueville and Beaumont.[36] The friendship and unity of thought between the authors affirms that, even if Tocqueville did not write the entire text of *On the Penitentiary System*, he certainly allowed his name to be affiliated with the ideas that were written and published therein.

The theme of this book, Tocqueville's understanding of and approach to penal reform in France as grounded in a moderate use of the imagination, also depends to some extent on the assumption that Tocqueville was a political philosopher.[37] Tocqueville's *On the Penitentiary System* represents a unique combination of penal praxis and theory. The judgments regarding prison disciplines and penal systems are not simply rooted in pragmatic or utilitarian principles, but instead flow from a cohesive philosophy of human nature and political society. Eduardo Nolla presents a wealth of evidence that Tocqueville himself did not want to be considered a philosopher, at least not a philosopher who lacked "contact with political life" (1992, p. xviii). Still, it cannot be doubted that Tocqueville continually asked questions regarding fundamental principles, even if he decided to reject any absolute answers to his questions. In that sense, Tocqueville can at least be said to have conducted philosophical inquiry. John Stuart Mill perhaps defined Tocqueville's method best when he said of Tocqueville's work in *Democracy in America*:

> He has applied to the greatest question in the art and science of government, those principles and methods of philosophizing to which mankind are indebted for all the advances made by modern times in the other branches of the study of nature [...] His method is, as that of a philosopher on such a subject must be—a combination of deduction with induction: his evidences are, laws of human nature, on the one hand; the example of America, and France, and other modern nations, so far as applicable, on the other. (1977, p. 156)

Mill recognizes the intellectual tendency driving Tocqueville's study of political institutions: a desire to moderately understand political institutions and public policy in light of both a universal human nature and changeable social conditions by martialing the evidence that both theory and practice afford. It is this tendency toward moderation that the book seeks to clarify in Tocqueville's penal thought through a close reading of *On the Penitentiary System.*

Organization of the Chapters

The following chapters are intended to answer the two primary questions posed at the beginning of this introduction: what is the meaning of *On the Penitentiary System*, and what is its purpose. To grasp the overarching purpose and theme of Tocqueville's and Beaumont's first work, the book relies on a close reading of the first published edition. Tocqueville and Beaumont published three editions of *Du Système Pénitentiaire aux États-Unis, et de son application en France: suivi d'un appendice sur les colonies pénales et de notes statistiques* during their lifetime (in 1833a, 1836, and 1845). In each subsequent edition, the main text remained substantively identical to the first edition, while Tocqueville and Beaumont expanded the introductions, added or deleted some appendices, and clarified footnotes. J.P. Mayer's definitive, annotated French text of Tocqueville's *Oeuvres Complètes, Écrits sur le système pénitentiaire en France et a l'étranger, Tome IV* contains a combined version of both the second and third editions (Tocqueville 1984a). Most of the chapters (with the exception of Chap. 5) in this book seek to interpret the 1833 text for two important reasons. First, understanding the purpose and meaning of the first edition will be most helpful to those who would like to compare the social and political ideas in *On the Penitentiary System* with those of *Democracy in America*, because it was the only edition published before Tocqueville's writing of *Democracy.*[38] The 1833 edition contains Tocqueville's fresh deliberation on both penitentiaries and American society; the later editions reflect his matured evaluation of penal problems in France. Additionally, in seeking to compare Tocqueville's penal thought with Francis Lieber's, a nineteenth-century American penal reformer who first translated *On the Penitentiary System*, it was necessary to interpret the same text that Lieber would most likely have received for translation in 1832.[39] While we cannot see all of Tocqueville's political thought in the 1833b text of *On the Penitentiary System*, since Tocqueville changed his mind over the course of his lifetime on some important issues, we can see some of the core principles and intellectual methods which guided his political activity and penal thought.

My interpretive method includes a literal reading of the original French text, assuming that the work is well-organized and is capable of guiding the reader to its meaning.[40] The methodological questions I rely on to conduct a close reading are: What are the words the authors use? What is the meaning of those words; that is, what are the main ideas dealt with in the text? And finally, how are those words used in the text? Hence, the book allows the text to interpret itself without overly situating its content in historical or intellectual contexts. Also, as will be shown, the only comparison between the ideas in *On the Penitentiary System* to alternative strands of political thought directly resulted from a need to disentangle the first English translation of the text performed by Francis Lieber. Otherwise, I do not attempt to situate Tocqueville's and Beaumont's penal thought within other theoretical precedents. The goal is to understand the penal work on its own terms.

To that end, Chap. 2 begins by understanding the principles of Tocqueville's moderate penal theory which he uses to evaluate the two competing penitentiary systems in America at the time, the Auburn and Philadelphia systems. According to Tocqueville, the choice between either system depends on a moderate vision of human nature and its potential for reformation. Chapter 3 deals with Tocqueville's and Beaumont's political purpose for *On the Penitentiary System*, and argues that they desired to moderately temper the risks involved in alternative penal theories being considered by the French public, namely agricultural colonies and penal colonies. Chapter 4 broadens the discussion of Tocqueville's penal theory by contrasting it with Francis Lieber's. By understanding the changes Lieber made to *On the Penitentiary System* during his translation efforts, we can see alternative uses of the political imagination in relation to penal reform. Chapter 5 conducts a brief historical review of Tocqueville's continued work in penal reform from 1833–1845 and analyzes the significant additions made to *On the Penitentiary System* in its second and third editions. Tocqueville's sustained attention to penal reform throughout his political career demonstrates how moderation allows a statesman to adapt to new circumstances and social needs while maintaining core political principles. Throughout the chapters, I attempt to draw out the primary principles guiding the authors' penal judgments and to broadly apply such principles to our contemporary liberal democracy and current penal reform movement in America.

Notes

1. The scope of the book limits itself to applying an understanding of *On the Penitentiary System* in light of Tocqueville's political thought, rather than in reference to Beaumont's, although both contributed to the writing of the report.
2. See, for example, Avramenko and Gingerich 2014; Boesche 1980; Schwartz 1985; Wolin 2001; Swedberg 2009; Drescher 1968; Keslassy 2010. There have been other studies which deal with Tocqueville's penal work more broadly; see, for example, Drolet 2003; Perrot 1984; Pierson 1938. Although quantitatively few in comparison to the amount of scholarship on larger works such as *Democracy in America*, all of these studies present qualitatively rigorous analysis of Tocqueville's penal work. My argument is not that a comparatively low amount of scholarship indicates insufficient understanding of a text, but that more work needs to be done to understand the primary political purpose and philosophical meaning of *On the Penitentiary System*.
3. Pierson was one of the first to suggest that the trip to America was conducted for political purposes, namely to preserve both authors' political careers after the rise of the July Monarchy in 1830 (1938, pp. 27–28, 31). See also Brogan 2006, pp. 143–145; Perrot 1984, p. 7; Sellin 1964, p. xv. Tocqueville himself partially affirms this view that his interest in penitentiaries was peripheral rather than primary when he writes to Charles Stoffels that their study of penitentiaries was "a very honorable pretext that makes us seem particularly to merit the interest of the government, whatever it may be, and that assures us its good will upon our return" (Letter of October 11, 1831, to Charles Stoffels. Yale Tocqueville Manuscripts. General Collection, Beinecke Rare Book and Manuscript Library, Yale University. A.VII, Box 1). Albeit acknowledging that the study of penitentiaries was a pretext, many scholars also affirm that Tocqueville's and Beaumont's interest in penal reform was genuine; see, for example, Wolin 2001, p. 102.
4. O'Brien 1982, p. 17; Forster 1991, p. 137.
5. Hence, a careful study of *On the Penitentiary System* also bears implications for Tocqueville's attitude toward imperialism, a topic sharply debated among commentators, as is explained in Chap. 3.
6. Drescher points out two common themes of the French penal reform movement: a notion "that a prison system was part of legislation for the poor, since poverty caused crime," and an increased emphasis on reformation to stem recidivism (1968, p. 133).
7. Thus, Wolin argues that *On the Penitentiary System* "was cast in a newer technical genre, with research as its starting point and policy recommendations as its goal," and resulted in "a radical transformation of the idea of culture from being an expression of traditionalism to becoming an object

of fabrication in the service of administrative control" (2001, p. 383). Wolin explicitly uses Foucault's analysis of early French penal reform to analyze Tocqueville's and Beaumont's work; see: Foucault 1995.

8. See Perrot 1984, p. 16. The brief duration of their observation periods should be kept in mind. Although Tocqueville and Beaumont visited only a few American penitentiaries, they gathered information on the following institutions: The Sing Sing prison in Ossining, New York; the Auburn Penitentiary in New York; Eastern State Penitentiary on Cherry Hill Street, Philadelphia; Walnut Street Prison, Philadelphia; prison in Pittsburgh; prison in Wethersfield, Connecticut; prison in Boston, Massachusetts; prison in Baltimore, Maryland; prisons in Kentucky, Tennessee, Ohio, Louisiana, Maine, and Vermont.
9. Tocqueville and Beaumont acknowledge such help in their Preface to *On the Penitentiary System*. Because the pair cut short their planned 18-month visit (for political and personal reasons), they sent a questionnaire to various penitentiary authorities with instructions for them to send answers to France, care of the Minister of France at Washington, before February 1, 1833. For a reprint of this letter, see Tocqueville 1984b, pp. 505–507.
10. The majority of these "statistics" are averages of data received from official reports of four different penitentiaries in New York, Pennsylvania, Connecticut, and New Jersey. Drolet provides an interesting study arguing that Tocqueville's interest in statistics was not only critical to *On the Penitentiary System*, but also "underscored the importance he attached to the social in his analysis of modern democracy" (2005, p. 451). Swedberg characterizes the appendices in *On the Penitentiary System* as presenting "moral statistics" with an economic dimension (2009, pp. 113–114). See also Hadari 1989 for a reconstruction of Tocqueville's scientific methodology.
11. Cary supports this inference in his argument that "Tocqueville and Beaumont tried to remain non-partisan and to avoid committing themselves to the support of either of the American prison disciplines. Actually, they gave their support to both" (1958, p. 192).
12. Pagination is based on the first French edition of *Du Système Pénitentiaire aux États-Unis et de son Application en France; suivi d'un Appendice Sur Les Colonies Pénales et de Notes Statistiques*, published by H. Fournier Jeune (1833a).
13. This book treats the appendices as extensions of the arguments of the main body and as equally important to understanding the whole of *On the Penitentiary System*. The original Table of Contents textually supports this use of the appendices; there, the main body of the text was labeled "No. 1," while the first appendix "On Penal Colonies" was labeled "No. 2," and so forth through the remainder of the appendices. Additionally, based on the almost equal page division of the text between the main

body and appendices, as well as the extensive nature of the appendices, my interpretation relies on a synthesis of the arguments in both the main text and appendices of the report.

14. Elam Lynds was the first warden of the Auburn penitentiary and famed creator of the Sing Sing prison in New York, one of the first prisons erected with prisoner labor. Martin Welles was instrumental in the establishment of the Wethersfield prison, a prison which garners much admiration from Tocqueville and Beaumont throughout *On the Penitentiary System*. Finally, Gerrish Barrett was chaplain of the Sing Sing prison in New York beginning in 1825.
15. The text itself gives no evidence that it is to be interpreted ironically as a dystopia.
16. Although much of the literature devoted to discussing the themes of *On the Penitentiary System* emphasizes the discussion of despotism, there are two notable exceptions. Joel Schwartz suggests that the work "represents Tocqueville's initial statement of his views concerning issues [...] such as the political roles of religion and intellectuals, and the relation of theory to practice" (1985, p. 7). Richard Swedberg analyzes *On the Penitentiary System* in terms of the political economy it evidences, arguing that the report gives us greater insight into Tocqueville's economic views of the poor and of prisoners (2009, pp. 56–63).
17. See Carrese 2016, p. ix. This study expands on previous studies confirming Tocqueville's fundamental methodology of moderation in his political science by applying this view of Tocqueville's moderation to his analysis of penal institutions. See, for example, Craiutu 2005, 2012; Eden 1990; Lawler 1989; Zetterbaum 1967. Carrese points out that to argue that Tocqueville fundamentally performs moderate political philosophy is to rightfully connect him to the Montesquieuean tradition (2011, p. 306). Montesquieu says in his *Spirit of the Laws* Book 29, Chap. 1: "I say it, and it seems to me that I have written this work only to prove it: the spirit of moderation should be that of the legislator; the political good, like the moral good, is always to be found between two limits" (1989, p. 602).
18. Throughout the work, I use the term "liberal democracy" broadly, since France was not a liberal democracy in the contemporary sense of the term during the time that Tocqueville lived and wrote. Tocqueville lived during a transition period between aristocracy and democracy and confronted the continuing effects of the French Revolution. Arguably, one of Tocqueville's main objectives was to spur France on to securing and extending the liberal democratic institutions it had begun to build.
19. My discussion of Tocqueville's use of imagination simultaneously builds upon and somewhat departs from Matthew Maguire's excellent analysis (2006). Maguire argues that while Tocqueville praises an exalted

imagination, connected to human pride and preserving true freedom, he simultaneously acknowledges the tension this imagination has with a democratic regime which emphasizes our natural equality. Such equality suppresses, or grounds, the imagination. I do not dispute Maguire's conclusion that "Tocqueville holds within himself an unprecedented range of the diagnostic and prescriptive alternatives for imaginative power in the nineteenth century;" rather, I am seeking to show how Tocqueville himself approached the use of imagination moderately, especially within the context of public policy crafting to remedy penal problems (Maguire 2006, p. 220).

20. Moderation thus does not represent attitudes of apathy or indecisiveness (Carrese 2016, p. xii, 1; Craiutu 2012, p. 248). Craiutu argues that moderates achieve prudential political action by pursuing three political goals: a defense of pluralism, preference for gradual reform, and an attitude of tolerance (2012, pp. 14–15). Similarly, Carrese teaches us that the moderate statesman avoids extremes, seeks breadth and balance among a variety of principles, and reconciles those principles upon a higher middle ground (2016, p. 2).
21. See for a further discussion of this attribute of moderation: Carrese 2016, p. 20; Craiutu 2012, pp. 3–4, 242.
22. Some might argue that Tocqueville's "moderation" in *On the Penitentiary System* was simply a posture rather than a sincerely exercised virtue. According to this argument, Tocqueville rhetorically portrays himself as a moderate by politically locating himself between two self-defined extremes. Tocqueville thus utilized a partisan tactic common during the July Monarchy, the *juste milieu*. See: "Juste Milieu" in *Trésor de la Langue Française informatisé* (2012). Additionally, scholars such as Brogan (2006), Boesche (1980), and Swedberg (2009) have argued that Tocqueville's proposals for penal reform are anything but moderate, particularly in their toleration of prison violence. The interpretation of *On the Penitentiary System* in the following chapters addresses both of these concerns.
23. See, for example, Boesche 2006, pp. 27–28; Clinton 2003, pp. 11–14; Lakoff 1998, p. 444, 446.
24. See for concurring arguments: Kahan 1992, p. 140; Pitts 2001, p. 3.
25. Duan 2010, p. 444; Wolin 2001, p. 6.
26. The following scholars have clarified the specific changes to classical liberalism: Welch 2001, p. 68; Merquior 1991, pp. 53–58; Adcock 2014, pp. 34–36.
27. For those who assert Beaumont as the primary author, see: Pierson 1938, p. 683; Drescher 1968, pp. 130–131; Jardin 1989, pp. 183–184; Swedberg 2009, p. 297.
28. Sellin 1964, p. xviii. Perrot attributes the appendices to Tocqueville and the main text to Beaumont (1984, p. 24).

29. Barnes 1966, p. 132. A study of J. P. Mayer's English translation of the notebooks reveals at least ten references to their study in penitentiaries. See Tocqueville 1971, pp. 5–6, 7–11, 56, 120–125, 167–168, 181, 207, 209–211, 215, 233–234.
30. Pierson 1938, pp. 681–682.
31. Letter de Tocqueville à Mignet, 26 Juin 1841. Yale Tocqueville Manuscripts. General Collection, Beinecke Rare Book and Manuscript Library, Yale University. D.III.a, Box 47.
32. Wolin agrees that "recent scholarship has restored Tocqueville as a genuine collaborator" (2001, p. 384).
33. As much as possible, these correspondences between *Democracy in America* and *On the Penitentiary System* will be indicated throughout the book. However, as explained above, the purpose of the work is to uncover the meaning of *On the Penitentiary System* apart from the lens of Tocqueville's thought expressed in his larger, and successive, works.
34. Both Brogan and Perrot agree that Tocqueville contributed almost one-third of the text (Brogan 2006, p. 226).
35. Perrot agrees; see 1984, p. 23.
36. Drescher 1968, pp. 201–217.
37. For those who argue that Tocqueville did, indeed, construct a unique political philosophy, see: Eden 1990; Mansfield 2009, 2010. Lawler says that Tocqueville's "task was to surpass the philosophers from a human perspective by teaching human beings how to live well as human beings" with the truth "of the fundamental uncertainty or contingency of human existence revealed by philosophic inquiry" (1990, p. 401).
38. For scholars who have argued that *On the Penitentiary System* can be seen as a potentially prefatory work to *Democracy in America*, see: Brogan 2006, p. 234; Dunn 1985, p. 401; Drolet 2003, p. 129. *Democracy* itself contains two brief references to penitentiary systems: Tocqueville 2000, p. 44, 238.
39. For textual indications that Lieber received the first edition, see Beaumont and Tocqueville 1833a, p. v.
40. All translations throughout the work are my own.

References

2012. TLFi: Trésor de la langue Française informatisé. *ATILF—CNRS & Université de Lorraine*. http://www.atilf.fr/tlfi. Accessed 13 November 2017.

Adcock, Robert. 2014. *Liberalism and the Emergence of Political Science*. Oxford: Oxford University Press.

Avramenko, Richard, and Robert Gingerich. 2014. Democratic Dystopia: Tocqueville and the American Penitentiary System. *Polity* 46: 56–80.

Barnes, Harry Elmer. 1966. Review of *On the Penitentiary System in the United States and Its Application in France. The Pennsylvania Magazine of History and Biography* 90 (1): 131–133.

Beaumont, Gustave de and Alexis de Tocqueville. 1833a. *Du Système Pénitentiaire aux États-Unis et de son Application en France; suivi d'un Appendice Sur Les Colonies Pénales et de Notes Statistiques.* Paris: H. Fournier Jeune.

———. 1833b. *On the Penitentiary System in the United States and Its Application in France, with an Appendix on Penal Colonies and also Statistical Notes*, trans. Francis Lieber. Philadelphia: Carey, Lea & Blanchard.

Boesche, Roger. 1980. The Prison: Tocqueville's Model for Despotism. *The Western Political Quarterly* 33: 550–563.

———. 2006. *Tocqueville's Road Map: Methodology, Liberalism, Revolution, and Despotism.* Lanham, MD: Lexington Books.

Brogan, Hugh. 2006. *Alexis de Tocqueville: A Life.* New Haven: Yale University Press.

Carrese, Paul. 2011. Tocqueville's Foreign Policy of Moderation and Democracy Expansion. In *Alexis de Tocqueville and the Art of Democratic Statesmanship*, ed. Brian Danoff and Louie Joseph Herbert, 299–322. Lanham, MD: Lexington Books.

———. 2016. *Democracy in Moderation: Montesquieu, Tocqueville, and Sustainable Liberalism.* Cambridge: Cambridge University Press.

Cary, John. 1958. France Looks to Pennsylvania: The Eastern Penitentiary as a Symbol of Reform. *The Pennsylvania Magazine of History and Biography* 82 (2): 186–203.

Clinton, David. 2003. *Tocqueville, Lieber, and Bagehot: Liberalism Confronts the World.* New York: Palgrave Macmillan.

Craiutu, Aurelian. 2005. Tocqueville's Paradoxical Moderation. *The Review of Politics* 67: 599–630.

———. 2012. *A Virtue for Courageous Minds: Moderation in French Political Thought, 1748–1830.* Princeton: Princeton University Press.

Drescher, Seymour. 1968. *Dilemmas of Democracy: Tocqueville and Modernization.* Pittsburgh, PA: University of Pittsburgh Press.

Drolet, Michael. 2003. *Tocqueville, Democracy and Social Reform.* New York: Palgrave Macmillan.

———. 2005. Tocqueville's Interest in the Social: Or How Statistics Informed His 'New Science of Politics. *History of European Ideas* 31 (4): 451–471.

Duan, Demin. 2010. Reconsidering Tocqueville's Imperialism. *Ethical Perspectives* 17 (3): 415–447.

Dunn, Thomas. 1985. Friendly Persuasion: Quakers, Liberal Toleration, and the Birth of the Prison. *Political Theory* 13: 387–407.

Eden, Robert. 1990. Tocqueville and the Problem of Natural Right. *Interpretation* 17: 379–389.

Forster, Colin. 1991. French Penal Policy and the Origins of the French Presence in New Caledonia. *The Journal of Pacific History* 26 (2): 135–150.

Foucault, Michael. 1995. *Discipline and Punish: The Birth of the Prison*, trans. Alan Sheridan. New York: Vintage Books.

Hadari, Saguiv. 1989. *Theory in Practice: Tocqueville's New Science of Politics*. Stanford: Stanford University Press.

Jardin, André. 1989. *Tocqueville: A Biography*, trans. Lydia Davis and Robert Hemenway. New York: Farrar, Straus and Giroux.

Kahan, Alan. 1992. *Aristocratic Liberalism: The Social and Political Thought of Jacob Burckhardt, John Stuart Mill, and Alexis de Tocqueville*. Oxford: Oxford University Press.

Keslassy, Éric. 2010. Tocqueville et l' 'Économie' Pénitentiaire. *Revue d'Histoire des Sciences Humaines* 2 (23): 175–202.

Lakoff, Sanford. 1998. Tocqueville, Burke, and the Origins of Liberal Conservatism. *The Review of Politics* 60: 435–464.

Lawler, Peter Augustine. 1989. Tocqueville's Elusive Moderation. *Polity* 22: 181–189.

———. 1990. Was Tocqueville a Philosopher? The Distinctiveness of His View of Liberty. *Interpretation* 17 (3): 401–414.

Maguire, Matthew. 2006. *The Conversion of Imagination: From Pascal Through Rousseau to Tocqueville*. Cambridge: Harvard University Press.

Mansfield, Harvey. 2009. Consequential Ideas: Exploring the Subtle Dangers of 'Soft Despotism' in Democracies. *Weekly Standard* 14 (38). http://www.weeklystandard.com/consequential-ideas/article/17705.

———. 2010. *Tocqueville: A Very Short Introduction*. Oxford: Oxford University Press.

Merquior, J.G. 1991. *Liberalism Old and New*. Boston: Twayne Publishers.

Mill, John. 1977. De Tocqueville on *Democracy in America*. In *The Collected Works of John Stuart Mill, Volume XVIII: Essays on Politics and Society Part I*, ed. John M. Robson, 47–91. Toronto: University of Toronto Press.

Montesquieu, Charles-Louis. 1989. *The Spirit of the Laws*, ed. Anne M. Cohler, Basia C. Miller, and Harold S. Stone. Cambridge: Cambridge University Press.

Nolla, Eduardo. 1992. Introduction. In *Liberty, Equality, Democracy*, ed. Eduardo Nolla, xv–xxiii. New York: New York University Press.

O'Brien, Patricia. 1982. *The Promise of Punishment: Prisons in Nineteenth-Century France*. Princeton: Princeton University Press.

Perrot, Michelle. 1984. "Tocqueville Méconnu." In *Œuvres Complètes: Écrits sur le système pénitentiaire en France et à l'étranger, Tome IV, Vols 1 and 2*, Michelle Perrot, 7-44. Paris: Gallimard.

Pierson, George. 1938. *Tocqueville in America*. Baltimore: The Johns Hopkins University Press.

Pitts, Jennifer. 2001. *Writings on Empire and Slavery*. Baltimore: Johns Hopkins University Press.

Schwartz, Joel. 1985. The Penitentiary and Perfectibility in Tocqueville. *The Western Political Quarterly* 38: 7–26.

Sellin, Thorsten. 1964. Introduction. In *On the Penitentiary System in the United States and Its Application to France*, ed. Thorsten Sellin, xv–xl. Carbondale: Southern Illinois University Press.

Swedberg, Richard. 2009. *Tocqueville's Political Economy*. Princeton: Princeton University Press.

Tocqueville, Alexis de. 1971. *Journey to America*, trans. George Lawrence, ed. J.P. Mayer. New York: Doubleday Anchor Books.

———. 1984a. *Œuvres Complètes: Écrits sur le système pénitentiaire en France et à l'étranger, Tome IV, Vol. 1*, ed. Michelle Perrot. Paris: Gallimard.

———. 1984b. *Œuvres Complètes: Écrits sur le système pénitentiaire en France et à l'étranger, Tome IV, Vol. 2*, ed. Michelle Perrot. Paris: Gallimard.

———. 2000. *Democracy in America*, trans. and ed. Harvey Mansfield and Delba Winthrop. Chicago, IL: University of Chicago Press.

Welch, Cheryl. 1984. *Liberty and Utility: The French Idéologues and the Transformation of Liberalism*. Columbia: Columbia University Press.

———. 2001. *De Tocqueville*. Oxford: Oxford University Press.

Wolin, Sheldon. 2001. *Tocqueville Between Two Worlds: The Making of a Political and Theoretical Life*. Princeton: Princeton University Press.

Zetterbaum, Marvin. 1967. *Tocqueville and the Problem of Democracy*. Stanford: Stanford University Press.

CHAPTER 2

Tocqueville's Moderate Penal Theory

Tocqueville's analysis of the theory of penitentiary systems acts as a case study on the character of the human soul and its relation to the material world.[1] *On the Penitentiary System* makes possible a detailed exploration of the human soul because the report deals with a political institution whose ostensible purpose is to morally or socially reform human beings. Whether human beings have the ability to change, or are capable of reform, is an important question in determining the power of political institutions over individuals. There are two main alternatives to consider when asking whether penitentiaries are capable of reforming individuals. Either human beings are capable of change and such change leads to perfection or greater disorder, or human nature has a universal and fundamental character that is, at least partially, unalterable. The extent of permanency within human nature places limits on government activity. Conversely, the question of whether the nature of human beings has a telos, or a final end of perfectibility, lies at the heart of deliberations about political possibilities. If one takes a middling position between both views, human nature can be understood as representing a tension between being and becoming, or between rest and motion.[2] Human beings are perhaps fundamentally good in their *being*, but capable of becoming better; on the other hand, human beings are perhaps fundamentally bad, but have aspects of their nature that can be improved. Depending on one's view of human nature, resolving the tension in favor of either being or becoming results in political

E. K. Ferkaluk, *Tocqueville's Moderate Penal Reform*,
Recovering Political Philosophy,
https://doi.org/10.1007/978-3-319-75577-9_2

activity directed either toward developing the potential virtue of human beings or limiting the potential evil in human beings.

In *On the Penitentiary System*, Tocqueville and Beaumont deal with the same apparent contradiction between being and becoming that lies at the heart of what it means to be human. The report implicitly asks the question of what goal to establish for any penal measure—whether to set the goal of reforming human beings, or of simply restraining the evil or antisocial actions of human beings, or of a possible combination of both ends. The same question lies at the root of current penal questions regarding classically understood functions of the American penal system such as deterrence, incapacitation, retribution, and rehabilitation in light of modern difficulties with incarceration. As will be shown, Tocqueville and Beaumont suggest that one's answer to the question of what goal to set for any penal system depends on one's understanding of the nature of human beings. Consequently, the purpose of this chapter is to piece together a deeper understanding of the components of human nature presented in *On the Penitentiary System* and thereby see how Tocqueville and Beaumont answer that overarching question of what sort of human end (perfection or restraint) should be established for penitentiary systems. *On the Penitentiary System* contains numerous accounts of the human body, soul, imagination, memory, senses, religious impulse, and innate love of honor. While each part of the human being is discussed in separate and isolated circumstances, the individual discussions can be combined to see a sketch of universal human nature.[3]

Ultimately, Tocqueville and Beaumont answer the question of what sort of human end should be established for political and social institutions by articulating a specific relationship between body and soul as the moderate limit to penal activity.[4] Fundamentally, Tocqueville and Beaumont assume that the human soul has a particular relationship to the material world, specifically to the human body.[5] This relationship between body and soul is best viewed when one recognizes that there is a difference between spiritual[6] and material causality.[7] Humans have bodies which are affected by the material or physical world, and souls which are affected by spiritual or psychological realities. Still, as will be shown, the body can be affected by spiritual realities and the soul can be affected by the material circumstances of the body, both via the imagination. Political and social institutions often neglect the interconnectedness between body and soul in the individual, instead appealing to one part of the human constitution as predominate so as to advance the institution's moral or material goals.

Tocqueville and Beaumont use this schema of the relationship between body and soul as a standard for evaluating French penal reform. They view the relationship between body and soul through three contrasting pairs of elements in the American penitentiary system: theory and experience, solitude and labor, and corporal punishment and religion. All three contrasting elements center on the authors' fundamental critique of immoderate penal imaginations which hinder the French from reforming the whole human being.[8] To simultaneously affect body and soul, the imagination must be properly directed.[9] Tocqueville and Beaumont thus blame the failure of French penal institutions to morally reform criminals on their inability to properly guide or limit the criminal imagination. In sum, *On the Penitentiary System* demonstrates a moderate or balanced vision of human nature, a form of self-knowledge that penal reformers need when attempting to morally reform an individual via an institution.

Theory and Practice: France's Indulgence in an Imaginative Theory of Reform

The report begins its Preface by articulating a bipartite distinction in causality to explain effects in human society. In particular, the report identifies the overarching problem it seeks to address as social unrest in France in view of the increasing failure of the criminal justice system. According to the authors, there is both a material and a spiritual cause to explain the failure of the French criminal system to remedy increasing recidivism.[10] Tocqueville and Beaumont claim:

> Society, in our time, experiences a restiveness that appears to us to have two causes: the one, wholly psychological; there is within intelligences an activity that does not know where to spend itself, in minds an energy that lacks sustenance, and that devours society, for want of other prey. The other, wholly material; it is the physical distress of the working population that lacks labor and bread, and whose corruption, beginning in distress, ends in prison. The first evil is due to the intellectual wealth of the population; the second, to the penury of the poor classes. (Tocqueville 1984, pp. 152–153)

Specifically, the material cause of increasing crime is an increase in poverty, while the spiritual or psychological cause is a disjunction between what is promised in theory and what is produced in experiment.[11] Tocqueville and Beaumont extend this distinction between both causes, used explicitly in the first lines of the text, throughout the argument of *On the Penitentiary System*. They indicate that good penal theory necessarily recognizes the influence of both types of causality upon human activity, without ignoring one or the other. Consequently, Tocqueville and Beaumont intend to reveal that although French philanthropists articulate ideal theories on how to morally reform human beings, they do not adequately understand the nature of the beings they intend to reform. French penal theories fail at reforming the individual because they are not moderated by experiment and therefore do not acknowledge spiritual causality.[12] There is instead a tendency to emphasize the import of material causes to the detriment of spiritual causes as explanations for human activity. Hence, the philosophical problem in France is the inability to view both material and spiritual causes as necessary to effect moral reform of criminals.

Importantly, a certain amount of attention to practical activity is necessary to see spiritual causes in human society; conversely, it is necessary to use theory to understand material causes. French penal reformers have lost a view of the necessity of spiritual causes because they have neglected to attend to the lessons of experimenting or practice. Tocqueville and Beaumont complain in their initial *Mémoire* to the French government, "Those who clearly indicate the evil do not clearly point out the remedy. Books with theories abound; practical works are nowhere: or if the means of execution are shown, they are presented with the disfavor which is attached to experiments that experience has not sanctioned, and are devoid of practical documents in which the happiest conceptions have the appearance of utopias" (Tocqueville 1984, p. 51). Theories do not necessarily result in the practical relief of poverty and crime, and experience demonstrates the material limits of our human efforts. Problematically, theorists do not turn to experience to validate their theories on human life.[13]

Tocqueville and Beaumont therefore find fault with immoderately imaginative philanthropy.[14] Tocqueville and Beaumont identify French philanthropists as men "whose minds are nourished with philosophical reveries and whose extreme sensibilities need illusions" (Tocqueville 1984, p. 197). Philanthropy is most often an "affair of the imagination" (Tocqueville 1984, p. 235). More specifically, such philanthropy is the result of a misdirected imagination.[15] The imagination must be directed by wholly factual data rooted in actual experience (Tocqueville 1984, p. 284). Tocqueville and Beaumont accuse French philanthropists of lacking practical engagement with penal solutions, resulting in delimited penal imaginations.

What specifically are the reveries and illusions that French philanthropists indulge in, which have led to such extremes? According to Tocqueville and Beaumont, intellectuals who do not sufficiently limit their imaginations deviate from reality in believing that:

> ...man, however far advanced he is in crime, as capable of being always brought back to virtue. They think that the most infamous being can in every case recover the sentiment of honor, and following the consequences of this opinion they anticipate a time when, every criminal being radically reformed, prisons will be entirely empty, and justice will no longer have crimes to punish. (Tocqueville 1984, p. 197)[16]

In particular, publicists such as Charles Lucas ascribed to the idea of "moral science," which "sought the improvement of society through the application of the scientific method in the development of institutions" (O'Brien 1982, p. 31). On the basis of such beliefs, publicists claimed that institutional penal reform would eliminate crime by morally reforming criminals. The ideal which philanthropists indulge in assumes that every individual can be morally reformed via institutional means, no matter how criminal their inclinations.[17]

Paradoxically, philanthropists seeking to accomplish their ideal of reforming prisoners rely on material, as opposed to spiritual, causes for reform. Thus, Tocqueville and Beaumont complain that "for a long time, those in France who raised their voices to ask for reforms in the prison discipline called public attention only to clothing, food, and to everything that can be added to the comfort of the convict. So that, in the eyes of many, the adoption of a penitentiary system that necessitates such innovations tends only to ameliorate the material discipline of the prison" (Tocqueville 1984, pp. 230–231). Although they are generous, sensitive to the needs of prisoners, and ardent to pursue humane treatment in prisons, the French philanthropists' focus on improving the material conditions of prisons "has neglected a more precious interest, that of their moral reformation..." (Tocqueville 1984, p. 236).[18] The actual penal reform accomplished in France has been focused on making the bodily state of prisoners more comfortable; consequently, recidivism is a growing problem.[19] Throughout his decades of political work in penal reform, Tocqueville consistently accuses luxuries in French prisons (such as cafeterias, alcohol, free access to visits and letters from outside society, and a stipend for any work performed in prison) of adding to the vices of prisoners, rather than to their morality.

The focus on the material aspects of penitentiary discipline is also evident in the extreme partisanship over penitentiary discipline among French publicists. Publicists claim that the discipline in penitentiaries is either too soft to achieve justice for society or too severe to provide justice for the prisoner, or that it is a "utopia [...] intended to enlarge the number of human aberrations" (Tocqueville 1984, pp. 230–231). Each argument criticizes the material alleviation of penal rigor, rather than criticizing the psychological or spiritual aspects of prison discipline. Indeed, publicists such as Bentham, Lucas, and Livingston, who each argue in favor of alleviating the material severity of imprisonment, are "too preoccupied with philosophical doctrines" and thus "have not guarded themselves against the dangers of a theory carried to its furthest consequences" (Tocqueville 1984, pp. 230–231). Above all, in focusing on the material aspects of penitentiaries (such as music in a panoptic prison or a system of prison education), they misunderstand the necessary balance between severity and indulgence in any penal system. Such a balance moderates the need to achieve justice for both the prisoner and society.

In answer to the publicists, Tocqueville and Beaumont assert that it is impossible to morally reform prisoners solely by improving the physical living conditions of prisons. The pursuit of complete redemption for the criminal using only material means results in no redemption at all. The key problem in French penal reform is the reformer's inability to recognize the real and critical importance of spiritual causality behind human action, a blindness which results from imaginative theories untethered by experiment. Experiments, albeit tangible and rooted in the physical world, demonstrate the natural limits of a materialist worldview to account for all human activity.

Nevertheless, Tocqueville and Beaumont do not denounce the attempt to apply a scientific knowledge of institutions to remedy social problems. For example, the authors argue that statistics on inmate mortality "are better answers than any possible arguments to the objections that have been made" against the discipline of solitary confinement (Tocqueville 1984, p. 196). Indeed, *On the Penitentiary System* is full of rough statistical tabulations, innovative interviews with prisoners and administrators, and survey results; all of which were new developments in both a quantitative and qualitative approach to understanding problems within institutions and society. Out of the 19 appendices, 4 are devoted to statistical comparisons of states, penitentiaries, prisoners (distinguished by, e.g., race, ethnicity, crime, gender), and nations.

While conceding the need for a "moral science," Tocqueville and Beaumont also articulate the limits of institutions to improving society and individuals. The primary limit to social science is human nature itself. Thus, they argue that statistics cannot tell us anything about souls, sentiments, or intentions (Tocqueville 1984, p. 204). Statistics are also useless if there are incomparable data sets, lack of parallel comparison, insufficient data, or if all influential factors are not controlled.[20] Hence, statistics rely on the limited variables that numbers can tabulate, rather than the wide range of factors implicit in any human association. Finally, a theoretical hope to improve human society via institutional reform can be taken to an immoderate extreme if not tempered by experience. Theories need experiments to reveal their natural limitations. Tocqueville and Beaumont thus insist on a moderate reliance upon scientific methods for studying human society, human beings, and human associations.

Importantly, theory without experiment is dangerous to a liberal democratic society because political change ought to be the product of public opinion.[21] The authors saw the danger of philosophy in terms of penal reform during their study of the United States, as they note: "There are in the United States a certain number of philosophical minds who, full of theories and systems, are impatient to put them into practice" so that "if they had power themselves to make the law of the country, they would efface by a stroke of the pen all the old customs, for which they would substitute the creations of their genius and the decrees of their wisdom" (Tocqueville 1984, p. 170). An immoderate reliance on theory has the potential to produce a unique form of tyranny over individuals within a liberal democracy. Because democracy relies to some extent on public debate and consensus on political activity, its public imagination is far more susceptible to the dangers of publicists in exaggerating or ignoring political realities when speaking in the public marketplace of ideas. Large assemblies of people need tighter control over their collective imagination, since it is harder to discern between truth and error. Yet the work of philosophy (or penal theory) is performed by an individual rather than the people. Philosophy thus has the potential to uproot public opinion expressed through customs, rather than conserve it.[22] To avoid this problem, the philosopher ought to work within the constraints of public opinion.

Time is one of the primary constraints public opinion places upon ardent penal reformers. The development of public opinion takes time. Time is the key factor because "rightly or wrongly, the people do not move as fast as they [penal reformers]; they [the people] consent to changes, but they want them progressive and partial" (Tocqueville 1984, p. 170). Changes to public opinion in a liberal democracy must therefore be fundamentally and moderately slow. Tocqueville and Beaumont praise the "prudent and reserved reform," which results when public opinion effects change in a nation "whose entire habits are practical." On the other hand, if those "seduced by theories" ruled, the nation would undergo "hasty trials." The practicality of the people is a means of slowing the implementation of theories of the elite, and thereby moderating their ideas.

The authors' criticism of French penal reformers, especially philosophers and philanthropists, is therefore intended to restore a measure of control over penal discourse to the public. Tocqueville and Beaumont seek to purify the intellectual influences upon public opinion in France. The authors complain that "all those who exercise some power over opinion, spend their intellectual energy in discussions useful to the government but sterile for social benefit."[23] Just a few sentences earlier, Tocqueville and Beaumont state that "every capacity, all intelligence is pointed towards a single object, the life of political society."[24] Political events in France, such as the July Revolution and the beginning of the conquest of Algeria (both occurring in 1830), preoccupy the French public so much that projects of interior amelioration are ignored. Yet Tocqueville and Beaumont suggest that local communities need to take on the responsibility for prisons because they can best feel and modify the results of the penal experiment.[25] By separating theory from experiment, philosophers and philanthropists cut off the role of local communities in enacting, moderating, and revising proposals for penal reform in France.

Hence, as a remedy to the disjunction between penal theory and practice, Tocqueville and Beaumont emphasize the need for localities to engage in practical penal reform. Decentralized experiments in penal reform will help to regain the balanced recognition of both material and spiritual causality for action.[26] By seeing the limited effects of material reform through experiment, reformers can begin to acknowledge the need for spiritual (or, psychological) effects on individuals. In other words, they will see the natural limits to reforming prisoners via physical means. Human beings thus need active engagement in the material realm as a boundary to their imaginations. Tocqueville and Beaumont are capable of seeing the excess in French penal imaginations because they have a fuller understanding of human nature and causality behind our actions. Such "self-knowledge" allows the pair to moderate theory with practice, a balance which results in moderating penal hopes against the actual potential for individual prisoner reform.

The moderation that Tocqueville and Beaumont seek between theory and practice also results in an equilibrium between the interest of society and that of the individual. This expression of intellectual moderation was well noted in a review of the first edition of *On the Penitentiary System* published by *The Law Magazine*. The review argued that the opinions expressed by Tocqueville and Beaumont find the middle ground between the indifference of fatalists, who assume that crime will always be present among human beings, and the fervor of "the blind philanthropy of pious persons" who only dream of alleviating the criminals' sufferings without thinking of the negative social consequences of crime.[27] Moderate penal reform needs to keep both a concern for the criminal and concern for society in view; it therefore needs to balance hope for reform of individuals and realistic notions of the source of and remedy for crime in society.

Additionally, Tocqueville and Beaumont make way for the activity of practical men when confronting the damaging effects of philosophic publicists. According to the authors, effective policy changes are the work of practical men, not philosophers. Tocqueville and Beaumont thus consistently defer to the opinions of practical men in making their own judgments (Tocqueville 1984, p. 191, 204, 220). Out of the nineteen appendices, 4 in *On the Penitentiary System* include interviews with superintendents, chaplains, and directors of penitentiaries and houses of refuge; their inclusion highlights the emphasis upon practical engagement within institutions as a standard of judgment. Indeed, Tocqueville and Beaumont claim to be such practical men: as they state in the very beginning of their report, "it is to practical observations above all that we give our attention" (Tocqueville 1984, p. 172). By attending to practical experiments of penal theories, Tocqueville and Beaumont expect the philanthropic imagination to regain a view of how human beings are affected by both material and spiritual causes.

Finally, the authors' description of houses of refuge as penal institutions provides an internal case study on how experience can teach lessons on the limits of penal theories and the need to acknowledge both types of causality. Houses of refuge were the earliest forms of juvenile detention centers. The institutions were created after realizing the need to separate juvenile offenders from adult criminals in prisons; however, houses of refuge did not only shelter juvenile offenders but also took in any child whose parents abandoned them in vagrancy. While penitentiaries are distinct from prisons in their goal to morally reform criminals, houses of refuge differ from penitentiaries in that they were created specifically for one class of offenders (children) and are a hybrid of school and prison. Although technically not classified as prisons, Tocqueville and Beaumont include houses of refuge within the category of penitentiary systems to emphasize their unique method of using experience as an educational tool.

Tocqueville and Beaumont praise the institution of the house of refuge throughout their report. The American houses of refuge rise to the fore as the "best penitentiary establishments that have been conceived by the genius of man" since they represent the proper separation between government and philanthropy and between centralized government and decentralized administration (Tocqueville 1984, p. 249). Houses of refuge were created and built by groups of private citizens, who contributed their own funds and time to the effort. Although houses of refuge are private institutions in their origin, they have the legal right to retain children in their custody via the sanction of the government. Moreover, Tocqueville and Beaumont commend the institutions because "the law does not interfere at all in their direction and surveillance," although "each year the State gives pecuniary help to aide in the expense of their maintenance." The state does not demand any official accounts of the activity or success of the houses of refuge. The independent house of refuge is thus able to moderate the role of the state in its localized social activity by incentivizing the state to both contribute monetarily and simultaneously give up the ability to control how the money is used.

The experience afforded by houses of refuge to juvenile delinquents educates the reader in how to achieve moderation between material and moral goals for social institutions. As will be argued in greater depth below, for Tocqueville, the moral goal of any penitentiary institution is to reform the prisoner's criminal inclinations to correspond to the *mores* or standards of morality established in a particular society. This goal is reached through a combination of affecting both the material circumstances and the minds of prisoners. The disciplinary regime at the house of refuge neither presents "the severity and the wholly material discipline of a prison" nor "the too indulgent and wholly intellectual discipline of a school" (Tocqueville 1984, p. 250). The time of the children is divided so that "their intellectual labors give to the establishment the appearance of a primary institution, and their labor in the workshop is the same as in a prison" (Tocqueville 1984, p. 252). By establishing both intellectual and material goals for children in houses of refuge, the discipline of the house of refuge balances both severity for offenders and mildness for children. Here we find the moderate balance of utilizing both material and spiritual causes to effect moral reformation: while a prison is nearly exclusively concerned with the body, a school is almost solely concerned with the intellect. Both concerns are combined in one penal institution to affect both body and soul simultaneously.[28] The experience of the house of refuge confirms what theory postulated, that moral reform of individuals is possible via institutional means but only by attending to both material and spiritual causes.

Solitude and Labor: France's Inability to Properly Direct the Criminal Imagination

After asserting the distinction between spiritual and material causality and the corresponding need to moderate theory with experiment to see both causes of human action, Tocqueville and Beaumont must next answer the question of how spiritual and moral causality contributes to the reformation of criminals. There are three questions to ask: whether human beings are capable of reform, whether there are any limits to such reform, and in what way human beings can be reformed.

Before beginning to answer the questions regarding the extent to which reformation of the individual can occur within a penitentiary, it is helpful to understand how Tocqueville and Beaumont define "reformation." Tocqueville and Beaumont draw a distinction between two types of reformation that can be established as ends of the penitentiary: moral (or, radical) and rational.

In the first instance, reformation can indicate the radical change of a wicked person into an honest human being by means of gaining virtue (Tocqueville 1984, pp. 200–201). This change constitutes moral reformation, or a regeneration of the human soul. Radical reformation necessitates consciousness of one's moral condition, whether measured against a social or religious standard. However, Tocqueville and Beaumont note that radical reformation of the depraved person is only an accident, rather than a rational consequence, of even the best political institution.[29] Radical reformation is accidental because it necessitates that both body and soul are acted upon, while human institutions rarely consider or have the ability to affect both simultaneously.

The second type of reformation is rational; it is to redeem a criminal's habits to become useful for society by training the body. Tocqueville and Beaumont state that the principal object of punishment in relation to the prisoner is "to give him sociable habits," foremost of which is obedience (Tocqueville 1984, pp. 175–176). Rational reformation comes by knowing or having an opinion of one's own social condition, or, one's rightful place and conduct in the social order (Tocqueville 1984, p. 257). Habits of order established while in the penitentiary influence moral conduct after the prisoner returns to society. Human beings can thus be reformed to act morally even though their soul is not completely or essentially reformed. The reformation that trains the body via habits can be distinguished from the reformation that changes the soul via virtue.

All three questions regarding the possibility and means of both radical and rational reformation are answered in Tocqueville's and Beaumont's examination of two modes of discipline in American penitentiaries. Tocqueville and Beaumont assume that human beings are capable of both types of reformation, but specify the limits to such reform based on the means of reform. As has been argued, penal reformers in France idealize the possibility for complete moral reform solely through material causality. By claiming to rely on affecting physical circumstances alone to radically reform criminals, French penal reformers assume that changes to the soul can be made by acting on the body. Therefore, part of Tocqueville's and Beaumont's task is to stress to the French public the importance of acting on *both* body and soul to achieve the moral goal of prison discipline—the reformation of the prisoner to abide by civic virtue.[30] By emphasizing the need to act on both elements of human beings, and by arguing that the soul can only be reached through a combination of material and spiritual causes, Tocqueville and Beaumont will restore balance to the ideals of French reformers and thereby make penal reform effective. Simultaneously, the authors will also point out the limited capability of institutions to effect radical reform. In their examination of the limits of institutional penal disciplines such as solitude and labor, Tocqueville and Beaumont reveal that penitentiaries need to look beyond their own walls to find an effective means of reaching prisoners' souls. The disciplines of solitude and labor imposed on prisoners for their reformation are practical, institutional, and limited means to keep both spiritual and material causes of the moral goal of the penitentiary in view.

Tocqueville and Beaumont can identify the French public's fundamental misunderstanding of the relationship between body and soul because they studied the history of the American experiment in reforming prison systems. In both America and France, penal theory initially ran ahead of penal practice, and so in both cases efforts needed to be made to accord practice with theory and vice-versa. America's work in undertaking such efforts, seen in the historical development of penitentiaries in the nation, reveals France's need to do the same. The American penitentiary system came through a three-step experiment to eventually conclude that both solitude and labor are necessary penitentiary disciplines by which to reform criminals. Each turn in the American experiment was caused by a new discovery in the relationship between body and soul. Thus, the development in American penal theory depended on an experimental education in the fundamental components of human beings, aspects of humanity which limited and reformulated reformers' understanding of the institutional processes touching the individual prisoner.

Prison reform in America began with a desire to abolish bodily harm toward criminals, particularly the death penalty. It is well documented that punishments in seventeenth- and eighteenth-century America included forms of whipping, burning, branding, hanging, and mutilation. Importantly, the penitentiary system was not initially a synonym for the prison system. The penitentiary was created as an alternative to the prison system, which stressed corporal punishment and was more commonly used as a holding place for criminals awaiting their sentence. Penitentiaries would go further than simply retaining convicted prisoners in their goal of morally reforming inmates. Further, penitentiaries generally avoided using bodily harm as punishments. The goal of the penitentiary was to morally reform prisoners through psychological rather than corporal means.

In their criticism of the French prison reform movement, Tocqueville and Beaumont suggest that French penal theory has not moved beyond the first step in the development of the theory of penitentiary systems. French penal reformers seek only to preserve the physical bodies of criminals. By defining discipline based on avoiding bodily chastisement or providing comfort for prisoners, France neglects directing prisoner's minds toward the good. Prisoners avoid physical pain and are prevented from conveying or receiving immoral communication while in prison, but they are not necessarily exposed to moral communication.[31] Tocqueville's and Beaumont's concern is to show what it would take to achieve the moral reformation of prisoners, rather than simply sparing their lives.

The second development in the theory of the American penitentiary system was to determine how best to reform the criminal whose life had been preserved. Initially, the experiment in reforming criminals relied on a seemingly pure intellectual means of punishment, isolation.[32] Solitary confinement and work in silence were proffered as a two-fold solution to the problem of evil human inclinations. Both the Pennsylvania and Auburn penitentiary systems rely on the same syllogism: if inclinations toward crime originate from within the soul of the human being, and if it is true that such inclinations are shared among human beings like a disease, then human relationships promote vice. Tocqueville and Beaumont describe the mutual education between prisoners that occurs in prisons as a "dangerous contagion" which threatens to harm society by producing "a special population of malefactors who become each day more numerous and more threatening" (Tocqueville 1984, p. 197). Hence, isolation, either by solitude or enforced silence, mitigates the danger of evil communication among prisoners by cutting off almost all human relationship, particularly dangerous relationships between prisoners.

Although based on the same theory of the character of evil inclinations, the two primary penitentiary systems in America (Auburn and Philadelphia) represent very different applications of isolation as a penitentiary discipline. Solitary confinement, represented by the Philadelphia mode of discipline, makes communication with another human being physically impossible. Proponents of the Philadelphia system argue that human interaction not only promotes vice but also precludes reformation (Tocqueville 1984, pp. 174–175). Thus, the Philadelphia system theoretically uses complete solitude to place prisoners in a "moral situation" which sensitizes prisoners to the influence of "wise counsels and pious exhortations" from prison chaplains (Tocqueville 1984, p. 199). Because of their extreme loneliness, prisoners become more apt to listen to the clergy who visit their solitary cells. The idea of solitary confinement also claims to temper the danger of evil from within the individual by forcing the prisoner to reflection and thereby to repentance. Solitude is a discipline of simplicity: "there is no punishment because there is no infraction" (Tocqueville 1984, p. 190). The punishment of solitary confinement purportedly takes the soul as its object by forcing the criminal into a state where disobedience to prison regulations is impossible and where self-reflection is the only permitted activity. Solitary confinement therefore seemingly acts only on the mind because it excludes the possibility of bodily interaction or harm between two or more individuals. It could be said, therefore, that the Pennsylvania penitentiary system relies on pure theory to guide its material limits on prisoners.

Whereas the Philadelphia system relies on the physical impossibility of communication, the Auburn system relies on the psychological (moral) impossibility of communication. The Auburn penitentiary also assumes that isolation is the key to preventing vice, but it uses silence, rather than solitude, as the mode of isolating prisoners. At Auburn, prisoners silently work together in common rooms during the day and enter solitary cells only at night. Tocqueville and Beaumont describe the prisoners' relationships to each other in Auburn thus: "Their congregation is wholly material, or, to put it better, their bodies are together and their souls [are] isolated; and it is not the solitude of the body that is important, it is that of the intelligence" (Tocqueville 1984, p. 176). Auburn's discipline rests on the assumption that material force alone is insufficient to cause human action. Psychological force, the uniting of minds, must be added to material force. Hence, although they are greater in number, the prisoners do not harm the guards at Auburn because they lack the power gained by conversation (Tocqueville 1984, p. 220).

Moreover, Auburn's discipline assumes that the prudential leadership of superintendents, rather than theory, must be the guiding factor in punishment. Superintendents are responsible for vigorously imposing silence when prisoners are gathered in common work areas. Complete silence during the day is enforced by armed guards who circuit a wooden gallery around the common workroom. The gallery allows guards to walk and hear all that occurs in the workroom without being seen by prisoners. Consequently, the prison director's presence was even more influential at Auburn than at Philadelphia due to the fear that prisoners had of their invisibility.[33]

When comparing both the Philadelphia and Auburn systems, Tocqueville and Beaumont argue that solitude enforced at Philadelphia forms habits rather than reforms the heart. The isolation created by solitary confinement has a moral influence on individuals but "deprive[s] the inmates' submission of its moral character."[34] In other words, the prisoner's actions are moral even if his motives for acting are not. Solitude can only create habits of obedience to authority by taking away the physical ability to rebel against authority. Thus, absolute solitude simply constrains bodily activity within certain material parameters rather than affecting the inclinations or the will of the criminal. Conversely, prisoners at Auburn still have a choice and ability to disobey the regulations; they are only prevented from disobedience by fear of the bodily pain (whipping) which will accompany their actions. Whereas Philadelphia closes off the possibility of the prisoner's exercise of free will, Auburn regulates the use of the free will via fear. Both penal disciplines, then, attempt to influence the moral nature of human beings via material constraints rather than purely theoretical means as purported by Philadelphia proponents.

Yet reformers moved too far in the opposite direction when initially departing from laws whose goal was to affect only the body. Only after seeing the harmful bodily effects of solitary confinement did the American theory of penitentiaries come to its final development by incorporating labor as a means of discipline. Solitude, if complete, "is beyond the strength of man; it consumes the criminal without respite and without pity; it does not reform, it kills" (Tocqueville 1984, p. 159). Although intended to force the mind into reflection, solitude instead destroys the physical strength of human beings. The body suffers when the mind suffers, and vice-versa. Thus, even when the body is not the direct object of punishment there are physical consequences. Most often, these physical consequences stem from mental health issues produced by solitary confinement. Without physical exertion, the human is subject to a state of depression, insanity, or despair, which are the results of debilitating passions such as "melancholy, chagrin…"[35] Thus, in the new American system of solitary confinement, prisoners attempted suicide by jumping out of windows or stopped eating due to the depression caused by solitary confinement.

The experiment in establishing a penitentiary system began with the discipline of solitude, with its unique effect on the mind, as a means of reforming the human soul; reformers added the discipline of labor only after solitary confinement failed its initial purpose.[36] The Auburn system included forced labor in common workrooms, while the Philadelphia system introduced labor for the individual prisoners within their solitary cells (such as shoemaking and carpentry). The added discipline of labor thus reflects a lesson taught by experiment that penal disciplines must act on both the body and mind of prisoners to effect moral reformation. The Philadelphia experiment of complete isolation without labor taught Americans that one cannot attempt to singularly affect the mind without also affecting the body.

Still, what is the link between the conditions of mind and body? As in the case of determining the balance between theory and practice, Tocqueville and Beaumont point to the imagination. The authors argue that each individual is naturally inclined either toward a lively imagination or to a tranquil mind undisturbed by the imagination. In both cases, the health of a prisoner depends to a certain extent on the exercise of their intellect, specifically the exercise of the imagination to conceive of one's own personal honor or position in society. The man with an elevated social position suffers from the infamy of entering prison more than the man of an obscure condition because his past experiences enable his imagination to assume the worst about his degradation in society. The body suffers in correlation to the lively imagination.

Tocqueville and Beaumont also argue that intellectual men suffer the most in absolute solitude because they lack proper companionship. Human relationships—the social context in which each individual finds themselves—shape the imagination. Consequently, "solitude becomes more painful in proportion to the greater needs of sociability" (Tocqueville 1984, p. 291). Prisoners in solitary confinement are led to believe that they are completely isolated from society, and thus permanently rejected by such society. Furthermore, prisoners in solitary confinement have no hope of successfully returning to society because they are isolated from proper *mores*, which are the "power of example and the influence of public opinion," and which train individuals in how to successfully navigate society's dictums by restraining human passions (Tocqueville 1984, p. 279). Human beings were intended to live together, and such togetherness innately holds benefits for moral human activity. Whether or not the prisoner's hypotheses of social alienation are true, the hopelessness produced by such imaginative extremes in solitary confinement prohibits rather than promotes moral reformation.

Notably, labor places boundaries around the human imagination that enable prisoners to overcome such detrimental extremes. Labor within the penitentiary mentally and physically prepares prisoners to successfully reenter society. Prisoners interviewed by Tocqueville at the Philadelphia penitentiary expressed gratitude for labor in their solitary cells because it distracted them from the terrors of their imagination (Tocqueville 1984, p. 175). Humans are intended not only to live in relationships with each other, but more specifically to work alongside each other. In other words, a fundamental part of the prospering human soul is the need to work with one's hands. Labor is good for human beings because idleness allows the imagination to go beyond bounds, whereas labor keeps the mind steady by exercising both the intellect and the body simultaneously.[37]

More specifically, although the punishment of labor takes the body for its object, rather than the soul, labor also provides rest for the human soul which solitude cannot by filling "the solitary cell with an interest" (Tocqueville 1984, p. 175). Labor is a self-interested pursuit on the part of the prisoner. Humans must be in motion, and the fundamental motion derives energy from self-interest. Yet the self-interest utilized by labor in American penitentiaries is not economic, since the prisoners do not receive a *pécule* (or, wage) as do prisoners in France. The lack of economic recompense removes the temptation to immoral conduct for criminals leaving the prison.

Rather than promote an economic self-interest, Americans interest the prisoners in their future or potential ability to become an active member of society. While still in the penitentiary, the self-interested labor of the individual is directed toward a profession that benefits society. The penitentiary demands that labor not be performed simply as a distraction or as an alternative to idleness within the prison. Instead, Tocqueville and Beaumont stress the principle "that by working the convict learns a profession whose exercise will support him when he leaves prison" (Tocqueville 1984, p. 187). Hence, Tocqueville and Beaumont reject the option of using treadmills to keep the prisoners active, a policy promoted in Britain. It is not mere activity that is the goal but activity toward the end of self-sufficiency in society. Motion should not occur without intelligent direction toward a sustaining profession for the individual. Labor is thus a means of engaging the human mind and self-interest in worthwhile pursuits which do not contradict society's goals for citizens.

More pointedly, American penitentiaries engage prisoners' imaginations to understand their own social obligation. The American penitentiary operates on the principle "that the criminal owes all his labor to society to indemnify it for the costs of his imprisonment" (Tocqueville 1984, p. 426). Through labor, prisoners gain an education in civil obedience and rights, in particular the right of society "to find in the work of the inmate the indemnity that it is due" (Tocqueville 1984, p. 426). Later, in their revised introduction to the second edition of *On the Penitentiary System*, Tocqueville and Beaumont will commend to the French: "Let us not forget, when philanthropy excites our pity for an unhappy man, to reserve some of our sympathy for a still greater interest, that of society as a whole" (Tocqueville 1984, p. 136). Tocqueville and Beaumont argue that any plan for penal reform needs a balanced, and therefore moderated, pursuit of two goals for punishment: rehabilitation of the individual and retribution for society. Through labor, the inmates learn not only of their own individual rights but the rights of society as a whole.

Further, penal labor becomes a tool of equality within a democracy. Tocqueville and Beaumont note that "there is even more equality in the prison than in society" because of enforced general labor (Tocqueville 1984, p. 183). Labor only allows for a distinction between natural capabilities in performing work; in every other way, individuals are considered equal. By teaching prisoners to labor, the penitentiary educates prisoners in their essentially equal responsibilities within democratic society.

The American penitentiary thus uses labor to engage the self-interest of individuals, not in profit, but in understanding and taking their own responsibility to promote social ends. The education that labor provides thereby tempers the imaginations of prisoners who despair of living honestly in society after completing their term of imprisonment. By laboring in prison, the inmate finds a means of enduring solitude, prepares to re-enter society as a self-sufficient citizen, and gains a better understanding of the right of society to punish disobedience to its laws. Ultimately, Tocqueville and Beaumont suggest that the disciplines of solitude and labor must be combined to lead prisoners toward their rational reformation. Both body and soul must be affected through proper control over the imagination.

Although prison labor can tame the imagination by giving the body an activity, and thereby calm the soul by reassuring the individual of his eventual re-entrance into human society, by itself labor cannot lead a criminal to radical reformation. It is possible to calm the soul without being able to direct it toward moral or virtuous ends. The relationship between solitude and labor therefore shows us the limits of political and social institutions in terms of moral reformation effected via material causality alone: such institutions can only prepare the conditions in which the individual is capable of reform. Political and social institutions cannot push the soul of the individual to complete reformation. In the end, political or social institutions have the greatest power to affect the exterior circumstances of human beings and thus shape their habits, not their hearts. Although human beings are capable of both radical and rational reformation, institutions are limited in pursuing radical reformation on behalf of individuals because of the inherent difficulty in affecting the minds of men.

Based on their study of the historical development of American penal systems and the necessary relationship between the body and soul which that study evidences, Tocqueville and Beaumont propose that the goal of French penal reform should be moderated to seek to achieve rational reformation, as opposed to radical reformation. French philanthropists should first cease aggravating social vice and "render it less deadly" in prisoners' habits, rather than attempt to make men virtuous (Tocqueville 1984, p. 153).

Nevertheless, although Tocqueville and Beaumont admit that rational reformation is easier to attain, they still hold out the possibility of radical reformation for prisoners. The goal of their report is to broaden the scope of public policy to consider both the good of the body and the good of the soul as two equal ends to political activity. In the final analysis, it is doubtful whether rational reformation is good for the criminal's soul. The last comparison between two types of honor proffered by corporal punishment and religion indicates that Tocqueville and Beaumont make the distinction between both types of reformation to demonstrate that religion is a necessary ancillary discipline to the penitentiary, a penal measure which enables the institution to achieve the moral reformation of prisoners. Without religion, penitentiaries are limited to acting only on the bodies of human beings; that is, they are limited to a material causality or to a combination of solitude and labor which can at best result in rational reformation. As will be seen, religion provides the type of spiritual causality which is necessary for complete moral reformation of the prisoner.

Corporal Punishment and Religion: France's Potentially Moderated Penal Imagination

Two remaining aspects of human nature remain to be shown through Tocqueville's and Beaumont's examination of the American penitentiary system. We have already seen that Tocqueville and Beaumont present human action as universally contextualized by both material and spiritual causes. When applied to penitentiary systems, this causal reality necessitates that theory is balanced with practice (or, experiment). Such a balance reveals to penal reformers how institutions can best utilize both kinds of causality to effect change within prisoners. Subsequently, we have seen that the human imagination connects soul and body within the individual. Hence, the penal disciplines of solitude and labor must be moderately balanced with each other to achieve the rational reformation of prisoners, even if such disciplines fall short of attaining radical reformation. Finally, Tocqueville and Beaumont show readers that human beings universally experience an innate desire for honor, as shown in the contrast between corporal punishment and religion as auxiliaries to prison discipline.[38] The contrast between both auxiliary penal disciplines shows what type of spiritual causality is necessary to lead prisoners to radical reformation: the spiritual cause of radical reformation is rightly incentivizing individuals to attain honor from God, rather than from society alone.

Not only do French penal reformers neglect acknowledging the need for a spiritual cause to morally reform individuals, but they also lack the social mores necessary to accomplish radical reformation. In America, rational reformation results from the disciplines of labor and solitude; Tocqueville and Beaumont see the ***auxiliaries*** of labor and solitude as the effective factors in radical reformation. Labor takes corporal punishment as an auxiliary in its work on the body, while solitude takes religion as an auxiliary in its work on the soul.[39] However, public opinion in France opposes both the aid of the whip and the assistance of religion.[40] Tocqueville and Beaumont therefore need to persuade the public of the necessary contribution of corporal punishment and religion to the success of penitentiaries in morally reforming the individual.

While decrying the excessive focus on the body in French punishment, specifically the indulgent interest in prisoner comfort, Tocqueville and Beaumont defend corporal punishment as an auxiliary to the discipline of labor. Notably, the authors deny their ability to solve the question of whether penitentiary discipline could "dispense with the help of corporal punishments," since they claim not to question society's right to punish the bodies of individuals (Tocqueville 1984, p. 193). Instead, Tocqueville and Beaumont want to know how useful corporal punishments are for attaining the radical reformation of the guilty. In Tocqueville's and Beaumont's words, "the sole question to examine" is whether mutilation of the body can or should morally reform human beings.[41] In a footnote to this discussion, Tocqueville and Beaumont quote Edward Livingston's succinct summary of the problem surrounding corporal punishment's usefulness:

> The question to resolve [...] is that of how to know if the whip is the most efficacious means to inculcate in the souls of the convicts religious and moral sentiments, the love of labor and science; and whether a man will love labor better because he has been coerced, by blows or by the terror of receiving them, to do the task each day that have been imposed on him. (Tocqueville 1984a, p. 194)

Thus, according to Livingston, penitentiaries aim to cultivate two different objects in prisoners: sentiments and love. Sentiments are both religious and moral, whereas the love of the prisoner is to be directed toward "labor and science." To attain these objects, the criminal must not only be habituated to a certain activity but must also gain a love for the activity. While habit can be inculcated simply by working upon the body of the criminal, love can be attained only by affecting the soul of the criminal. The question, posed in terms of punishment, asks whether punishment of the body affects the soul in the "most efficacious" way; in other words, whether corporal punishment eventually turns habits into love. Additionally, Livingston's question implicitly asks whether corporal punishment can be expected to attain *all* the necessary goals of the penitentiary system. For example, it remains an unanswered question whether punishing the body leads human beings to religious and moral sentiments.

In answer to Livingston's question, it could be argued that corporal punishments are the *only* means of correcting the human soul. Tocqueville and Beaumont present this viewpoint by citing Gershom Powers, an American penal reformer who argues that all punishment is bodily. There is no alternative to reaching the soul other than through physical punishment. As an example, Powers states that even if a penitentiary refused to exercise the whip it would turn to reducing food as the principal means of controlling the prisoner; thus, "by humane motives [...] one will make them die by starvation" (Tocqueville 1984, p. 194). Powers views all penal action as fundamentally corporal; there can be no other means available to penitentiaries for punishing or reforming prisoners.

Notably, however, the arguments that corporal punishment can cure the soul are given as a defense of whipping. Francis Lieber argues that whipping is as much a psychological punishment as it is a corporal one, since it "effects immediately the submission of the delinquent," does not interrupt labor, and does not affect overall health in the long term (Tocqueville 1984, p. 190). According to Lieber, the efficacy of the whip comes not from the pain it inflicts, but rather in that it is based on the principle "active in all men, that the present evil is always the greatest [...] if, then, punishment is *certain* of falling *immediately* upon the offender, it has the greatest effect" (Beaumont and Tocqueville 1833, p. x). The whip relies on a psychological anticipation of pain to incentivize criminals to avoid breaking the rules. When used regularly, the infliction of corporal punishment thus becomes a "law of right" in the penitentiaries; inflicting cruel pain is a "powerful means of acting on the prisoners" psychologically (Tocqueville 1984, pp. 190–191). Lieber thus defends the use of the whip (or corporal punishment) because of its psychological immediacy rather than the extent to which it harms the body.

Still, Tocqueville and Beaumont reject both Powers' and Lieber's defense of bodily punishment because they assert that human beings are fundamentally motivated by a desire for honor. Importantly, the effectiveness of corporal punishment in reforming human beings in French prisons finds its limit at the bestowing of infamy. Tocqueville and Beaumont ask,

"How can we hope to reform the morality of a man who carries on his body indelible signs of his infamy, either because the mutilation of his limbs incessantly reminds him of his crime, or because the mark imprinted on his forehead perpetuates its memory?" (Tocqueville 1984, p. 169). Corporal punishments leave marks upon the bodies of prisoners which they will carry with them after returning to society. The authors declaim such long-term consequences of corporal punishment which prohibit the former prisoner from successfully reintegrating into society.

Specifically, infamy represents a dangerous use of the function of memory in the human mind. Corporal punishments do not direct the thoughts of a criminal toward the goal of living an honest life, but instead continually remind both the criminal and society of their crime. Branding, whipping, and other corporal punishments leave the mark of a bad memory of a past event which is often difficult or impossible to erase. Infamy is consequently a permanent reputation affixed to a prisoner whom society hopes to redeem. Tocqueville and Beaumont argue that there is an extent to which corporal punishments are incompatible with the moral object of the penitentiary system. The governing principle of the penitentiary system seeks to restore the criminal to society by redeeming the prisoner, which demands a certain elevation not just of the prisoner's morals but also of his reputation in society.

Tocqueville and Beaumont thus call into question the legitimacy of punishing by shame. Whipping is problematic for the French penal system not because it inflicts bodily pain or psychological fear, but because the results induce a sometimes permanent sense of shame. According to the authors, shame incorrectly motivates human beings to do the good. Shame is not a natural consequence of all punishments. It is intrinsically public in nature and depends on tight communal attachments that are central to individual identity. Shame as part of punishment can be produced only within a strongly knit community that has standards for honor or dishonor which are projected on wrongdoers. Thus, in America whipping is not connected to shame because it is equivocated to the rights of fathers, teachers, masters, and captains in the Navy (Tocqueville 1984, p. 194). In France, on the other hand, society views whipping as a mark of shame (Tocqueville 1984, p. 234, 237). Ultimately, then, shame represents the (sometimes permanent) destruction of an individual's reputation. Shame lowers a person in the eyes of others. To shame an individual is to indicate that their character or actions lie outside the norms of society. To be effective, shame depends upon a community's memory of the individual's past both at the time of punishment and in the future life of the individual. Shame thus prevents an individual from gaining the type of social honor which is necessary to reintegrate well in a democracy.

The problem of shame points to the need to effectively use honor when attempting to morally reform criminals. The question of honor, or inversely of infamy, lies at the heart of Tocqueville's and Beaumont's defense of both corporal punishment and religion as auxiliary disciplines. Honor motivates human beings to act on principles. Yet honor depends to a certain extent on the work of the imagination: an individual must be able to perceive some form of self-interest, that is, have the ability to imagine honor being bestowed, when exercising their free will. In terms of the prisoner, they must be able to imagine a restoration of honor given to them by society. Tocqueville and Beaumont see corporal punishment as effectively cutting off the possibility of regaining honor in French society. Because the bodily scars of corporal punishment kindle memory of a past dishonor, the imagination cannot conceive of potential future honor. Therefore, to avoid the potential for recidivism it is necessary to know how to direct the prisoner's imagination to conceive of the possibility of regaining his own personal honor in society after his release.

What is honor according to Tocqueville and Beaumont?[42] Honor (*honneur*) is used in three senses in the text of *On the Penitentiary System*.[43] First, there is the honor given to an individual in recognition of a great action. This first type of honor can be afforded by society. Problematically, Tocqueville and Beaumont suggest that such honor in a democracy sometimes does not belong to a single individual because innovation is a product of the progress of time and simultaneous efforts (Tocqueville 1984, p. 160). For example, when recounting the historical development of the penitentiary system in America, the authors have difficulty identifying a single person who ought to be praised for creating the penitentiary because the invention occurred over such a long time.

In the second use of the word *honneur*, we see that honor can be found in living an honest life. Rather than gaining honor by great political or social actions on behalf of the community, the democratic individual gains honor by his degree of conforming to conventions. The *Dictionnaire de l' Académie française* (1835) defines *honnête* (honesty) as "conforming to reason, decency, suitable to the age and profession of the people."[44] The *Trésor de la langue Française informatisé* (2012) defines *honnête* (honesty) as "conforming (whether by probity or virtue) to a socially recognized moral norm"; similarly, it defines *honneur* (honor) as "principal moral action which leads a person to have conduct conforming (either by probity, virtue, or courage) to a social norm and which permits them to enjoy the esteem of others and the right to moral dignity." Honor can be understood as the principle by which one lives an honest life. So too, often it is not great individuals who gain honor, but great citizens—persons who demonstrate their ability to live a quiet, productive life on behalf of society and in accordance with the rules of society. Tocqueville and Beaumont thus speculate that the practical and achievable reformation of a criminal is not to make him an honest man, but to have enabled him to contract honest habits which will garner him honor in a commercial society.[45]

What are these honest habits in a democracy? Obedience to the laws by working knowledgeably and diligently, detesting crime for its legal consequences, and being a reasonable, self-interested human being. Patricia O'Brien adds that nineteenth-century prisons in France "were intended to instill the virtues of the workplace: productivity, thrift, punctuality, discipline, and order" (O'Brien 1982, p. 14). Notably, these honest habits do not necessitate that a human being love the good, act virtuously or morally, or have a lively and deep religious faith. Rather, the honest life is encapsulated in America by self-sufficiency. The first two uses of honor are therefore defined in reference to the relationship between the individual and society; the goal of any penal system, according to Tocqueville and Beaumont, is to restore the prisoner's ability to live an honorable life as a citizen; to achieve a right relationship between the individual and their society.

The third sense in which *honneur* is used in the text designates the honor which the individual gains in relation to God. Tocqueville and Beaumont argue that the prisoner's soul needs not only labor and solitude, but most importantly moral pardon which only God can provide (Tocqueville 1984, p. 204). To be completely reformed, the soul needs to regain its original purity.[46] Remember that Tocqueville and Beaumont identify two forms of reformation: radical (or, moral) and rational (or, habitual). Tocqueville and Beaumont define moral regeneration in the prisoner as the restoration of "primitive purity to a soul that crime has defiled."[47] While the authors do not give us a formal definition of "primitive purity," they argue that the individual's return to such a state is almost impossible because "whatever his efforts, [the prisoner] will never regain that delicacy of honor that alone gives an unblemished life. Even when he takes the part of living honestly, he cannot forget that he has been a criminal; and this memory, which deprives him of self-esteem, also deprives his virtue of reward and guarantee" (Tocqueville 1984, pp. 203–204). Thus, the state of primitive purity consists in part of an honor that gives satisfaction to living virtuously and provides the individual with a sense of self-respect or worth. These internal measures of one's actions are necessary to living an honest life.

Despite its best efforts, society is incapable of restoring such purity to the prisoner. Tocqueville and Beaumont preface their discussion of primitive purity by stating: "It would have been much easier for the guilty to remain honest than for him to rise again after his fall" (Tocqueville 1984, p. 203). They further argue that "when society pardons, it puts the man in liberty; that is all: it is only a material fact. When God pardons, he pardons the soul. With this moral pardon, the criminal regains *self-respect, without which honesty is impossible*" (Tocqueville 1984, p. 204; emphasis added). The authors suggest that to act honestly it is necessary to have pardon from God; civic virtue cannot be held otherwise. Moral pardon must come from a source outside of society (God) and is conveyed through religion.[48]

Tocqueville and Beaumont contrast pardon from God with pardon from society throughout their report. Pardon from society increases dishonesty. Indeed, by allowing the possibility of legal pardon from the governor of a state, criminals always retain some hope of escape which distances them psychologically from their present circumstances. This false hope works against the efforts of religious persons in the penitentiary, since the criminal will show to the chaplain (one of the only persons allowed to visit the prisoner in solitary confinement) "a deep remorse for his crime and a lively desire to return to virtue" even if such sentiments are a lie.[49] Problematically, the chaplain thus gains the illusion of the prisoner's reformation, an illusion that often leads to the actual legal pardon of an unreformed offender. Such illusions are destructive to society because they increase pardons and thereby allow for potential recidivists to return to society. Legal pardon creates hypocrites, rather than penitents. State pardons are thus too often based on dishonesty by encouraging the criminal to imagine an escape from the consequences of their action, as well as encouraging the chaplain to imagine a moral reformation which has not yet taken place in the criminal. Most of all, state pardons do not give opportunity for the prisoner to become honest by rightfully fulfilling the sentence for their crime.[50]

Further, legal pardon fails to support prisoner reformation because the authorities who are given the pardon power do not have the attributes of

God. Statistical notes in the appendices of *On the Penitentiary System* show that pardon is most often extended to those convicted for life. Criminals convicted for life have the greatest interest in beseeching the governing authority for pardon, since they cannot hope in any other means of escape and cannot rely on any other alleviation of their fears. Thus, the power to pardon garners the interest of the most unpardonable. The abuse of the pardon power results from according such power to politically lower officials who are more dependent on public opinion, and thus more susceptible to the pleas of prisoners and their family or friends (i.e., the governors of states) (Tocqueville 1984, pp. 378–381). In light of this reasoning, Tocqueville and Beaumont suggest that the power to forgive ought to come from those capable of correctly making the judgment of who ought to be forgiven, namely, those with attributes like God: those of highest authority and complete social independence. It is questionable whether any human being can possess such attributes.

Tocqueville and Beaumont further argue that moral reformation in prisons is infrequent because it is a reformation of the conscience.[51] The conscience is the place of remorse.[52] Yet the conscience is hidden from human eye and action. The difficulty of attaining radical reformation within the penitentiary results from the incapacity of society to touch the interior of human beings. Tocqueville and Beaumont assert that "human institutions, powerful on the actions and the will, have no power over consciences" (Tocqueville 1984, p. 204). Nor can the outside individual "descend into the conscience of the prisoner in order to see his repentance" (Tocqueville 1984, p. 230). Thus, even if a criminal has experienced radical reformation, the difficulty remains of "how to demonstrate by statistics the purity of the soul, the delicacy of sentiments, and the innocence of intentions? Society, powerless to effect this radical regeneration, is no more capable of proving it when it exists. It is in both cases an affair of the heart of hearts..." (Tocqueville 1984, p. 204). Society can neither see into the conscience nor act upon it.

Because the conscience is hidden from human beings and human institutions, the conscience is much harder to reform. Tocqueville and Beaumont bemoan the fact that "in vain society pardons [the prisoner]: his conscience does not give grace" (Tocqueville 1984, pp. 203–204). Tocqueville and Beaumont make the case that moral reformation of a single individual cannot be the object of a politician's focus, since "an institution is political only if it is made in the interest of the masses" (Tocqueville 1984, p. 205). Only the religious man can appreciate the moral reformation of an individual soul; the politician must focus his attention on the civic habits necessary for all citizens. The political institution is therefore limited. Moral reform is possible, but only by turning to religion as a social institution.

To achieve this third form of honor which makes possible the honest life, Tocqueville and Beaumont evaluate the use of religion within American penitentiaries.[53] The reformation aimed at is fundamentally radical under the Pennsylvania system, targeting men's hearts, whereas the Auburn system seeks to reform the criminal's mind via punishment of the body. Both systems employ chaplains and Bibles, not only to impart religious conviction but also to provide elementary education to the prisoners. The majority of prisoners interviewed by Tocqueville in the Philadelphia prison expressed gratitude for such religious elements of solitary confinement, explaining that the visits of the chaplain and reading of the gospels were some of their greatest consolations. Additionally, prisoners often learned how to read by utilizing the Bibles provided by the penitentiary or by attending the elementary schools hosted after Sunday chapel services.

Religion is not simply a disciplinary measure used to encourage and educate men on how to live honest lives. Rather, religion is a natural impulse in the human heart.[54] The religious impulse is an impulse to hope—for the prisoner, religion provides hope in the possibility of reform.[55] By giving prisoners hope of internal reformation, religion affords human beings the opportunity to gain honor from outside the context of society. In seeking pardon from God, rather than from a governor, the criminal cannot hope to escape the social and legal punishment for his crime, but he can hope that his forgiveness from God will prevent future recidivism.[56] The criminal's imagination is turned toward a desire to live honestly after punishment has been fulfilled. Consequently, the defense of religion as an auxiliary to solitude can be made by expanding the view of honor from merely being defined and awarded by society to being defined and awarded by God.

Religion has the power to effect radical reformation because it has the ability to act upon men's consciences. Tocqueville and Beaumont assert, "If society is powerless to reprieve consciences, religion has the power to do so" (Tocqueville 1984, p. 204). Through the enlightened conscience the heart can be touched (Tocqueville 1984, p. 202). Religion calms the conscience by giving knowledge of God's moral pardon of the soul. God alone has the ability to effect moral reformation, and God alone can judge whether or not such reformation has taken place. Religion, as the institution entrusted with knowledge of God, can thus touch the conscience by bringing individuals into contact with God. When the social institution of the penitentiary allows for a role of organized religion in punishment, it opens the possibility of regaining honor for the individual.

Hence, while the penitentiary is a political institution, it depends upon the religious person's involvement to effect moral change within the individual. Tocqueville and Beaumont conclude that "the movement that has determined the reform of prisons has been essentially religious. It is religious men who have designed and accomplished everything that has been undertaken [...] thus, religion is still one of the fundamental elements of discipline and reform in every new prison today" (Tocqueville 1984, p. 236). Moreover, religion which actively participates in morally reforming individual prisoners is not connected to the formal institution of the church. Rather, "the society of the United States is itself eminently religious," and thus an informal religious influence would continue in penitentiary establishments by "a crowd of charitable persons" even if no chaplain was present. Even the guards and those employed at the prisons are religious. As a result, "the inmate in the United States thus breathes a religious atmosphere in the penitentiary that comes to him from every part" (Tocqueville 1984, p. 236). Respect for religion is the habit of the masses which political institutions must protect, or at the very least tolerate, to ensure the moral reform of the individual. Thus, religion in the United States' penal system does not depend wholly upon the clergy, nor does it depend on the clergy's relation to or estrangement from political power.

Consequently, Tocqueville and Beaumont suggest that to attain the true end of the penitentiary system, the moral reform of the individual criminal, the French populace would need to restore a form of Christian civil religion as a pervasive influence within society. Tocqueville does not think this restoration of respect for religion a hopeless endeavor among the French. Tocqueville asserts later in his 1843 speech to the Chamber that the greatest glory of the French Revolution was to have taken the maxims of Christianity "from the religious sphere in order to make them inform the practical sphere of legislation," especially the Christian belief in the possibility of individual reformation (Tocqueville 1968, p. 80). In the same speech to the Chamber, Tocqueville claims to want penitentiaries to become "sanctuaries where repentance and morality can penetrate" as a result of the mutual work of philanthropic and religious morality (Tocqueville 1968, p. 83). Both state and society need to coordinate a healthy support for Christian principles in order to achieve the moral reformation of the individual in penitentiaries, and France's secularization of Christian principles does not preclude the efforts of religion in its society.

The penitentiary system in America, attracting to itself popular consent yet springing from the efforts of an unpopular religious sect, thus demonstrates the tangential effect a specific religion can have within a democracy. Religion infuses democracy with the import of the value of the human being disconnected from the value of that being's particular activities in society. Religion, in other words, gives the criminal's imagination a reprieve from shame and enables them to conceive of successful re-entrance into society. Honor in terms of religion also refers to the innate dignity of the human being. Honor is not always earned: it must sometimes be given unmerited. In that sense, honor represents a form of grace that religion, not society, affords. The individual dignity of the human being comes through an act of the religious imagination to conceive of each person's relationship to God, rather than a political understanding of man in relation to society (Tocqueville 1984, p. 193). By rejecting a purely materialistic view of human beings in their insistence on the reality of the human soul and its connection to the body, and by insisting on the necessity for penitentiary institutions to affect the soul in order to morally reform prisoners, Tocqueville and Beaumont open the logical pathway to argue for the benefits of civil religion in penal reform.

Moderation as the Means of Reform in a Liberal Democracy

Can human beings, then, be morally reformed through the thoughtful structuring of penal systems and laws? According to Tocqueville and Beaumont, only to a limited extent. Tocqueville admits such in a letter to his father before returning home, saying that they learned two important lessons regarding American penitentiaries: first, penitentiaries are more economical than the French penal system; second, the men who undergo punishment in penitentiaries do not leave the prison more corrupt than when they entered. However, Tocqueville asks: "But do they actually reform? I know no more here on this point than you do sitting by your fire; what is certain, is that I will not entrust my purse to these honest people."[57] *On the Penitentiary System* teaches us that the possibility of complete moral reformation must be tempered by a realistic expectation that preventing prisoners from becoming more corrupt might be the more achievable goal. Restraint, rather than perfection, ought to be the guiding theme of institutional penal reform.

Additionally, Tocqueville's moderate view of human nature which led him to reject a materialistic view of penal reform also allowed him to see the danger of pursuing penal theories without proper experiments. Penal theories without practice pose a danger in liberal democracies to both the freedom of the public and the freedom of the individual prisoner. In the case of French penal reform, untested theories led reformers to believe that moral regeneration of the prisoner was possible only through material and institutional means rather than accounting for the need to affect both body and soul through tools such as religious education. Immoderate theories also cut off the proper role of the public in democratic penal reform. The extremes that Tocqueville and Beaumont address in nineteenth-century French penal reform are warnings to any future penal reformers of the need to moderate theory with practice.

Finally, Tocqueville's moderate penal theory shows us how to balance competing arguments for prison disciplines through a moral lens. Tocqueville shows us who we are as human beings, composites of body and soul linked by our imaginations. Such self-knowledge allows us to restrain our efforts in and expectations of reforming prisoners via institutional means. By understanding the moral nature of human beings as affected not only by our physical circumstances but also by spiritual (or, psychological) realities, we can then evaluate the disciplines and institutions that are best equipped to shape that nature for successful reintegration into society and prevention of crime. For example, deciding whether prisons should include forced labor depends on an understanding of how bodily action affects the mind (i.e., whether it soothes or exasperates the prisoner). Similarly, determining whether prisons should include religious components depends on an evaluation of whether Tocqueville and Beaumont were correct in their assumptions regarding the relationship between the prisoner's conception of honor and their future ability to live an honest life in society. We, too, need to renew a rigorous view of the moral nature of human beings and the moral needs of prisoners. Even if complete moral reform lies outside the bounds of prison possibilities, it is a goal worth striving for within proper limits. Such a goal necessitates a measure of consensus on what constitutes civic morality in our society, and a collective willingness to hold persons accountable to achieving those standards by surrounding the individual with a community that will support and strengthen their moral efforts.

Notes

1. As the following argument will make clear, for Tocqueville, the "soul" (*l'âme*) is an element of the human being distinct from both mind (*l'esprit*) and body. Still, the mind is part of the soul and certain functions of the intellect (such as the imagination) are crucial to understanding the relationship between soul and body.
2. For an extended analysis of Tocqueville's understanding of the human oscillation between rest and motion in connection to Augustine's formulation of the tension, see Mitchell 1995, pp. 40–87.
3. Tocquevillian scholarship has generally asserted that Tocqueville does not present a universal view of human nature. See, for example, Levin 2008, p. 143; Maletz 2010, pp. 183–202; Manent 1998, pp. 79–84; Tocqueville 2000, p. xxvi; Zuckert 1993, p. 7. Zetterbaum points out that "Tocqueville's approach to the study of political things appears as a departure from the method of those political writers of the seventeenth and eighteenth centuries who began their inquiries with the study of man simply, irrespective of his citizenship in a particular regime. For Tocqueville, the study of politics begins with an inquiry into social condition" (1987, p. 761). Alternatively, Jech argues that by considering the human being's "generative conditions" Tocqueville does present a vision of man alone (2013, pp. 84–93). See also: Salomon 1935.
4. Tocqueville sees the relationship between body and soul as dependent; the soul does not exist independently of the body, and vice-versa. This is an anti-Cartesian position. Moreover, the soul cannot be reached solely through the body. There must be a spiritual means to reach the soul in addition to the material or corporal means. This view of the relationship between body and soul corresponds to Tocqueville's understanding of the role of religion within a society, as discussed later in the chapter.
5. According to Lawler, Tocqueville thinks "there is a closer connection than is supposed between the soul's improvement and the betterment of physical conditions" (1993, p. 63). I argue that *On the Penitentiary System* shows us the nature of that "closer connection." Tocqueville and Beaumont reject the ontology of man as machine and the notion of a historical progression of human beings, yet those rejections do not exclude an alternative relationship between the soul and the material world.
6. I am using the term "spiritual" to represent the French word *morale*, which has two primary meanings: "That which concerns the mind, psyche, or which is of a spiritual nature," and that which pertains "to the mores, customs, traditions and habits specific to a society during an epoch." Throughout *On the Penitentiary System*, Tocqueville uses *morale* in the first sense, but also suggests that both senses are intimately connected to

each other. In other words, the human mind is affected by the *mores* of the society in which the individual lives. For that reason, I use the term "spiritual cause" throughout the chapter to designate both senses of the term (that is, as a psychological cause which affects criminals' minds in order to promote moral behavior as defined by the surrounding social order). See: "morale" in *Trésor de la langue Française informatisé*. Hereafter cited as TLFi (2012).

7. In the chapter, "causality" denotes the older meaning of "explanation." To find the cause of civilization or crime, it is necessary to see what is responsible for its change or motion. According to TLFi (2012), "causalité" means "relation of cause to effect," where "cause" is the primary term and means "the necessity of each part, because of what is outside it, to be other than if it were alone." The *Dictionnaire de l'Académie Française* defines "causalité" as "manner in which a cause produces an effect." The main causality that must be discovered is what motivates change from criminal to moral inclinations within a human being, and whether political or social institutions can utilize or effect that cause.
8. My argument will proceed by drawing out these three contrasting pairs posed within the text. These three pairs of contrasting elements are not simply dualisms, but have a specific relationship to each other. This interpretive method follows Nolla's and Jaume's understanding that Tocqueville's philosophical method is to maintain contradictions (Nolla 1992, p. xxvi, xxiv; Jaume 2013, p. 174).
9. Imagination doesn't fit nicely into the distinction between body and soul because it is a mental (or, spiritual) faculty that requires bodies (or, physical objects). The presence of imagination in human beings prompts the questions: How is imagination connected to our physical experiences? Do penitentiary systems in general require a certain use of the imagination, and can they manipulate imagination through physical circumstances in order to effect reform? Tocqueville's and Beaumont's arguments through the progression of the series of contrasts answer these questions.
10. Mitchell argues that Tocqueville has a circular notion of cause and effect, rather than a unilinear one (1995, p. 18). Mansfield and Winthrop point out that Tocqueville deliberately confused causality in terms of politics and society to avoid returning to either a "classical founding" or a liberal "state of nature" (Tocqueville 2000, p. xliii).
11. In contrast to the dearth of penal experimenting in France, the American penitentiary in Philadelphia was primarily the result of experiments by a Protestant religious group to prove theoretical social inquiry. Adamson argues that "Quaker experimentalism fueled rational inquiry into the causes of crime" (2001, p. 38). If Adamson is correct, Tocqueville's and

Beaumont's emphasis on experiment might have been influenced by viewing a uniquely religious application of science to society.

12. The contradiction between material and spiritual causality can also be understood as that between nature and nurture. Tocqueville and Beaumont do not argue against philosophy as a whole; they draw a distinction between good philosophy and bad, where good philosophy acknowledges that human beings are contextualized throughout their lives by both material causes stemming from an environment (nurture) and spiritual causes that stem from the exercise of free will (nature).
13. Throughout *On the Penitentiary System*, Tocqueville and Beaumont identify three types of persons—the politician, the philosopher, and the philanthropist—who have the ability to direct society by influencing public opinion. The authors' arguments effectively re-balance political power between all three types of persons. Nolla argues that Tocqueville rejects the work of philosophers, particularly political philosophers, because their work does not belong to reality and lacks contact with political practice (1992, pp. xviii–xix). The arguments in *On the Penitentiary System* suggest that, at the very least, Tocqueville calls political philosophers to take account of political practice and policy, without necessarily rejecting their role in society.
14. Perrot states that "*Le Système Pénitentiaire* marks, in a certain way, the end of the philanthropic prison era whose "illusions" Tocqueville and Beaumont vigorously denounced" (Perrot 1984, p. 25; my translation). Wolin argues that there is a "distinctively modern or liberal temptation" toward democratic despotism which arises from "enlarged conceptions of power characteristic of the modern imagination and assumed by it to be available in reality [...] in imagination modern notions of experimentation were joined to modern forms of power—technological, military, and administrative—to support a claim that conditions (social and economic) could be effectively controlled so that "pure" solutions to carefully delineated problems were possible" (2001, p. 385).
15. Lawler asserts, "For Pascal and Tocqueville, imaginative deceit is as much a part of the human condition as the restless mind [...] the existence of human life depends upon "perpetual illusion," which is mostly self-flattery" (1993, p. 76). Maguire argues that for Tocqueville, the imagination was a medium for human freedom: an exalted imagination extends human pride toward great undertakings (2006, pp. 187–189).
16. Tocqueville 1984, p. 197. Tocqueville's American notebooks clarify his belief that it is almost impossible to morally reform human beings who are habituated in crime. After a conversation with Mr. Maxwell, the founder of the New York House of Correction, Tocqueville notes: "This belief in the uselessness of the penitentiary system as far as moral reform is concerned

seemed to us to be shared by a great number more of able men, among others those with practical experience" (1971, p. 6, 211). Human beings are therefore more capable of moral reform during their childhood than in adulthood. Tocqueville tends to agree with superintendents of the houses of refuge when they say that there is little hope of reform for boys after the age of 15, and for girls after the age of 14 (1971, p. 168). Yet he does not address the question of whether the moral lessons learned in childhood are kept through the duration of adulthood. Finally, Tocqueville's emphasis on the limits of moral reformation via institutions recurs throughout his political career, and evidences itself practically in his limited application of penitentiary systems to petty or first-time offenders who are not habituated to a lifestyle of crime.

17. Lawler connects the problem of social unrest to extreme philanthropic ideals: "Extreme mental disorder or restlessness, the inability of the mind to perceive any order at all and hence to find any rest, leads the imagination to generate misanthropic ideals, ones which oppose human liberty or distinctiveness" (1993, pp. 64–65). Similarly, Maletz derives from his study of Tocqueville that "those who resort to abstract theory as an imaginative substitute for real political life may paint glorious pictures of utopia, but the literature they produce has become exceptionally harmful when carried over into programs of public action" (2010, pp. 196–197).
18. Notably, Tocqueville and Beaumont suggest that the focus on material improvement results from a lack of religious motivation in French penal reform.
19. For a more in-depth description of the corruption that occurs in French prisons as a consequence of focusing on material comforts for prisoners, see Tocqueville's and Beaumont's case study on the life of the criminal Lacenaire in their revised Introduction to the second edition of *On the Penitentiary System* (Tocqueville 1984, pp. 117–118). Lacenaire's public reputation grew in inverse proportion to his repentance for his crime because of free communication and easy access to a cafeteria while in prison.
20. Tocqueville 1984, p. 214. See especially the discussion of the limits of statistics in I.3.2, beginning on pp. 207–218; and Statistical Notes No. 17, pp. 411–421.
21. Tocqueville 1984, p. 169. Francis Lieber, a contemporary of Tocqueville's, also emphasizes the role of experience in human life (1911, pp. 63–65).
22. Plato's *Republic* suggests *how* philosophy tends to uproot public opinion in the formulation of the contradiction inherent in the philosopher-king: philosophers are the most qualified to rule because they are freed from public opinion yet must be forced to rule because ruling does not contribute to the completion of the philosophic self. The philosopher pursues through

dialectic what is true, whereas the city-state does not depend on what is true but on a unified understanding of the good life. The best way of life (philosophy) thus undermines the stability of the best city (1991, pp. 151–161). Notably, Tocqueville and Beaumont seem to suggest that philosophy uproots public opinion simply by force of its speed in enacting legislation, rather than through any contradiction between truth and necessary "noble lies."

23. Tocqueville 1984, p. 234. Earlier, Tocqueville and Beaumont asserted that theoretical questions such as whether society has the right to do all that is necessary to punish recalcitrant criminals "are rarely discussed, to the interest of truth and human society" (Tocqueville 1984, p. 193). Both truth and human society, then, demand a measure of ignorance: human beings cannot know all things without harmful consequences to some good things. Experience, or common sense, filtered through public opinion indicates which things are necessary to question and which must be simply accepted. Additionally, here we see Tocqueville's and Beaumont's distinction between government and society which is vital to keep in mind. How can certain discussions be useful to the government, but problematic to society? The assertion assumes that both government and society are separate and independent realms whose goals can sometimes be opposed to each other. The government is a type of "political society" (*la société politique*), operating within the context of general society. Based on the context of the phrase, theoretical discussions are useful to the government if they contribute to governmental organization or control of political power, as opposed to policy recommendations.
24. Lieber translates this sentence: "Talent and capacity are directed towards one single object—politics" (Beaumont and Tocqueville 1833, p. 91).
25. Ceasar argues that Tocqueville's political science as a whole acts as an alternative to both philosophic rationalism and traditionalism, which includes an emphasis on habit in order to limit the influence of intellectuals on political culture (1985, pp. 656–672).
26. Levin formulates the benefit of political activity more narrowly as countering particular modern ideas: "political activity is at the heart of the cure to simultaneously oppose excessive individualism and overpowering collectivism so the souls of free individuals may flourish. This is because inactivity is what threatens democratic societies" (2008, p. 144). More deeply, however, Tocqueville's and Beaumont's inquiry into practical politics ultimately deals with universal human motivation. The authors implicitly question what motivates humans. The account that is given expands beyond security or fear, including honor, shame, profit, rest, and a desire for God.

27. See: Tocqueville 1984, p. 443. The excerpt from the journal was included by Tocqueville and Beaumont in an appendix to their second edition of *On the Penitentiary System*.
28. After returning from America, Tocqueville visited the Hôtel de Bazancourt, which operated as a house of correction for 25–30 young children sent there by their parents. Following the publication of the first edition of *On the Penitentiary System*, France saw an increased use of houses of refuge for juvenile delinquents. Tocqueville and Beaumont note in their Introduction to the second edition that the success of such institutions occurred mostly in eastern France, which evidenced greater industrialization (Tocqueville 1984, pp. 82–83, 116).
29. See: Tocqueville 1984, p. 206. Boesche argues that Tocqueville "views mere change in the external behavior of the criminal as insufficient, and he seeks a reformed prison that can transform [...] the ideas, habits, and even instincts" of human beings (1980, p. 555). In contrast, my argument takes into consideration the nuances in Tocqueville's approximation of whether such reform is possible.
30. Tocqueville expands his criticism of a wholly materialistic worldview in *Democracy in America* (2000, p. 517–520). As Lawler points out, Tocqueville criticizes "not materialistic doctrine but the materialists themselves who are infected with vanity" (2001, p. 220).
31. Note that Tocqueville and Beaumont use "communication" to refer not only to verbal messages, but also to lifestyles and the characteristics which define them. This double usage indicates that there is a connection between language and the body. Bodies present problems for discipline not because it is the flesh which contains the seed of corruption, as in a biblical sense, but because bodies are a means of communication even when language is prohibited. Bodies communicate by two means. First, men can develop body language to externally and physically communicate with each other. This physical language by its nature prevents the development of moral ideas, since it cannot release itself from its particular mode of communication to deal wholly with content. In other words, body language greatly narrows the content of information communicated, notably excluding moral ideas which are intangible. Morality thus requires a kind of verbal deliberation. The second means by which bodies "communicate" is inwardly with the self. Physical actions can support or strengthen pre-existent motives, intentions, purposes, and sentiments within an individual.
32. See: Tocqueville 1984, p. 197. As will be shown, absolute solitude can be said to be "purely intellectual" in that it results from an extreme theory that solitude only affects the minds of prisoners (not their bodies), and that it allows for human beings to guide themselves to reform when left completely alone.

33. A more detailed description of the wooden gallery was given in a letter from Tocqueville to the Ministry of the Interior while on the American journey; see Tocqueville 1984, p. 22.
34. For further discussion on this idea, see: Tocqueville 1984, p. 176, 184, 190, 197–199.
35. See: Tocqueville 1984, p. 159, 287–288. The quote comes from alphabetical note (c), which attempts to provide a more detailed explanation for the medical link between absolute solitude and pulmonary diseases afflicting prisoners in such conditions.
36. Notably, the French penal system already included what are called "central houses of hard labor," established since 1808. These were originally located in Poissy, Melun, Beaulieu, Gaillon, Fontevrault, Rion, Nimes, Thouars, Loos, Clairvaux, and three locations for women (Clairmont, Rennes, Montpelier). See: Roth 2006, p. 108.
37. Compare to Tocqueville's description in *Democracy in America* of the American southerner: "... the American of the South is not preoccupied with the material needs of life; someone else takes charge of thinking of them for him. Free on this point, his imagination is directed toward other greater objects, less exactly defined. The American of the South loves greatness, luxury, glory, noise, pleasures, above all idleness; nothing constrains him to make efforts in order to live, and as he has no necessary work, he falls asleep and does not even undertake anything useful" (Tocqueville 2000, p. 360). On the other hand, the Northerner is absorbed by material cares and so "his imagination is extinguished, his ideas are less numerous and less general, but they become more practical, more clear, and more precise [...] he understands marvelously the art of making society cooperate for the prosperity of each of its members and for extracting from individual selfishness the happiness of all" (Tocqueville 2000, pp. 360–361).
38. Not all political philosophers have acknowledged this "innate desire for honor" which Tocqueville and Beaumont assume. For example, Hegel argues that because all citizens are equal before the Emperor in China, no honor exists, and consequently "no one has an individual right in respect of others" (1956, p. 131). Hence, it is not the individual conscience or sense of honor "which keeps the offices of government up to their duty, but an external mandate and the severe sanctions by which it is supported" (Hegel 1956, p. 127). Additionally, punishments in China "are generally corporal chastisements. Among us, this would be an insult to honor; not so in China, where the feeling of honor has not yet developed itself. A dose of cudgeling is the most easily forgotten; yet it is the severest punishment for a man of honor [...] the Chinese do not recognize a subjectivity in honor; they are the subjects rather of corrective than retributive punishment" (Hegel 1956, p. 128). Notably, Hegel argues that "despotism is necessarily

the mode of government" in China due to the lack of an internal sense of honor and the total equality of the citizens (Hegel 1956, p. 124). Hegel's depiction of China resembles the critiques of *On the Penitentiary System* made by Avramenko, Boesche, Gingerich, and Wolin, who each assert that Tocqueville and Beaumont recommended penitentiaries despite their despotic qualities, most particularly their use of corporal punishment and extreme equality. Indeed, Hegel's description closely resembles the culture described in the Auburn prison system. Yet Tocqueville and Beaumont do not support such despotism as necessary to the "sub-culture" of the penitentiary. Instead, they stress the honor of the individual prisoner because it is the key to curbing the seeming despotism of penitentiaries.

39. Lieber notes in his Translator's Introduction, "if the whip is mentioned as a disciplinary measure, we must also mention labor as such, and if I mistake not it contributes much more to maintain order than the whip. That labor has a powerful disciplinary effect with criminals (it is the same with all men) the reader will find asserted by a high authority in the course of this book [...] it calms and assuages the mind of the irritated convict" (Beaumont and Tocqueville 1833, p. ix).
40. See: Tocqueville 1984, p. 236, 245, 237. Drolet argues that because "French sensibilities were at odds with a prison system that relied on physical coercion," Tocqueville and Beaumont suggested that "France adopt prisons like Wethersfield as a model" (2003, p. 129). While Tocqueville and Beaumont certainly elevate Wethersfield as the best possible penitentiary in the text, I am arguing that the discussion of corporal punishment in the text has a broader import than simply determining which penitentiary model France ought to use.
41. See: Tocqueville 1984, p. 169, 193, 234, 237.
42. See also *Democracy in America* II.3.18, "On Honor in the United States and in Democratic Countries." There, Tocqueville notes that there are two senses of the word "honor" in the French language. Honor signifies the esteem and glory attained from those like oneself, as well as "the sum of rules with the aid of which one obtains this glory, esteem, and consideration" (Tocqueville 2000, p. 589). Mitchell argues that Tocqueville saw honor "as the currency by which inequalities [...] are delineated" (2008, p. 551). Honor thus cannot be easily supplanted by love of commerce and equality.
43. According to the *Dictionnaire de l'Académie française*, "honneur" signifies variously: "the esteem, reputation which a person enjoys in the world," or "virtue, probity; quality that leads us to do noble, courageous, loyal deeds." In the plural, *honneur* can mean: "the action, the exterior demonstration by which one makes known the veneration, respect, esteem that one has for the dignity or merit of someone." The synonym of *honneur* is, notably, *honnête*.

44. Translation my own.
45. See: Tocqueville 1984, p. 206. Similarly, Lieber declares in his preface: "Let a former convict but acquire habits of honesty, and he will also gradually acquire honest views and feelings. Let him obey the just laws of our country, and he will soon love them" (Beaumont and Tocqueville 1833, p. xxiii).
46. Brogan criticizes Tocqueville and Beaumont for holding such an "extreme" view, rather than adhering more limitedly to the idea "that society's only right and interest is to require not that a former prisoner shall have saved his soul, but that he obey the laws..." (2006, p. 227). Brogan also criticizes Tocqueville for immoderation in extending sympathy toward prisoners, yet does so through a Foucauldian lens (2006, pp. 228–229). My argument in this work suggests the opposite, that Tocqueville and Beaumont attempted to balance the rights of society with those of the individual prisoner. This balance can be seen in how Tocqueville and Beaumont bifurcate the types of possible individual reformation and moderately evaluate their potential success. The balance between the rights of individual and state in penal reform leads to a moderated view of the purposes of the prison, namely one that includes retribution, prevention, *and* both social and spiritual redemption.
47. Note that by using the word *render*, as opposed to *donner*, Tocqueville and Beaumont imply an originally pure state of the soul. Tocqueville 1984, pp. 203–204.
48. Notably, there is no discussion in *On the Penitentiary System* of what *kind* of religion performs the task of bringing individuals to accept moral pardon from God; however, given the context of penitentiary reform as stemming from Quakerism, it could be argued that Tocqueville and Beaumont assumed that the religion would be, at the very least, a form of Christianity, if not Protestantism more particularly.
49. See: Tocqueville 1984, p. 205. See also Tocqueville's note in his interviews with prisoners No. 47 and No. 00 (Tocqueville 1984, pp. 336–341). Elam Lynds articulates the same opinion in his interview with the authors (Tocqueville 1984, pp. 342–345).
50. Out of 26 prisoners pardoned in the early stages of the American penitentiary reform, 14 returned to prison (Tocqueville 1984, p. 22). See also the statistics given in Appendices No. 16 §2 and No. 11 (Tocqueville 1984, p. 389, 413).
51. Catherine Zuckert suggests that religious belief in Tocqueville's thought is reduced to "the sanctity of the human being or freedom of conscience" in order to be useful for democracy (1981, p. 279).

52. Appendix No. 13, concerning the Boston House of Refuge, includes the regulation that tattle-tales will only be allowed if it is evident that the child acts for the sake of their conscience (Tocqueville 1984, pp. 369–370).
53. The following argument contributes to the ongoing debate in Tocquevillian scholarship over whether Tocqueville considered religion in a purely utilitarian light, as opposed to considering the merits of the particular content of religious belief as fundamental to the good of individuals and societies. As will be presented, the argument in *On the Penitentiary System* seems to bridge both sides of the debate by not only presenting religion as socially useful in encouraging the moral reform of criminals, but also as necessary for the individual to regain self-esteem which is vital for successfully operating within a commercial democratic society. For those who argue that Tocqueville emphasized the social and political utility of religion, see Koritansky 1990; Lively 1962, p. 183; Zetterbaum 1967. Mansfield presents a convincing argument that, in terms of the structure of *Democracy in America*, Tocqueville "considered religion's utility to democracy" in Volume 1 and "the truth of religion" in Volume 2 (2010, p. 61). Tessitore also attempts to argue a middle course when he says that Tocqueville saw Protestantism as moderating the extremes of religious sectarianism and godless secularism (2002). But compare with: Kessler 1992. For scholars who argue that Tocqueville respected the content of religion, see Deneen 2005; Goldstein 1975; Hancock 1991; Mitchell 1995, pp. 183–187; Sloat 2000, p. 775.
54. Lawler argues that "Tocqueville follows Pascal in showing that the need for faith is at the core of man's true greatness" based on man's hope for resolution to the contradictions of human existence (1993, p. 145). For others who argue that Tocqueville viewed religion as innate to human beings, see: Galston 1987; Mansfield 2010, p. 53; Mitchell 1995, pp. 183–187; Yenor 2004, pp. 10–17.
55. Tocqueville says later in *Democracy in America*: "The short space of sixty years will never confine the whole imagination of man; the incomplete joys of this world will never suffice for his heart [...] religion is therefore only a particular form of hope, and it is as natural to the human heart as hope itself" (Tocqueville 2000, pp. 283–284).
56. Kahan argues that, "for Tocqueville, human nature has a natural tendency toward belief in God and spirituality, regardless of the social context" (2015, p. 105). In the context of my argument, although each individual is naturally aware of their relationship to God, religion supplies the particular knowledge of God necessary to confirm their human dignity.
57. The word for "honest men" here is: *honnêtes gens*. Letter de Tocqueville à son Père, Hartford, 7 Octobre 1832. Yale Tocqueville Manuscripts. General Collection, Beinecke Rare Book and Manuscript Library, Yale University. B.I.a.2, Box 4.

References

1835. *Dictionnaire de l'Académie française*, 6th ed. Vols. 1 and 2. The ARTFL Project. http://artfl-project.uchicago.edu/node/17. Accessed 24 March 2016.

2012. TLFi: Trésor de la langue Française informatisé. *ATILF—CNRS & Université de Lorraine*. http://www.atilf.fr/tlfi. Accessed 13 November 2017.

Adamson, Christopher. 2001. Evangelical Quakerism and the Early American Penitentiary Revisited: The Contributions of Thomas Eddy, Roberts Vaux, John Griscom, Stephen Grellet, Elisha Bates, and Isaac Hopper. *Quaker History* 90 (2): 35–58.

Beaumont, Gustave de and Alexis de Tocqueville. 1833. *On the Penitentiary System in the United States and Its Application in France, with an Appendix on Penal Colonies and also Statistical Notes*, trans. Francis Lieber. Philadelphia: Carey, Lea & Blanchard.

Boesche, Roger. 1980. The Prison: Tocqueville's Model for Despotism. *The Western Political Quarterly* 33: 550–563.

Brogan, Hugh. 2006. *Alexis de Tocqueville: A Life*. New Haven: Yale University Press.

Ceasar, James. 1985. Alexis de Tocqueville on Political Science, Political Culture, and the Role of the Intellectual. *American Political Science Review* 79 (3): 656–672.

Deneen, Patrick. 2005. The Only Permanent State: Tocqueville on Religion and Democracy. In *Democratic Faith*, 214–239. Princeton: Princeton University Press.

Drolet, Michael. 2003. *Tocqueville, Democracy, and Social Reform*. New York: Palgrave Macmillan.

Galston, William. 1987. Tocqueville on Liberalism and Religion. *Social Research* 54 (3): 499–518.

Goldstein, Doris. 1975. *Trial of Faith: Religion and Politics in Tocqueville's Thought*. New York: Elsevier.

Hancock, Ralph. 1991. The Uses and Hazards of Christianity in Tocqueville's Attempt to Save Democratic Souls. In *Interpreting Tocqueville's "Democracy in America"*, ed. Ken Magusi, 348–393. Savage: Rowman and Littlefield.

Hegel, Georg Wilhelm Friedrich. 1956. *The Philosophy of History*, trans. J. Sibree. New York: Dover Publications.

Jaume, Lucien. 2013. *Tocqueville: The Aristocratic Sources of Liberty*, trans. Arthur Goldhammer. Princeton: Princeton University Press.

Jech, Alexander. 2013. 'Man Simply': Excavating Tocqueville's Conception of Human Nature. *Perspectives on Political Science* 42 (2): 84–93.

Kahan, Alan. 2015. Checks and Balances for Democratic Souls: Alexis de Tocqueville in Democratic Societies. *American Political Thought* 4 (1): 100–119.

Kessler, Sanford. 1992. Tocqueville's Puritans: Christianity and the American Founding. *The Journal of Politics* 54 (3): 776–791.

Koritansky, John C. 1990. Civil Religion in Tocqueville's *Democracy in America. Interpretation* 17: 389–401.

Lawler, Peter Augustine. 1993. The Restless Mind. In *Tocqueville's Defense of Human Liberty: Current Essays*, ed. Peter Augustine Lawler and Joseph Alulis, 63–85. New York: Garland Publishing.

———. 2001. Tocqueville on Pantheism, Materialism, and Catholicism. *Perspectives on Political Science* 30 (4): 218–226.

Levin, Yuval. 2008. Democracy and Human Nature: Lawler and Tocqueville on the Modern Individual. *Perspectives on Political Science* 37 (3): 142–146.

Lieber, Francis. 1911. *Manual of Political Ethics*, 2nd ed., ed. Theodore D. Woolsey. Philadelphia: J. B. Lippincott.

Lively, Jack. 1962. *The Social and Political Thought of Alexis de Tocqueville*. Oxford: Clarendon Press.

Maguire, Matthew. 2006. *The Conversion of Imagination: From Pascal Through Rousseau to Tocqueville*. Cambridge: Harvard University Press.

Maletz, Donald. 2010. Tocqueville on Human Nature and Natural Right. *Interpretation* 37 (2): 183–202.

Manent, Pierre. 1998. Democratic Man, Aristocratic Man, and Man Simply: Some Remarks on Equivocation in Tocqueville's Thought. *Perspectives on Political Science* 27 (2): 79–84.

Mansfield, Harvey. 2010. *Tocqueville: A Very Short Introduction*. Oxford: Oxford University Press.

Mitchell, Joshua. 1995. *The Fragility of Freedom: Tocqueville on Religion, Democracy, and the American Future*. Chicago: University of Chicago Press.

———. 2008. Tocqueville for a Terrible Era: Honor, Religion, and the Persistence of Atavisms in the Modern Age. *Critical Review* 19 (4): 543–564.

Nolla, Eduardo. 1992. Introduction. In *Liberty, Equality, Democracy*, ed. Eduardo Nolla, xv–xxiii. New York: New York University Press.

O'Brien, Patricia. 1982. *The Promise of Punishment: Prisons in Nineteenth-Century France*. Princeton: Princeton University Press.

Perrot, Michelle. 1984. "Tocqueville Méconnu." In *OEuvres Complètes: Écrits sur le système pénitentiaire en France et à l'étranger, Tome IV, Vol. 1*, ed. Michelle Perrot, 7–44. Paris: Gallimard.

Plato. 1991. *The Republic of Plato*, 2nd ed., trans. Allan Bloom. New York: Basic Books.

Roth, Mitchel P. 2006. France. In *Prisons and Prison Systems: A Global Encyclopedia*. Westport, CT: Greenwood Press.

Salomon, Albert. 1935. Tocqueville, Moralist and Sociologist. *Social Research: An International Quarterly of Political and Social Science* 2 (4): 405–427.

Sloat, James M. 2000. The Subtle Significance of Sincere Belief: Tocqueville's Account of Religious Belief and Democratic Stability. *Journal of Church and State* 42 (4): 759–779.

Tessitore, Aristide. 2002. Alexis de Tocqueville on the Natural State of Religion in the Age of Democracy. *The Journal of Politics* 64 (4): 1137–1152.

Tocqueville, Alexis de. 1968. *Tocqueville and Beaumont on Social Reform*, ed. and trans. Seymour Drescher. New York: Harper Torch Books.

———. 1971. *Journey to America*, trans. George Lawrence, ed. J.P. Mayer. New York: Doubleday Anchor Books.

———. 1984. *Œuvres Complètes: Écrits sur le système pénitentiaire en France et à l'étranger, Tome IV, Vol. 1*, ed. Michelle Perrot. Paris: Gallimard.

———. 2000. *Democracy in America*, ed. and trans. Harvey Mansfield and Delba Winthrop. Chicago: University of Chicago.

Wolin, Sheldon. 2001. *Tocqueville Between Two Worlds: The Making of a Political and Theoretical Life*. Princeton: Princeton University Press.

Yenor, Scott. 2004. Natural Religion and Human Perfectibility: Tocqueville's Account of Religion in Modern Democracy. *Perspectives on Political Science* 33 (1): 10–17.

Zetterbaum, Marvin. 1967. *Tocqueville and the Problem of Democracy*. Stanford: Stanford University Press.

———. 1987. Alexis de Tocqueville: 1805–1859. In *History of Political Philosophy*, ed. Leo Strauss and Joseph Cropsey, 3rd ed., 761–784. Chicago: University of Chicago Press.

Zuckert, Catherine. 1981. Not by Preaching: Tocqueville on the Role of Religion in American Democracy. *The Review of Politics* 43 (2): 259–280.

Zuckert, Michael. 1993. On Social State. In *Tocqueville's Defense of Human Liberty: Current Essays*, ed. Peter A. Lawler and Joseph Alulis, 1–17. New York: Garland Publishers.

CHAPTER 3

Tocqueville's Moderate Penal Activity

Within contemporary American political culture, growing affirmation of diversity often increases our difficulty to achieve consensus on what is the common good. Democratic pluralism can lead to political and intellectual polarization; it thus imposes upon us a responsibility to resist the temptation of extreme ideology and instead seek to achieve a moderated consensus on certain political policies and issues. One example of the effect of democratic plurality on our public discourse surrounding the common good can be seen in recent scholarly interpretations of the works of Alexis de Tocqueville. Our understanding of the political philosophy of Tocqueville has of late become entangled in a dispute over American exceptionalism.[1] Tocqueville has sometimes been cited as the source of American exceptionalism, supplying the idea that the United States possesses unique liberal characteristics which account for the success of its democracy.[2] On the other hand, some argue that Tocqueville's political thought includes important deviances from liberal principles, namely racism as a justification for French colonialism in Algeria.[3] Indeed, part of the complication in understanding Tocqueville's liberalism arose with the publication of Tocqueville's newly translated works on the colonization of Algeria and Ireland in 1958 and 2001 (Tocqueville 1958, 2001). While early scholars downplayed Tocqueville's support for French colonialism, others have since criticized Tocqueville's involvement in Algerian colonization as an apparent refusal to apply liberal principles to his evaluation of unjust imperial measures.[4]

E. K. Ferkaluk, *Tocqueville's Moderate Penal Reform*,
Recovering Political Philosophy,
https://doi.org/10.1007/978-3-319-75577-9_3

Tocqueville's entanglement in the issue of American exceptionalism evidences as much about our current intellectual spirit as it does about Tocqueville. It reveals a certain immoderation that contradicts the true root of American exceptionalism per Tocqueville's analysis. American democracy is exceptional because it balances various facets of democratic pluralism that act as the animating principles of the American way of life. That Tocqueville recognized this type of moderate balance as a political virtue in the American liberal democracy is revealed in his proposed solution to France's political problem of how to best remedy the failure of their criminal justice system.[5] Exploring how Tocqueville moderately pursued penal policy in France against the backdrop of British imperialism through the text of *On the Penitentiary System* helps us to both moderate our view of Tocqueville's political philosophy and understand the importance of moderation to public policy crafting in liberal democracies.

Was Tocqueville a Moderate, or an Imperialist?

In general, scholars give four answers to the question of why Tocqueville supported Algerian colonization. Either Tocqueville supported French colonialism as a means to enliven French nationalism at home, to establish France as a legitimate power in the international scene (thus offsetting Britain's growing imperialism), because he agreed with the ideal of *mission civilisatrice* (the justification of colonization on the basis of the spread of civilization), or finally because he deluded himself in turning a blind eye to the moral problems of colonization.[6] These answers typically portray Tocqueville's support for imperialism as antagonistic toward any classical liberal principles he seems to have held.

Four exceptions to the consensus that there is an inconsistency or tension between Tocqueville's support for colonialism and liberalism can also be noted. Tzvetan Todorov argues based on social contract theory that Tocqueville's colonialism is an extension, rather than a contradiction, of his liberalism (1988). More recently, Jennifer Pitts argues that Tocqueville supported French imperialism out of a desire to sustain the liberal order in France; hence, Tocqueville's liberalism necessitates the material support of empire (2005, pp. 230–240). Refuting Pitts' argument, Demin Duan attempts to resolve the tension between Tocqueville's liberalism and imperialism by arguing that Tocqueville supports imperialism as a balance of power at the international level (2010, p. 444). Finally, Paul Carrese suggests that Tocqueville's work on Algeria reflects a moderated understanding of what can be politically achieved in an era of increasing globalization, since "France must have both the soft power or attractive prestige of liberal principles and the hard power of arms and credible threats in order to steer affairs toward liberal ends" (2011, p. 311). In sum, these scholars mediate the apparent antagonism between Tocqueville's liberalism and imperialism by arguing that imperialism is, in part, an outgrowth of classical liberal or republican principles.

Notably, *On the Penitentiary System* was published far before Tocqueville's substantial involvement in shaping France's Algerian policy. Tocqueville published his first and second editions of *On the Penitentiary System* in 1833 and 1836; his first visit to Algeria was in 1841. Although the work ostensibly analyzes the American penitentiary system, it is also intended to address the French political problem of instituting a just domestic penal policy against the backdrop of Britain's imperial foreign colonialism (Brogan 2006, p. 263). At the time, the French public faced a growing problem of recidivism and a choice between three penal solutions: agricultural colonies, penitentiary systems, or penal colonies. Fears of criminal recidivism led the public to call for a seemingly easy but immoderately risky policy of penal colonies from the national government.

As the following sections will demonstrate, Tocqueville and Beaumont intend to moderate the French public's fears through a two-part argument. The authors seek to prove France's incapacity to successfully pursue a policy of penal colonization which promotes material and moral immoderation. Instead, Tocqueville and Beaumont attempt to persuade the French to adopt penitentiary systems because they promote a balance between centralized and decentralized political power. By choosing penitentiary systems as the best possible mode of penal reform, Tocqueville and Beaumont seek to strengthen public opinion against a potentially confrontational international policy of establishing foreign French penal colonies.[7] *On the Penitentiary System* teaches the French public how to be moderate in penal reform to both obtain justice for the criminal (understood as moral reformation of the individual) and avoid a reputation for injustice garnered by imperial actions. Tocqueville thereby preserves the justice of French liberalism by pursuing a policy of moderate penal reform.

France: Recognizing the Need to Moderate Public Fear of Criminals

Tocqueville and Beaumont undertook their study of penitentiaries on behalf of the French government, but they published *On the Penitentiary System* on behalf of the French public. The authors take care to indicate their intended audience within the Preface. Since the French government had already received the report well before the publication of the manuscript, *On the Penitentiary System* was published as "an account of our [Tocqueville's and Beaumont's] labors" to French citizens.[8] Hence, the report is not simply a technical work intended to guide policy discussion within the government. *On the Penitentiary System* is a political work intended to also moderate public opinion by enlightening French citizens on the exigencies and complications in justly resolving the problem of crime.

Public opinion needs moderated because collective fear is the primary passion governing France's discussions of crime. The Preface begins by stating that there are two million paupers and forty thousand liberated convicts in France, a fact that provokes fear in the public (Tocqueville 1984, p. 153). Freed convicts are proper objects of fear since they are corrupted further during their stay in prison (Tocqueville 1984, p. 246). The public fears that released convicts will commit more injustice after returning to society.

Fear of recidivism is rooted in two assumptions related to the justice of the nation. First, the public assumes that moral reformation of human beings is impossible, or at least, improbable. Justice toward prisoners includes the idea that it is the state's responsibility to reform criminals of their lifestyle or habit of crime. The growing problem of recidivism thus reflects a lack of concern for the justice of the penal system to prisoners; released criminals evidence the moral neglect of French prisons. Second, the public assumes that the presence of ex-criminals is always an immutable and unjust danger to society. The policy of establishing penal colonies reflects an impulsive resolution to the problem of recidivism, since deporting criminals immediately mitigates the danger of freed criminals. Tocqueville and Beaumont admit that "the deported person reappears only rarely on the native soil; with him departs a fertile seed of disorders and new crimes" (Tocqueville 1984, p. 267). Yet the idea of deportation is simplistic and designed for mass consumption, rather than as a moderate and just solution to a long-term problem. Tocqueville's and Beaumont's use of moderation thus aims at both justice in terms of the treatment of prisoners and justice as the international reputation of France's burgeoning liberal democracy. Tocqueville and Beaumont want to give the public the ability to deliberate on alternative methods of penal reform so that they will be able to make an informed, moderate decision on the relative justice of penal options.

Tocqueville and Beaumont not only acknowledge the problem of public fear in response to increased criminality, but also the problematic public reaction to such fear. The authors address the French public because they see the French public as the proper actors in resolving the problem of crime (Tocqueville 1984, p. 247). Penal reform is not simply a political affair; it is also a social problem needing local care. Yet "political events cause such preoccupation that even the most important questions of interior improvement but feebly excite public attention" (Tocqueville 1984, p. 234). Instead of taking responsibility for increased recidivism rates, the French public has incorrectly asked the centralized French government to supply a remedy to the issues of poverty and crime. Penal colonies are a convenient solution predicated on the power of national centralization. To persuade the public away from penal colonies, Tocqueville and Beaumont will need to convince local governments of their own responsibility in effecting penal reform. Hence, Tocqueville and Beaumont must seek to establish a moderating tension between centralization and decentralization of administrative power over penal systems in France.

In response to the need to moderate public fear and over-centralization, Tocqueville and Beaumont attempt the task of educating the public on all of the options for penal remedies available to France. Tocqueville and Beaumont seek to give self-knowledge of France's political capacities to the French public by demonstrating which penal institution can be best established within France, given French resources and circumstances (Ossewaarde 2004, p. 2). The authors thereby seek to teach the French public two maxims for greatness in both nations and individuals: to undertake "not all that one desires but all that one is capable of" and to judge self "without weakness, all the while preserving the correct confidence of our powers" (Tocqueville 1984, p. 284). Greatness comes through self-moderation, and such moderation can be achieved by knowing the limits of one's capabilities. Tocqueville and Beaumont therefore deliberately balance the different penal options to temper or avoid the risks involved in each of them.

Importantly, penitentiaries are the best possible penal solution, rather than the ideal. In the early arguments of *On the Penitentiary System*, agricultural colonies appear superior to both penitentiaries and penal colonies. Experience shows that stagnant lands become productive with sufficient capital and effort; hence, transporting otherwise unemployed persons to agricultural colonies ostensibly benefits the nation (Tocqueville 1984, p. 309). Agricultural colonies are also seemingly superior to penitentiary systems because they do not necessitate "administrative surveillance whose consequences are almost all disastrous" to the freed convicts.[9] Whereas penitentiary systems comprise an elaborate administrative structure, forced labor at agricultural colonies relies on the inability of colonists to return to society by uniting them in a single location, giving them all restrictive clothing "in order to make flight less easy," and forcing them to work under the direction of a guardian (Tocqueville 1984, p. 311). Monitoring the daily work of prisoners in agricultural colonies does not require the complicated bureaucratic system of inspectors, superintendents, contractors, and wardens that penitentiary systems necessitate.

Likewise, Tocqueville and Beaumont argue that agricultural colonies rely upon a different form of surveillance from that of penitentiaries. Agricultural colonies enable the government to use police surveillance upon freed convicts and the poor classes (Tocqueville 1984, p. 244). In France, *surveillance de haute police* had a particular penal meaning up until 1885: "Penal accessory in criminal and correctional matters, whose effect is to give to the government the right to determine the residence of the criminal and to require him to present himself to the authority at fixed times."[10] Agricultural colonies were thus designed as a semi-permanent type of parole system for criminals, rather than as a temporary place of imprisonment.

Further, the surveillance of agricultural colonies differs from that of penitentiaries because the institutions extend their influence over different types of people. Penitentiaries are confined to influencing only those persons who enter their walls; society in general cannot be reformed through penitentiary discipline. On the other hand, agricultural colonies are a governmental means of supplying labor to the poorest of the nation. Forced agricultural colonies include the innocent poor person as well as the criminal.[11] Thus, agricultural colonies have the opportunity to affect a wider range of persons than penitentiary systems.

Indeed, to some degree the authors equate the problem of crime with the problem of poverty. Tocqueville and Beaumont identify the material problem contributing to rising recidivism in France as the physical discomfort experienced by the poorest classes in society. Because the poor lack "labor and bread," they commit crimes. The punishment for crime, imprisonment, subsequently solidifies their corruption by creating communities of inmates who influence each other (Tocqueville 1984, p. 152). Still, how do Tocqueville and Beaumont make the connection between poverty, which is sourced in deficiency of material goods, and crime?[12]

The relationship between poverty and crime can be understood through the use of the word *misère* in the text of *On the Penitentiary System*. There are two important senses to the French word *misère*. In the first sense, *misère* can mean an unhappy state, extreme poverty, or deprivation of things necessary to life. Yet *misère* can also "express the weakness and nothingness (*le néant*) of man."[13] More broadly, Tocqueville and Beaumont assume that misery in the second sense, not just poverty, is a compelling human motivation behind crime.[14] Tocqueville and Beaumont use *misère* in this second sense by arguing that without physical labor the human being gains a view of his "nothingness."

To begin to understand the use of *misère* in the text, it is helpful to see that Tocqueville and Beaumont present work and misery as binary opposites. The authors claim that a nation increases its poverty (*misère*) by disturbing industrial manufacturing and business through political divisions, thereby augmenting crime.[15] Conversely, work is sought as a distraction from misery (Tocqueville 1984, p. 189). Impoverishment can be remedied by industries such as farming (Tocqueville 1984, p. 309). Poverty thus results from lack of honest work.

Specifically, Tocqueville and Beaumont reveal that poverty promotes restlessness in the soul as a consequence of lacking industry, rather than lacking material goods which are the products of work. Poverty represents the moral difficulty that results from a deficiency of bodily work (Tocqueville 1984, pp. 394–395, 401). Human beings would still be miserable if they had every necessary material good but no labor to occupy their time. Such is the condition of prisoners in solitary confinement, who are materially cared for yet miserable if not laboring in their cells. Thus, Tocqueville and Beaumont argue: "It seems to us that in such matters it is necessary to carefully distinguish the poverty that is born from a physical and material incapacity from the one that comes from other causes" (Tocqueville 1984, p. 320). Bad social habits are one cause of the second type of poverty. Tocqueville and Beaumont argue that "the true pauper has almost always contracted habits of sloth that are difficult to change"

(Tocqueville 1984, p. 319). The impoverished person in both senses of the word *misère* lacks orderly habits of labor that would give them the skill of foresight. Habitual laziness reinforces to the individual what they lack, or, their weakness in securing the necessary items of life. Laziness leads to poverty, and poverty results in crime.[16]

A second cause of poverty is ill-conceived poverty laws. A poverty law that becomes a regular form of assistance, outside of providing for those who physically cannot help themselves, "always depraves the population that it is expected to relieve" because it underpins the poor moral and social choices of the impoverished. Tocqueville argues that the poor cannot have an open right to receive provision from the state simply because their circumstances are miserable.[17] Charity should not become a political right implemented through social institutions such as almshouses because it thereby tends to increase the number of poor persons as well as social tension between the unemployed poor and honest workers (Tocqueville 1984, pp. 320–321).[18] Because it is also laziness that leads to poverty, rather than mere physical incapacity, the law cannot effectively seek to directly remedy the "misery" of the people by providing the material necessities of human life such as food and housing. Human beings must be taught that the true source of happiness and relief from poverty lies in an honest life of labor rather than in a corrupted lifestyle that seeks to gain material well-being outside of the law. Consequently, poverty laws need to teach human beings the dignity and benefits of desiring to labor, rather than simply giving the benefits of labor to the impoverished.

Nevertheless, those who experience poverty due to laziness create a peculiar administrative difficulty for penal legislation. The only way to educate the citizenry to love labor is to enable them to labor. Yet the poor man "contests the right of society to force him by violence to a fruitless labor and to hold him against his will" (Tocqueville 1984, pp. 319–320). In its simplest terms, the problem for the government is that the lazy person does not desire and cannot be legally forced to work. Nevertheless, those who are poor because of moral choice have the same habits as criminals (namely, an inability or lack of desire to profit society through honest work) which give the government an interest in reforming them, since they pose a danger to the rule of law and social order. The conflict boils down to a contradiction between the lack of individual rule and order possessed by an impoverished person, in the case of poverty caused by laziness, and the rule of law necessarily extending from the government.

Based on this understanding of poverty, Tocqueville and Beaumont argue that agricultural colonies are the solution to resolving the administrative difficulty involved in legally addressing poverty. Agricultural colonies "make arms useful" and provide the opportunity for labor that the poorest classes need to stay out of crime (Tocqueville 1984, p. 153). Further, agricultural colonies incentivize the poor to relocate and work by choice, rather than by force, since they allow the colonist to own their own farm after a certain number of years. For this reason, Tocqueville and Beaumont recommend that not only convicted criminals be sent to agricultural colonies, but also those in poverty who are tempted by crime. The report argues that if agricultural colonies were established on the uncultivated soil of France, "no idler would complain of lacking work without the government offering it to him; beggars, vagabonds, paupers, and all free prisoners whose number, always growing, incessantly threatens the safety of individuals and even the tranquility of the State would find a place in the colony, where they would work to augment the wealth of the country" (Tocqueville 1984, p. 244). By incentivizing vagrants to work, the government addresses laziness as one cause of poverty while avoiding the administrative conflict of the poor individual's claim to be free from government's coercion.

Finally, in weighing the benefits of agricultural colonies, Tocqueville and Beaumont note that agricultural colonies do not necessarily harm manufacturing industries within the country, whereas penitentiary systems have the potential to negatively compete with free market manufacturing (Tocqueville 1984, p. 320). Agricultural colonies could become economically useful to the state by enriching unused land and creating work that only contributes to sustaining the laborer, rather than enabling the laborer to enter the free market.[19] Farming does not directly compete with manufacturing. Tocqueville's *Memoir on Pauperism* helps us to understand this argument in support of agricultural colonies in *On the Penitentiary System*. In his *Memoir*, Tocqueville contrasts agriculture with manufacturing industry:

> The farmer produces basic necessities. The market may be better or worse, but it is almost guaranteed; and if an accidental cause prevents the disposal of agricultural produce, this produce at least gives its harvester something to live on and permits him to wait for better times. The worker, on the contrary, speculates on secondary needs which a thousand causes can restrict and important events completely eliminate. However bad the times or the market, each man must have a certain minimum of nourishment.... (Tocqueville 1968, p. 9)

Thus, agriculture provides a certain economic independence to the individual that is beneficial for the government to promote. Additionally, the authors clarify that agricultural colonies can accomplish the same goal the public expects from penal colonies without the expenses or difficulties involved in establishing the latter: to keep freed criminals away from general society.

In contrast to agricultural colonies, penitentiaries create new market difficulties in a commercial society. Penitentiaries have the option of forcing prisoners to build their own prisons, thereby utilizing labor outside of the free market. Moreover, manufacturing labor is given to the prisoners in penitentiaries in part to repay society the costs of maintaining prisoners who broke social laws. Yet the prisoner's labor injects more manufactured goods into the free market. Not only does inmate labor inflate market supply, but the penitentiary also has the advantage of being able to sell those manufactured goods at a lower price than those produced by free laborers, since the prisoners do not need to be reimbursed as highly, if at all. Additionally, penitentiaries have the potential to negatively affect the free market by introducing more workers—either those who work cheaply or at no cost in prisons, or those who otherwise would not have entered the market as a skilled laborer on their own power.[20]

Hence, in their support for agricultural colonies Tocqueville and Beaumont present an alternative to an international form of colonization (penal colonies) but espouse a domestic form of colonization. As will be shown below, Tocqueville and Beaumont argue that deportation of prisoners to a penal colony is not a penal system designed to justly punish, rehabilitate, or reintegrate prisoners; it is instead a deficient mode of colonization (Tocqueville 1984, p. 271). In contrast to penal colonies, agricultural colonies are to be located on unused French land as opposed to foreign territory (Tocqueville 1984, p. 320). It is therefore clear that Tocqueville and Beaumont support some forms of colonization.[21] Colonization is not necessarily a form of international imperialism. Rather, colonization can occur domestically to resolve internal national problems without the intent to conquer foreign peoples.

Despite the advantages of agricultural colonies over both penitentiary systems and penal colonies, in the end Tocqueville and Beaumont suggest that agricultural colonies are to act as a corollary penal institution to the penitentiary rather than as an alternative. Agricultural colonies pick up where the influence of the penitentiary ends in the life of the criminal.

Since they utilize police surveillance, agricultural colonies can be used to supply freed convicts with jobs and to continue to keep such convicts separate from general society. In this way, Tocqueville and Beaumont can support both agricultural colonies and penitentiary systems as viable penal alternatives to establishing penal colonies. The emphasis of the report remains on convincing the French public of the need to erect penitentiaries, not to establish agricultural colonies.

In light of the many benefits of agricultural colonies compared to penitentiary systems, Tocqueville's and Beaumont's support for penitentiary systems represents their moderation as statesmen as well as the moderating effect statesmen can have upon public opinion. Notably, penitentiary systems have a humanitarian goal that is absent from both agricultural and penal colonies. Tocqueville and Beaumont thus choose to promote the policy most likely to persuade the public against penal colonies, while also pointing out the benefits of an equally effective alternative in agricultural colonies. By focusing on the benefits of penitentiaries, Tocqueville and Beaumont appear to seek a penal solution to recidivism with an understanding of what is the best possible solution given French circumstances, rather than appealing to a potentially unachievable political ideal. Tocqueville and Beaumont hence turn to compare the American experience of domestic penitentiary systems with the British experience of penal colonies located on foreign territory to determine the best policy option for remedying France's problem with crime.

Britain: Justly Avoiding the Material and Moral Extremes of Imperialism

Tocqueville and Beaumont attempt to moderate the French public's inclination toward imperial action by arguing against an attractive but mistaken solution modeled on British penal colonialism. According to the authors, the establishment and maintenance of penal colonies is more difficult than publicists dare convey to the French public.[22] Specifically, the success of imperial endeavors such as penal colonies depends on material and moral extremes. A liberal nation should attempt to avoid such extremes to preserve its reputation for justice. However, the French public mistakenly believes they can successfully establish a penal colony without realizing their limitations or the potential unintended consequences. Thus, Tocqueville and Beaumont accomplish the first step in pursuing moderation in penal policy: they give the French public self-knowledge of their incapacity to successfully establish penal colonies, thereby avoiding the material and moral risks associated with this penal option.[23]

Britain's experience reveals three material extremes associated with penal colonies. First, the British colony at Botany Bay (now Australia) was almost destroyed by famine and disease, indicating the topographical difficulties in finding a suitable location for the colony (Tocqueville 1984, p. 271). An extreme geographical specificity is necessary for penal colonies to be successful. The soil on the new land must be healthy and fertile; therefore, the land must have been inhabited with persons who know how to cultivate the earth. Similarly, the climate must be like Europe's to prevent disease or death among the deported criminals; therefore, the land must be located within certain points of latitude (Tocqueville 1984, p. 273).

Additionally, there is the material difficulty of maintaining order and preventing revolts among prisoners who are not confined within the walls of a prison. On the Island of Van-Diemen (later known as Tasmania, now part of Australia), British prisoners escaped and became dangerous enemies to the penal colony by living with natives. Eventually, semi-civilized tribes grew from intermarriage and continually threatened the stability of the colony. Even if escaped prisoners cannot return to their homeland, they can still threaten the success of the nation if they find a means to live outside of the colony.

Most importantly, there are extreme economic risks involved in establishing penal colonies. British experiments in penal colonization prove that such colonies are expensive to both establish and maintain (Tocqueville 1984, p. 273, 283). In the British colony of Australia, prisoners become hired servants upon arrival, thus raising the costs of maintenance and decreasing potential profits for the colony. Further, Britain's experience demonstrates that penal colonies as a form of punishment are not a sufficient deterrent to crime and thereby raise the total costs of the national penal system. Tocqueville and Beaumont argue that "deportation is nothing but immigration to Australia undertaken at the expense of the State" (Tocqueville 1984, p. 275). Britain could easily establish a penal colony because it was proficient in maritime commerce, from which it could draw resources for transporting criminals. Further, Britain's "empire of the sea" was acquired over a long period and was therefore "less subject than any other kind of empire to the sudden vicissitudes of fortune" (Tocqueville 1984, p. 283). The French navy, in contrast, would need considerable increase to its budget, while "French commerce, for its part, presents few resources for expeditions of this kind." France does not have either the material resources or the military force necessary to support a new colony positioned far from the mother country. Hence, Tocqueville and Beaumont argue that the policy of establishing a penal colony should not be pursued because France doesn't have the material resources to see it succeed. By referring to Britain's example, the authors present the geographic, militaristic, and economic extremes involved in maintaining a penal colony. They also show that the French people do not have the resources or capabilities to successfully overcome such extreme obstacles. This self-knowledge is a crucial step toward acting in moderation.

Not only are there material extremes to be avoided, but there are also moral extremes involved in establishing penal colonies that France should not risk. Tocqueville and Beaumont identify imperialism as not simply a material force that conquers land to expand national boundaries, but also as a moral force with the potential to undermine a certain set of mores from within a nation. Because establishing penal colonies is a form of imperial action, it has the potential to provoke the envy of other imperial nations. Even if France could somehow obtain land for the purposes of a penal colony, Britain's cupidity would pose a threat to the colony (Tocqueville 1984, pp. 284–285). Tocqueville and Beaumont assume that imperialism stems from greed, rather than necessity, and that such greed ultimately encourages envy in other nations. Hypothetically, even if a French colony made considerable growth so that Britain neither wanted to nor could seize it physically, Britain could still interfere with the success of the colony by isolating it from the mother country. Deprived of communication with the mother country, the colony would decay. Successfully maintaining a foreign colony requires a highly centralized national government which can defend the maritime pathway between the mother country and the colony.

Moreover, the discussion of slavery in *On the Penitentiary System* evidences the authors' understanding that modern imperialism finds its root in an immoral love of commerce, which represents a second moral risk inherent to penal colonies. Tocqueville equates the moral extremes of imperialism and slavery by finding their common foundation in democratic materialism. In America, Tocqueville says, "slavery, that shame of a free people, sees each day some territories over which it extended its empire escape its yoke…" (Tocqueville 1984, p. 170). Slavery thus represents an empire, one with disastrous consequences for the ethic of work in the regions where it exists. Tocqueville and Beaumont later explain, "especially in the States where slavery still exists, there are fewer men belonging to the white race who consent to subject themselves to the duties of domesticity or to the harder labors of agriculture and industry. To the [emancipated] black race is reserved pain as well as poverty. In the South, one mistakes labor as a servile work" (Tocqueville 1984, pp. 394–395). In contrast, northern states in which slavery was abolished allow necessity to force white persons "to engage in the hardest professions," yet that labor is considered honorable. Slavery denigrates the honor accorded to honest work in a society and unjustly segregates work based on race.

Tocqueville and Beaumont similarly warn against the potential "empire" a contractor can gain within a penitentiary which produces inhumane treatment of the prisoners. If unregulated, "The contractor sees in the inmate only a laboring machine, dreaming, in serving him, only of the profit that he wants to draw from him; everything appears good to him to stimulate his [the prisoner's] industry; and he worries very little if the expenses for the convict are made to the detriment of the order [of the penitentiary]" (Tocqueville 1984, p. 185). The northern prison contractor and the southern slave owner are parallel individuals within the text of *On the Penitentiary System*: one poses a problem to the moral direction of the prison, while the other poses a problem to the moral direction of the nation.

Just as the contractor works within the prison solely for his own profit (often at the expense of individual prisoners), the penal treatment of slaves is based on profit. Because imprisonment of slaves would be too expensive, death and whipping (methods which cost nothing) are preferred. Punishing a slave by selling them, an effective exile, also yields a material profit for the slave owner (Tocqueville 1984, p. 168).[24] Tocqueville and Beaumont argue that "every place where one half of society is cruelly oppressed by the other one must expect to find in the law of the oppressor a weapon always ready to strike nature that revolts or humanity that complains. The death penalty and blows; here is the whole penal code for slaves" (Tocqueville 1984, p. 168). Hence, the parallels between the penitentiary contractor and slavery illustrate the dangers of commerce to the moral status of a people. In both cases, inordinate love of the material benefits afforded by commerce results in viewing humans as only material, or bodily, beings.

Ultimately, a narrow focus on the physical condition of humanity motivates imperial activity. Just as the empire of slavery and the contractor reduce human beings to material objects in their tyranny over individuals, the British empire deals only with the material needs of human beings. Britain harbors the belief that to dry up the source of crime, it is necessary to give the poor either labor or money—both of which are material rather than moral goods. Yet Britain's experience demonstrates that the number of those in poverty increases each year that such a welfare policy is in effect. Furthermore, Britain's laws afford the most liberty to the individual, yet make the greatest use of the prison as a punishment (Tocqueville 1984, p. 323). Greater individual liberty leads to a rapid and progressive increase of criminals in Britain because the only repercussions for crime are those inflicted on the body (Tocqueville 1984, p. 276). Additionally, the type of labor Britain offers prisoners aims only at forcing activity rather than reforming the soul. Britain invented the treadmill to keep prisoners active; yet the treadmill encourages pointless rather than productive labor (Tocqueville 1984, p. 184, 295). The insufficient focus of Britain's domestic laws on the moral needs of human beings reflects the imperial tendency to view the world in "commercial" or material terms. Democratic materialism indulges a foreign penal colony model out of majoritarian greed rather than a temperate understanding of the human condition as both bodily and spiritual.

The third moral extreme that must be overcome for the French to successfully implement penal colonization is that of the unmoderated imagination. Plans for deportation are the product of an imagination unhindered by fact and unrealistically dependent on limiting the imaginations of others. Tocqueville and Beaumont ironically argue that France's hope for establishing a penal colony is rooted in the idea that "the universe is still divided by the imaginary line that the Popes had once drawn, and as though beyond it unknown continents extend where the imagination can go lose itself in liberty" (Tocqueville 1984, p. 281). This hope to find "unknown continents" is impracticable; the authors discredit any possibility of unclaimed land that also suits the French temperament and constitution.

Indeed, in some manuscript notes to *On the Penitentiary System* Tocqueville expands the thesis that the French are unsuited to holding good colonies. Within the notes, Tocqueville argues that France's "genius" is not apt for maritime enterprises because it depends on land, rather than the sea, as the "natural theater of her power and glory" (Tocqueville 2001, p. 1). Moreover, the French national character is a blend of "domestic tendencies and passion for adventure" that becomes savage if uprooted from "quiet habits" (Tocqueville 2001, p. 2). Finally, French centralization poses a difficulty to colonization because the government has habituated the public to political dependence rather than entrepreneurial individualism. Hence, the idea of penal colonies depends on igniting the imagination of the public to dream of the potential success of a penal colony without proper reliance on knowledge of their own national limitations.

Penal colonies also immoderately incite the criminal's imagination. The idea of deportation flatters the imagination of the poor person by offering the opportunity to make a new life as a colonist (Tocqueville 1984, p. 275). Thus, more citizens commit crimes to escape poverty in the mother country. This passion to escape poverty is not easily controlled and ultimately works against the needs of the mother country. Tocqueville and Beaumont argue that it is very hard to give a new future to human beings far from their home. The imagination galvanized by the idea of deportation can take two turns. Once in exile, the slightest hope of leaving the colony and returning home could trouble the imagination of the exile (Tocqueville 1984, p. 270). Tocqueville and Beaumont note, "Nothing is tenderer in general than the sentiment that binds colonists to the soil on which they were born. Recollections, habits, interests, prejudices, everything still unites them to the mother country, despite the ocean that separates them" (Tocqueville 1984, p. 277). Deported prisoners who are eventually freed in the penal colony often have a burning desire to return to their mother country and a consequent willingness to commit new crimes toward that end (Tocqueville 1984, p. 269). Thus, the passion to escape poverty could direct deported criminals toward excessively troubling the stability and order of the colony.

On the other hand, the passion aroused in the imagination of the deported person could direct penal colonists toward unhealthy independence from the mother country. Although the sentiment of patriotism gives a great source of power and glory to the mother country, that sentiment doesn't exist for some of the deported prisoners because they only recollect experiencing "sometimes unmerited misery" in the mother country. Moreover, the penal colony "is the only place where [the criminal's] history is known and where his shame has been divulged." Hence, for some deported prisoners the new colony fulfills their desire to start a new life, yet such a life includes complete rejection of their homeland.

The deported criminal thus often falls into extremes when imagining their relationship to the mother country. Either turn of the criminal's imagination is not politically helpful, since the mother country neither wants criminals to return to her soil nor to completely forsake loving her in principle. Instead, the penal colony seeks to re-make prisoners into productive social members by encouraging criminals to view their forced labor as contributing to the good of both the colony's society and that of the mother country. Further, the economic success of the penal colony depends on the mother country's ability to attain the benefits of free colonist labor. Such labor is possible only if the colonist understands their relationship to the mother country in a moderate way. The prisoner colonist must understand that the best life available to him lies in benefiting the mother country from afar. Thus, the passion each deported prisoner has for the mother country must be moderate, neither too strong nor too weak. Tocqueville and Beaumont argue that penal colonies are ineffective in correctly moderating the colonist's imagination.

Additionally, penal colonies cannot reform human beings because they immoderately work upon the moral imagination of human beings. For both the criminal and society in general, the principle of penal colonies rests on escaping the social consequences of wrong action. Society desires an easy riddance of criminals; prisoners desire an easy (and sometimes self-interested) punishment for their crime. By inciting a passion that cannot be properly moderated, the mother country loses not only a potential source of national income and relief from crime, but also the opportunity to restore citizens as honest contributors to society. Penal colonies thus fall short of the standard established by Tocqueville and Beaumont for penal justice: the moral reformation of criminals. Penal colonies give corrupt human beings an escape from the consequences of their actions, whereas the penitentiary first forces human beings to confront their crimes in solitude and then offers grace upon their return to society.

Most importantly, failing to avoid the material and moral risks involved in penal colonization would eventually undermine France's international reputation. The potential failure of a French penal colony because of maritime war with imperial Britain would result in more than simply needless expense. France must consider how "to make at all times the justice of its rights respected" (Tocqueville 1984, p. 284). Specifically, penal discipline in any form represents the justice of the unique rights of citizens in a nation, in contradistinction to other nations. Tocqueville and Beaumont assert that France must uphold a liberal reputation for justice in the international world (Clinton 2003, p. 43). The potential for eroding the justice of a nation is particularly high in establishing penal colonies.

Again, Britain provides the perfect example of the consequences of imperial activity for a nation's international reputation for justice. Notably, "of all the British colonies, Australia is the only one that is deprived of those precious civil liberties that have been the glory of England and the strength of her children in all parts of the world" (Tocqueville 1984, p. 283). The colonies in Australia do not have juries because they include warring classes of persons with prejudices against each other. Additionally, the risk of death either by nature (due to the climate or famine) or by criminal aggression unjustly sentences some criminals to death. Deportation is proportionate as a punishment only to those criminals already sentenced for life. Since the criminal cannot return from his exile without further expense to the state, deportation would be an unjust exile to criminals who could be released after a number of years but have no way to return home (Tocqueville 1984, p. 268). The example of deprivation of civil liberties within British colonies, the attribute of disproportionality common to penal colonies as a punishment, and the unintentional death penalty associated with penal colonies confirms that the penal method does not conform to the rigors of justice. This injustice toward criminals undermines the legitimacy of the nation's justice and acts as a moral reason for rejecting imperialism.

Overall, Britain's experience in establishing penal colonies reveals that imperial activity necessitates a combination of material resources that France does not have and moral activities that France should not desire. The public's demand for penal colonies as the solution to recidivism is fundamentally immoderate. Attempting to establish penal colonies will consequently result in negative repercussions, namely undermining France's international reputation for justice. Tocqueville and Beaumont seek to temper the material and moral risks of imperialism, and in so doing protect a moderate justice for both criminals and the community.

America: Moderately Balancing the Extremes of Centralization and Decentralization

Instead of advocating for the British model of penal colonies, Tocqueville and Beaumont argue for a penitentiary system following the American model. Penitentiaries will work to reduce recidivism because they necessitate a balance of centralization and decentralization as modes of administrative power in prison management.[25] The success of the American penal system demonstrates that the failure of French penal institutions results in large part from the overcentralized control of the penal system by the national government.[26] Tocqueville and Beaumont complain that the French are habituated to seeing the "central government attract all to itself and to imprint a uniform direction on all parts of administration in the diverse provinces" because administrative centralization is codified into the legal system and political society (Tocqueville 1984, p. 165, 238). Administrative centralization in France kills penal innovation because it suppresses any spirit of competition between departments.[27] Departments are ultimately subject to the central government and denied discretionary ability when executing national laws. Consequently, the problem of recidivism and lack of moral reform of the individual in the French penal system results partially from an excess of governmental centralization over penal institutions. Immoderate centralization needs to be balanced with a renewed emphasis on decentralization.

In contrast to French departments, the American states evidence the penal benefits of administrative decentralization. Tocqueville and Beaumont explain, "These States, bound together by their common federal tie, are, in respect to everything that concerns their common interests, subjected to a single authority. But outside these general interests they preserve their personal independence, and each of them is sovereign master to govern itself as it pleases" (Tocqueville 1984, p. 165). American prisons are consequently "almost as independent of each other as the States are among themselves" (Tocqueville 1984, p. 167). Such individuality produces a spirit of productive competition; for example, New York was eager to enact penal reform because it directly competed with Pennsylvania for the status of being the "leading" state in the Union (Tocqueville 1984, p. 157).

In particular, the American experiment shows Tocqueville and Beaumont that the success of penitentiaries depends on decentralization in two areas: national governmental administration over penal institutions, and penitentiary contracts governing labor by prisoners for both state profit and the profit of private contractors (Tocqueville 1984, p. 225).[28] As will be argued below, the moderate balance of administrative centralization and decentralization has two direct positive consequences within the American criminal justice system. By finding the right middle ground between using centralization and decentralization in different institutional contexts, Americans justly balance economy with efficiency and stability with progress. Most importantly, the moderate balance between centralization and decentralization contributes toward the justice of the penal system in morally reforming individuals. The arguments on centralization and decentralization in *On the Penitentiary System* therefore evidence the constant need for balancing modes of administrative power within a democracy when designing penal policy. The successful example of American penitentiaries demonstrates that centralization and decentralization are not inherently superior or inferior modes of organizing administrative power, and sometimes both must be used jointly in a democratic society to offset their independent risks.

First, centralization and decentralization differ in their economic costs to political society and thus must be balanced with each other. In terms of building penitentiaries, administrative centralization allows for efficiency, but not economy. Centralization decreases the nation's prosperity when it is "applied to objects of local interest" (Tocqueville 1984, p. 239). The comparison of America and France illustrates the economic differences: "[French] prisons, created and governed entirely by the central power, are expensive and powerless to reform the inmates; we have seen in America cheap prisons raised in small States under the influence of localities, in which every corruption has been avoided" (Tocqueville 1984, p. 241). Tocqueville and Beaumont complain most often of the expense of hiring engineers who wish to secure a reputation for grand architecture rather than for cheap, useful buildings. Such a mistake can be avoided if a smaller government undertakes building penitentiaries; because local governments have fewer funds, they are more careful about how such monies are spent. Further, a centralized government acts uniformly and thus does not have the necessary flexibility to "subject the penitentiary system to the modifications that are necessary because of mores and local needs" (Tocqueville 1984, pp. 240–241). Centralization incurs a higher economic cost because the government cannot properly oversee the details of the construction. In contrast, decentralization within the penal system would ensure better economy in erecting the prison. Because municipalities are closer geographically to the site of construction, local administration would allow for a closer watch over where and why money is spent during the building process.

Still, after the penitentiary has been built it takes a combination of both centralization and decentralization to secure profitable maintenance. Penitentiaries are more economical if there is a centralized person controlling the contracting power of the penitentiary (Tocqueville 1984, p. 186, 239). The penitentiary utilizes unique penal disciplines such as solitude and labor to achieve its goal of morally reforming criminals. Morally reformed criminals are less likely to fall into recidivism after leaving prison, thereby decreasing the long-term cost of the American penal system. To effectively employ such penal disciplines, the penitentiary relies on a wide scope of various contracts. The superintendent must organize hiring private contractors to oversee and educate convicts in labor, provide services for essential items such as food or hygienic supplies, and sell goods created by prisoners in the general market. Yet there is a two-fold problem with the contracting system in the penitentiary. Contractors who oversee prison labor do not necessarily contribute toward the moral reformation of the prisoner because their goal is profit, rather than benevolence. Additionally, the contract made between a penitentiary and contractor to sell goods manufactured by prisoners has the potential to be unjust to the honest worker outside the prison because those goods can be sold more cheaply by not paying for labor costs (Tocqueville 1984, pp. 255, 294–296).

To solve both problems with the penitentiary's contracting power, American penitentiaries first decentralize power within the penitentiary and then re-centralize it in the person of the superintendent. In the first place, penitentiaries limit a single contractor's power by distributing that power to several individuals. When employing multiple contractors, the penitentiary "can stipulate the fairest conditions for each industry" and ensure that prisoners are experiencing solitude which will lead them to moral reformation (Tocqueville 1984, p. 186). Next, the power belonging to a single contractor to stipulate the terms of contracts, oversee prisoner labor, and decide how monies are spent on market goods recentralizes in the person of the superintendent. To sustain multiple and often overlapping contracts, superintendents must be extra-vigilant to oversee and manage the industry of the prison (Tocqueville 1984, p. 226). The superintendent must seek to prevent contractors from imposing disadvantageous conditions on the penitentiary such as longer work hours for prisoners, lower wages paid by the contractor to the penitentiary for prisoner labor, and a longer term for the contract itself. These contractual stipulations have the potential to financially harm the penitentiary by decreasing the profit gained from prisoner labor and the flexibility needed to compete in the free market. In sum, decentralization often leads to recentralization of power elsewhere, implying a necessarily continuing balance between the different modes of distributing power.

Second, centralization and decentralization must be balanced because they differ in the nature and amount of national progress they allow. Decentralized political activity evidences "a prompter and more energetic progress in the direction it freely follows" (Tocqueville 1984, p. 167). Decentralization allows for more progress to be accomplished because it acts with greater force upon individuals than centralized government.

Furthermore, decentralization engages the self-interest of the people. To enact reform, democratic governments depend on a high amount of public involvement in the creation and maintenance of an institution. Again, Tocqueville and Beaumont use their own nation as an example of the problems with centralization:

> The French government, acknowledging how necessary local direction and surveillance are to the prosperity of prisons, has tried at several times to interest the departments in the administration of their prisons; but its attempts in this respect always remain without success. Whatever the government may do, the localities will never assume interest in what they have not made themselves. (Tocqueville 1984, p. 241)

In contrast, the authors see in America that the same persons "who have put a lively interest in its creation are occupied with ardor at putting it into action; and even after the system that they have introduced there is in force they do not cease to monitor its execution. They are preoccupied with it as with a thing that is their own work and in whose success their honor is interested" (Tocqueville 1984, p. 239). Self-interest of the people is necessary to complete political reform in a liberal democracy, and decentralization in terms of establishing penitentiaries does a superior job of conscripting self-interest in comparison to centralization.

Yet decentralized administration of a policy also inherently holds the danger that some individuals, namely those who do not live within the confines of the local community, will not benefit from progress. In terms of penal reform, Tocqueville and Beaumont point out that decentralized administration of penitentiaries encourages reforming only the worst criminals, the equivalent of attempting to heal only the sickest (and perhaps incurable) patients in a hospital (Tocqueville 1984, p. 290). Local governments must focus their comparatively limited resources on those prisoners who are considered most dangerous, often neglecting prisoners incarcerated for petty crimes, as witnesses, or simply accused but not yet prosecuted. Decentralization accomplishes progress more quickly but less universally than centralization of administrative power.

Additionally, although administrative power is stronger when decentralized from national to local governments, it is also much less stable. Tocqueville's mention of his study on the American penitentiary system in *Democracy in America* I.2.7, "On the Omnipotence of the Majority in the United States and its Effects," helps to further explain why the type of progress that results from decentralization is problematic (Tocqueville 2000, pp. 235–239). In the chapter, Tocqueville argues that the progress of penal reform in America reflects the evil of legislative instability because of the omnipotence of majority rule. The case study on American penitentiaries reveals this effect: "the majority, preoccupied with the idea of founding the new [penal] establishment, had forgotten the one that already existed" and thus "alongside the prison, lasting monument to the mildness and the enlightenment of our time, was a dungeon that recalled the barbarism of the Middle Ages" (Tocqueville 2000, p. 239). Tocqueville references the majority in a local community, since *On the Penitentiary System* reveals that American penitentiaries were purely local initiatives (at the most rising to the state level, never the federal or national sphere). The disparity between old and new prison systems in America produced by local majoritarianism can be explained by noting, as above, that decentralization allows for "much more zeal and activity [to be] brought to certain improvements," but also for all action to cease "from the moment that its [the majority's] attention goes elsewhere." Both legislative instability and lack of universal progress result from administrative decentralization and the subsequent increase to local majoritarianism.[29]

In contrast to decentralization of administrative power, centralization provides slower, more stable, and more universal progress. Tocqueville notes that centralized national European governments have "a social force infinitely less great, but more continuous" in governing penal systems (Tocqueville 1984, p. 239). In Europe, "the administrative power has an independent existence and a secure position," so that it can continue to execute "the will of the legislator" even when the majority has moved on to focus on a different policy issue. For example, a central authority allows the government to obtain statistical data necessary to evaluate whether penitentiaries reduce recidivism rates (Tocqueville 1984, pp. 207–208). Centralization thereby contributes to data necessary to achieve and confirm moral reformation of prisoners. Conversely, decentralization hinders progress that is based on data. Because "the link that ties the United States together is purely political," rather than administrative, local police officers and criminal tribunals have difficulty "knowing the true name and still less the history of the guilty" (Tocqueville 1984, p. 167). Decentralization thus makes re-committals difficult to prove and success in terms of reducing recidivism difficult to track. The comparison of decentralization and centralization in terms of national progress reinforces the notion that both methods of distributing power must be balanced. By implication, France should not cede all its centralized authority over penal institutions, even if it decentralizes part of the establishment and administration of those institutions to local departments.

Ultimately, America's successful penal reform maintains a constant balance of centralization and decentralization as modes of power and by extension balances the political values of economy, efficiency, stability, and progress (Tocqueville 1984, p. 186, 225). The American penitentiary system teaches Tocqueville and Beaumont that both administrative centralization and decentralization are necessary but not mutually exclusive. The tension between decentralization and centralization is therefore never permanently resolved in the text. Indeed, the goal is not to resolve the conflict. Instead, America shows Tocqueville and Beaumont the need for balance. Hence, Tocqueville and Beaumont advise the French government to adopt a moderate policy, the reasonable middle ground: the "system of a general prison for each department," a form of decentralization that will provide better discipline to the prisons and ensure the potential success of the American penitentiary system in France. Such decentralization will temper over-centralization in France and secure the success of penal reform.

Moderation as the Sustainer of Liberal Democracies

In conclusion, the rhetorical argument of *On the Penitentiary System* gives us Tocqueville's principle of moderation as the means he used to address problems within liberalism in a liberal way. Tocqueville and Beaumont specifically address the problem of French fears about increasing criminal recidivism. Fear led the public to desire a risky and immoderate policy of penal colonization. Tocqueville and Beaumont therefore argue against the attractive but dangerous solution modeled on British penal colonization. Penal colonies are risky because they promote and depend on material and moral extremes that would be difficult to moderate and that would potentially undermine France's reputation for justice as a liberal nation. Instead, Tocqueville and Beaumont argue for penal reform modeled on American penitentiaries, which will work because penitentiaries depend on a balance of centralization and decentralization of political power. In his discussion of the success of American penitentiaries, Tocqueville's comparison between centralization and decentralization demonstrates the need to sometimes temper risks by balancing opposing principles. Conversely, the discussion of the material and moral extremes of penal colonies, and France's incapacity to moderate those extremes, demonstrates the need to sometimes avoid risk altogether. Risks can be moderated or avoided if grounded in an honest self-assessment of a nation's capabilities and the principles needing to be balanced.

Tocqueville's later arguments in support of colonization evidence the same concern for finding a moderate solution to temper or avoid risks, given French circumstances. Just as Tocqueville looked to the particular circumstances of the French penal system to determine the moderate policy course for resolving recidivism, Tocqueville's later recommendations for colonizing Algeria are moderate because they are conditioned by his understanding of the particular circumstances of the native people, the land, and the risks involved in the project (Tocqueville 2001, p. 91). Further, Tocqueville advocates for French colonization in Algeria out of an identical concern for his nation's international reputation for justice that first motivated his arguments against penal colonization. From the perspective of moderation, although Tocqueville rejects a policy of foreign imperialism in 1833 because it does not preserve the proper conflict between centralized and decentralized political power necessary to secure individual freedom and a liberal international reputation, he later supports the French colonization of Algeria for the same reasons.

Importantly, Tocqueville does not advocate a foreign penal colony model in his later writings on Algeria. Colonization in Algeria was not intended to be penal, that is, populated by deported convicts. Tocqueville's arguments in *On the Penitentiary System* do not evidence distaste for colonization in general, but a wariness of the pitfalls that foreign colonization with convicts, rather than an invested middle class, poses. Additionally, France had already invaded Algeria when Tocqueville began his political involvement in colonization; thus, Tocqueville did not consider Algeria an off-shore (or "foreign") colony, but instead an effort most closely resembling domestic agricultural colonies. The policy problem was not whether to imperially pursue new areas of colonization, as was the case in *On the Penitentiary System*, but how best to colonize an already conquered territory given the unique challenges and exigencies Algeria presented to the French (Tocqueville 2001, p. 25; Welch 2011, p. 319).

Additionally, Tocqueville's involvement in Algerian colonization is characterized by a call for moderation between imperial rule and colonization. For Tocqueville, French governance of Algeria hinged on introducing "the establishment of a European society in Africa," particularly an agricultural society (Tocqueville 2001, p. 122). Military dominance ("ruling a defeated people") must be moderated by domestic agricultural colonization ("displacing or replacing a part or the whole of that population") to successfully establish governance and order in the colony (Welch 2011, p. 314, 317; Tocqueville 2001, pp. 61–62, 66). Tocqueville's recommendations for Algerian colonization are intended to balance the strength of the localized political force of the natives with the centralized political power of France. The failure of the French government to consolidate power in the colony resulted from lack of sufficient administrative centralization in Algeria, which in turn created anarchy (Tocqueville 2001, p. 93). That anarchy threatened the exercise of individual liberties that are necessary to incentivize the French people to take part in an agricultural colony in Algeria. By centralizing the government at Algiers and decentralizing the power of Paris over the colony (i.e., rebalancing modes of power), France would secure a greater guarantee for individual liberty in Algeria that was crucial to the success of its efforts in colonization (Tocqueville 2001, pp. 16, 95–96, 100).

Further, successfully establishing an agricultural colony in Algeria was necessary to reinforce and justify France's reputation among world powers as a liberal political order. Tocqueville saw a need for a liberal nation such as France to "balance the influence of the other [world] powers" and provide an example of humane rule to less civilized peoples through its successful effort at colonization (Tocqueville 2001, pp. 59–60; Welch 2011, p. 331). Tocqueville, in other words, sought a highly moderated imperialism that would in turn allow France to act as a moderating international force. In the end, Tocqueville's later attitude toward colonization is rooted in his understanding of the need for moderate policies to address specific but changing national circumstances, rather than in a moral valuation of the activity of imperialism itself.

Thus, throughout his political career Tocqueville approaches different political problems that arise within France's liberal political order, such as penal reform and colonization, from the perspective of moderation. Moderation helps Tocqueville remedy problems that emerge within liberalism, such as a desire to establish penal colonies that would be unjust to the individual rights of criminals and threaten France's liberal reputation for justice internationally. Yet moderation also helps Tocqueville temper these potential failures of liberalism in way that remains liberal, such as decentralizing prison control by establishing penitentiaries.

A fresh reading of *On the Penitentiary System* therefore reminds us of the importance of the political virtue of moderation to our own liberal political order. Three lessons for liberal democracies emerge from the rhetorical argument in *On the Penitentiary System*. First, by explicitly addressing French fear as one reason for publishing their report, Tocqueville and Beaumont remind us that democratic passions can sometimes get the best of liberal principles. In response to their fear of criminal recidivism the French public asked the centralized government to pursue a risky course of penal policies without considering either the nation's capacity to establish successful colonies or their own responsibility to enact penal reform through self-government. Hence, democratic passions need to be moderated by statesmen who are willing to seek out and choose the best possible policy course.

Second, the liberal statesman not only needs to moderate democratic passions, but also needs to enact moderate policies. Statesmen in liberal nations need to consider how the content of their policies promotes moderation that protects individual liberties and the nation's international reputation for justice. In 1833, when Tocqueville and Beaumont first sought a solution to recidivism in France, penal colonies promoted material and moral immoderation that endangered France's international reputation for justice, whereas penitentiaries depended on moderating modes of power to give the people greater involvement in the penal system. Thus, the content of institutional policies needs to be evaluated based on the principle of political moderation.

Finally, maintaining liberal principles depends to a certain extent on recognizing the democratic tendency to drift toward increasing centralization. Centralization threatens individual liberties by training citizens to excessively rely upon the national government to accomplish for them what they ought to accomplish themselves. Conversely, too little centralization (too much decentralization) also threatens individual liberties by stagnating national progress and destabilizing the legislative process. Tocqueville's consideration of the benefits of decentralization and centralization within a liberal democracy alert us to see the need to constantly balance both modes of power. Such a balance tempers the risks to liberal nations that both excessive decentralization and excessive centralization pose. Moderation is, in the end, an important virtue to sustain the excellence of liberal democracies.

Notes

1. See discussions in: Caesar 2012, p. 5; Smith 1993; Dahl 1985.
2. Most notably, Lipset 1996, p. 18.
3. See: Smith 1993, 1997; Olson 2004; Turner 2008; Kohn 2002; Janara 2004.
4. See, for example, Berlin 1965; Boesche 2005; Jardin 1989; Richter 1963.
5. *On the Penitentiary System* addresses two causes of increasing recidivism in France through its analysis of American penitentiaries: a philosophical problem of the imaginative abuse of theory that has led reformers to costly but ineffective penal institutions, and the political problem of determining which system best mitigates criminality. The philosophical problem was explored in Chap. 2; this chapter will limit itself to understanding how Tocqueville and Beaumont address the political problem.
6. Different scholars argue for different combinations of these hypothetical motivations for Tocqueville's support of French colonialism. According to Atanassow, Tocqueville thinks of Europe's expansion as an inevitable consequence of democracy's irresistible growth, since democracy casts doubt on the shared cultural identity of honor (2013). Clinton argues that Tocqueville supported French imperialism on the grounds of civilizing the conquered and to secure France's role in international politics (2003, p. 27). See also: Prasad 2009, p. 94. Kahan attempts to distinguish between Tocqueville's seemingly contradictory attitudes toward British imperialism in India (which he condemned) and France's imperialism in Algeria and Ireland (which he supported). Ultimately, Kahan argues that Tocqueville saw colonization as an unfortunate necessity stemming from his nationalism (2012, p. 152, 160). Similarly, Kohn suggests that Tocqueville held a pragmatic and contextual view of rights and the rule of law that allowed him to support French colonialism (2008). Welch provides a psychological reading of Tocqueville, concluding that Tocqueville used irony to avoid confronting the moral ambiguities in colonization, particularly the conflict between liberalism and domination (2003). According to Frederickson, Tocqueville maintained a tension between his liberalism and a "quasi-determinism" that explains the influence of "ethnocentrism and imperialism" in his thought (2000, pp. 101–104; see also: Bathory 1980; Strout 1980). Finally, Tracz-Tryniecki argues that Tocqueville's support for Algerian conquest represents his most serious theoretical mistake, an unresolved tension between human dignity and greatness in Tocqueville's thought (2014, pp. 126–127). Additionally, most scholars agree that Tocqueville did not support colonialism on the basis of biological racism. See, for example, Stokes 1990; Gershman 1976; Mitchell 2006.

7. The fact that Tocqueville and Beaumont focus not simply on penitentiaries but also on penal colonies is evident in their complete title of the published report, which draws attention to the chaptered appendix on penal colonies. Additionally, Drolet notes that Tocqueville later inspected France's largest domestic penal colony at Toulon, situated on the Mediterranean coast, thus suggesting Tocqueville's continued interest in the institutions (2003, p. 130). Indeed, Tocqueville inspected the *bagnes* in the midst of crafting *On the Penitentiary System*, after coming to the realization that they had no idea of the discipline of the *bagnes* despite its importance to the French penal system (Tocqueville 1984, pp. 20–22). The *bagnes* were key penal institutions to the penal debate in France because they sparked the most controversy over dangerous recidivists, the *forçats* (Forster 1991, p. 137). Tocqueville's later tours of French prisons will be discussed in Chap. 5.
8. Tocqueville 1984, p. 153. The *North American Review* pointed out that the report is a "general statement [...] addressed to the public in Europe and America" (1833, p. 118). I do not exclude the possibility that Tocqueville and Beaumont desired Americans to read the report, since they requested it to be translated and published in America; however, as will be shown, the author's primary concern is with guiding French public opinion using American democratic principles.
9. See: Tocqueville 1984, p. 244.
10. In a historical-political sense, *surveillance* meant "political control under the monarchical power." In its general and current sense, *surveillance* means the action of watching a person over whom one has responsibility or in whom one is interested; or, constant police activity to watch suspects or those who pose a risk so as to prevent criminal activities and guaranty public safety. See *Trésor de la Langue Française informatisé* (2012), "surveillance." Translation my own.
11. Mancini also states that *On the Penitentiary System* "was in some respects an early foray into the problem" of pauperism, but does not expand on his statement (2005, p. 192).
12. Drolet identifies three reasons for the relation between poverty and crime: first, "economic crises precipitated severe increases in unemployment;" second, a growing vagrant population including many ex-convicts; finally, a lack of education among the poor (2003, p. 135). Drescher notes that at the time of Tocqueville's and Beaumont's initial study, "there was universal agreement [...] that a prison system was part of legislation for the poor, since poverty caused crime [...] crime, though arising from poverty, was a social disease that might be cured by an intensive system of desocialization for every convicted criminal" (1968, p. 133).
13. See *Trésor de la Langue Française informatisé* (2012). Translation my own.
14. For example, see: Tocqueville 1984, p. 161, 206, 250, 338.

15. This claim is often repeated; see: Tocqueville 1984, p. 215, 231, 250.
16. See, for example, passages that draw these links: Tocqueville 1984, p. 175, 215, 231, 241, 250.
17. In 1835, Tocqueville repeats his criticism of legally treating public charity as a "right," since such laws result in an increase to poverty rather than a decrease (Tocqueville 1997, p. 3). Tocqueville views "rights" as a means for society to extend honor, rather than as intimately connected to justice (See: Tocqueville 2000, pp. 227–229). Public charity should not be treated as a "right" since it "publicizes inferiority and legalizes it" (Tocqueville 1997, p. 17). Rather than elevating the person receiving the charity, public charity degrades them and therefore cannot be correctly termed a "right." Notably, Tocqueville's *Memoir on Pauperism* contains an account that closely mirrors the "state of nature" narrative presented by Rousseau. Tocqueville "return[s] for a moment to the source of human societies" to see the progress of private property in relation to equality or inequality. Progress is driven by a desire for comfort, rather than basic necessities. According to his narrative, "inequality was legalized; it became a *right* after having been a fact" (Tocqueville 1997, p. 14). Tocqueville appears to be afraid that a second and similar shift would occur in making public charity a "right," since it is a right not founded on justice as proportional equality but on desire. Tocqueville says, "Any measure which establishes legal charity on a permanent basis and gives it an administrative form thereby creates an idle and lazy class, living at the expense of the industrial and working class" (1997, p. 17). In other words, the "right" to public charity is fundamentally connected to a sense of entitlement, rather than responsibility. Further, such a right creates a new type of inequality, rather than fulfilling "the idea of right which [...] places the one who claims it on the same level as the one who grants it" (Tocqueville 1997, p. 17).
18. Despite their denunciation of welfare, or governmental charity, Tocqueville and Beaumont do specify that penal law should include concessions to the poor for imprisonment of debts and imprisonment of witnesses. In terms of these two penal legislations, the authors criticize England and America for the severity of their laws in making utmost provision for the wealthy and providing almost no legal guarantees for the poor (Tocqueville 1984, p. 326). Tocqueville repeats his criticism of the unfair advantages afforded to the rich in English and American penal laws in *Democracy in America*. There, Tocqueville argues that the Americans simply inherited the punishments of imprisonment and bail from the English and did not bother to revise them because "civil laws are familiar to jurists [...] the bulk of the nation hardly knows them" (Tocqueville 2000, p. 45). Even though the poor "make the law" in America, the poor classes enact legislation directed against themselves, laws that favor "only the rich" (Tocqueville 2000, pp. 44–45).

19. Notably, this scenario works only if the lands are free to cultivate and assuming persons are available to populate them.
20. There is thus a tension in the very beginning of America between a completely capitalist society and the efforts a government can make to improve such a society. The beneficence of the government in tension with the self-sufficiency of the free market prompts the question: what are the economic problems involved in making men moral? Does the overall success of American commerce rely on a certain morality or immorality? In contemporary discourse surrounding penal reform, Thorpe gives an example of the complicated relationship between punishment and the free market when she suggests that penal laws punishing urban crimes with incarceration ultimately create a principal source of jobs and revenue for rural areas (2015, p. 619). According to Thorpe, "what began as a politically expedient wave of rural prison development may have inadvertently unleashed a self-reinforcing punishment discipline that is uniquely resistant to self-correction."
21. This distinction between colonization and imperialism is often lacking in secondary scholarship on Tocqueville's support for France's colonies in Algeria.
22. Many of Tocqueville's and Beaumont's criticisms of Britain's colonization at Botany Bay, Australia mirror the criticisms of François de Barbé-Marbois published in 1828 (Forster 1991, p. 140).
23. Drescher notes that Tocqueville rejected the idea of penal colonies only because he considered them as permanent settlements and extensions of the mother country (1968, pp. 134–135).
24. Tocqueville's and Beaumont's explanation of the punishments meted out to slaves is contained in a footnote, accented by a rare exclamation point in the book, suggesting a somewhat ironic or dismissive tone.
25. Here I build on the large amount of literature dealing with Tocqueville's insights into administrative centralization; see, for example, Pittz 2011; Commager 1993; Drescher 1964, 1968; Lamberti 1989; Pope 1986. Craiutu helpfully compares the ideas on centralization between Tocqueville and other French doctrinaires, demonstrating Tocqueville's close intellectual agreement with men like Guizot in this area (1999, pp. 479–483).
26. For further discussion of French centralization, see Drolet 2003, p. 133.
27. Departments are the legally defined administrative areas of France which somewhat parallel the American states.
28. Keep in mind Tocqueville's distinction between two kinds of centralization, governmental and administrative. America has a governmental centralization represented by its national government and federal system. However, "when the central government that represents [the national majority] has sovereignly ordained, it must rely for the execution of its

commandment on agents who often do not depend on it, and whom it cannot direct at each instant. Municipal bodies and the administrations of counties therefore form so many hidden shoals that delay or divide the flood of the popular will" (Tocqueville 2000, p. 250). See also the discussion of administrative power in Tocqueville 2000, pp. 75–79. Pope articulates Tocqueville's distinction as: "Government is centralized when common national interests are controlled by a single center and decentralized when such control resides in different, possibly competing centers [...] Administration is centralized when matters of primarily local concern are decided nationally, and decentralized when such matters are controlled locally" (1986, p. 55). The discussion of centralization in this chapter deals with administrative, rather than governmental, centralization.

29. Notably, Drescher argues that Tocqueville's silence on the problem of centralization in liberal democracies in later parliamentary debates on penal reform indicates an acquiescence "in the centralizing consensus of their contemporaries" (1968, p. 149). He surmises that Tocqueville was later willing to quell concern for overcentralized administration in return for innovative speed and uniformity of application.

References

1833. De Beaumont and De Tocqueville on the Penitentiary System. *The North American Review* 37 (80): 117–138.

2012. TLFi: Trésor de la langue Française informatisé. *ATILF—CNRS & Université de Lorraine*. http://www.atilf.fr/tlfi. Accessed 13 November 2017.

Atanassow, Ewa. 2013. Nationhood—Democracy's Final Frontier? In *Tocqueville and the Frontiers of Democracy*, ed. Ewa Atanassow and Richard Boyd, 178–201. Cambridge: Cambridge University Press.

Bathory, Peter Dennis. 1980. Tocqueville on Citizenship and Faith: A Response to Cushing Strout. *Political Theory* 8 (1): 27–38.

Berlin, Isaiah. 1965. The Thought of de Tocqueville. *History* 50: 199–206.

Boesche, Roger. 2005. The Dark Side of Tocqueville: On War and Empire. *The Review of Politics* 67: 737–752.

Brogan, Hugh. 2006. *Alexis de Tocqueville: A Life*. New Haven: Yale University Press.

Ceasar, James W. 2012. The Origins and Character of American Exceptionalism. *American Political Thought: A Journal of Ideas, Institutions, and Culture* 1: 1–25.

Carrese, Paul. 2011. Tocqueville's Foreign Policy of Moderation and Democracy Expansion. In *Alexis de Tocqueville and the Art of Democratic Statesmanship*, ed. Brian Danoff and Louie Joseph Herbert, 299–323. Lanham, MD: Rowman and Littlefield.

Clinton, David. 2003. *Tocqueville, Lieber, and Bagehot: Liberalism Confronts the World*. New York: Palgrave Macmillan.

Commager, Henry Steele. 1993. *Commager on Tocqueville*. Columbia, MO: University of Missouri Press.

Craiutu, Aurelian. 1999. Tocqueville and the Political Thought of the French Doctrinaires (Guizot, Royer-Collard, Rémusat). *History of Political Thought* 20 (3): 456–493.

Dahl, Robert Alan. 1985. *A Preface to Economic Democracy*. Berkeley, CA: University of California Press.

Drescher, Seymour. 1964. *Tocqueville and England*. Cambridge: Harvard University Press.

———. 1968. *Dilemmas of Democracy: Tocqueville and Modernization*. Pittsburgh: University of Pittsburgh Press.

Drolet, Michael. 2003. *Tocqueville, Democracy, and Social Reform*. New York: Palgrave Macmillan.

Duan, Demin. 2010. Reconsidering Tocqueville's Imperialism. *Ethical Perspectives* 17 (3): 415–447.

Forster, Colin. 1991. French Penal Policy and the Origins of the French Presence in New Caledonia. *The Journal of Pacific History* 26 (2): 135–150.

Frederickson, George. 2000. *The Comparative Imagination: On the History of Racism, Nationalism, and Social Movements*. Berkeley: University of California Press.

Gershman, Sally. 1976. Alexis de Tocqueville and Slavery. *French Historical Studies* 9 (3): 467–483.

Janara, Laura. 2004. Brothers and Others: Tocqueville and Beaumont, U.S. Genealogy, Democracy, and Racism. *Political Theory* 32 (6): 773–800.

Jardin, André. 1989. *Tocqueville: A Biography*, trans. Lydia Davis and Robert Hemenway. New York: Farrar, Straus and Giroux.

Kahan, Alan. 2012. Tocqueville: Liberalism and Imperialism. In *French Liberalism from Montesquieu to the Present Day*, ed. Raf Geenens and Helena Rosenblatt, 152–168. Cambridge: Cambridge University Press.

Kohn, Margaret. 2002. The Other America: Tocqueville and Beaumont on Race and Slavery. *Polity* 35 (2): 169–193.

———. 2008. Empire's Law: Alexis de Tocqueville on Colonialism and the State of Exception. *Canadian Journal of Political Science* 41 (2): 255–278.

Lamberti, Jean-Claude. 1989. *Tocqueville and the Two Democracies*, trans. Arthur Goldhammer. Cambridge: Harvard University Press.

Lipset, Seymour Martin. 1996. *American Exceptionalism*. New York: W.W. Norton & Co..

Mancini, Matthew. 2005. *Alexis de Tocqueville and American Intellectuals: From His Time to Ours*. Lanham, MD: Rowman and Littlefield.

Mitchell, Harvey. 2006. *America After Tocqueville: Democracy Against Difference*. Cambridge: Cambridge University Press.

Olson, Joel. 2004. *The Abolition of White Democracy*. Minneapolis, MN: University of Minnesota Press.

Ossewaarde, M.R.R. 2004. *Tocqueville's Political and Moral Thought: New Liberalism*. New York: Routledge.

Pitts, Jennifer. 2005. *A Turn to Empire: The Rise of Imperial Liberalism in Britain and France*. Princeton: Princeton University Press.

Pittz, Steven. 2011. Providential Partners? Tocqueville's Take on Equality and Centralization. *The Journal of Politics* 73 (3): 787–807.

Pope, Whitney. 1986. *Alexis de Tocqueville: His Social and Political Theory*. Beverly Hills: Sage Publications.

Prasad, Pratima. 2009. *Colonialism, Race, and the French Romantic Imagination*. New York: Routledge.

Richter, Melvin. 1963. Tocqueville in Algeria. *The Review of Politics* 25: 362–398.

Smith, Rogers M. 1993. Beyond Tocqueville, Myrdal, and Hartz: The Multiple Traditions in America. *American Political Science Review* 87 (3): 549–566.

———. 1997. *Civic Ideals: Conflicting Visions of Citizenship in U.S. History*. New Haven: Yale University Press.

Stokes, Curtis. 1990. Tocqueville and the Problem of Racial Inequality. *Journal of Negro History* 75: 1–15.

Strout, Cushing. 1980. Tocqueville and Republican Religion: Revisiting the Visitor. *Political Theory* 8 (1): 9–26.

Thorpe, Rebecca U. 2015. Perverse Politics: The Persistence of Mass Imprisonment in the Twenty-First Century. *Perspectives on Politics* 13 (3): 618–637.

Tocqueville, Alexis de. 1958. *Journeys to England and Ireland*, trans. George Lawrence and J.P. Mayer. New Haven: Yale University Press.

———. 1968. *Tocqueville and Beaumont on Social Reform*, ed. and trans. Seymour Drescher. New York: Harper Torch Books.

———. 1984. *Œuvres Complètes: Écrits sur le système pénitentiaire en France et à l'étranger, Tome IV, Vol. 1*, ed. Michelle Perrot. Paris: Gallimard.

———. 1997. *Memoir on Pauperism*, trans. Seymour Drescher. Philadelphia: Coronet Books.

———. 2000. *Democracy in America*, ed. and trans. Harvey Mansfield and Delba Winthrop. Chicago: University of Chicago.

———. 2001. *Writings on Empire and Slavery*, ed. and trans. Jennifer Pitts. Baltimore: Johns Hopkins University Press.

Todorov, Tzvetan. 1988. Tocqueville et la Doctrine Coloniale. In *De la colonie en Algérie*, 9–36. Paris: Éditions Complexe.

Tracz-Tryniecki, Marek. 2014. Human Dignity Versus Greatness: Tocqueville's Dilemma. In *Tocquevillian Ideas: Contemporary European Perspectives*, ed. Zbigniew Rau and Marek Tracz-Trynieck, 111–130. Lanham, MD: University Press of America.

Turner, Jack. 2008. American Individualism and Structural Injustice: Tocqueville, Gender, and Race. *Polity* 40 (2): 197–215.

Welch, Cheryl. 2003. Colonial Violence and the Rhetoric of Evasion: Tocqueville on Algeria. *Political Theory* 31: 235–264.

———. 2011. Out of Africa: Tocqueville's Imperial Voyages. *Review of Middle East Studies* 45 (1): 53–61.

CHAPTER 4

Tocqueville's Moderation and Lieber's Idealism in Penal Reform

Upon returning to France, Tocqueville and Beaumont asked Francis Lieber to translate their report and publish it in America. The three had been introduced in Boston toward the conclusion of Tocqueville's and Beaumont's travels, and would meet again in Paris in 1844. They maintained correspondence with each other throughout their lives.[1] At the time of their first meeting, Lieber was a recent immigrant to America, born in Berlin around 1800 to a large merchant family. Intellectually, Lieber's status as a nationalistic German liberal twice led to his imprisonment in Germany (in 1820 and 1823). Lieber fought in the Prussian army against Napoleon and in the Greek War of Independence before settling in Boston in 1827.[2] In 1835, Lieber was offered a faculty position at the University of South Carolina, where he would write his most famous works and become the "first" political scientist in America.[3] According to historian George Pierson, Lieber, "more than any other publicist in the United States, would parallel Tocqueville's political philosophy in his own writings" (Pierson 1938, p. 376). Indeed, Lieber sought to promote the claim that he was part of a trio of "historico-philosophical publicists," which included Montesquieu and Tocqueville.[4] Most importantly, at the time of Tocqueville's and Beaumont's tour of America, Lieber was heavily involved in the American debate surrounding which penitentiary system—Auburn or Philadelphia—was best for penal reform. Lieber's translated text of *On the Penitentiary System* therefore evidences early American

E. K. Ferkaluk, *Tocqueville's Moderate Penal Reform*,
Recovering Political Philosophy,
https://doi.org/10.1007/978-3-319-75577-9_4

penal thought understood from both a European and an American perspective and offers us an alternative to Tocqueville's moderate pursuit of penal reform.[5]

We have an ability to compare Tocqueville's and Lieber's penal thought because of the evident differences between their two versions of the same text, *On the Penitentiary System*.[6] Lieber opens his Translator's Preface by acknowledging a lack of accuracy and linguistic precision in his translation, which he attributes both to the authors' prioritization of content over conveyance and to his own difficulty with the English language. Lieber's excuse regarding his difficulty with English is plausible, given that he immigrated to America from Prussia only five years prior to translating the text. Still, Lieber claims that his translation is clear, intelligible, and faithful. This chapter challenges and explores Lieber's latter claim.

During translation, Lieber altered the original French text in three substantial ways. First, Lieber complicated the presentation of Tocqueville's and Beaumont's original thoughts with numerous additions in both footnotes and appendices. Lieber added a "Preface and Introduction of the Translator," an appendix on the Pennsylvania penitentiary system, and lengthy additions to the appendices and footnotes throughout the main text which often contradicted Tocqueville and Beaumont in both opinion and fact. Second, Lieber altered the text through omission by explicitly replacing some of the original appendices with his own wording rather than a translation.[7] Finally, Lieber made significant translation choices for certain French words, which will be discussed throughout the chapter.[8] The result of Lieber's efforts is a text that stands on its own and in contrast to the original report drafted and published by the two Frenchmen.[9]

The omissions and additions to the text lead us to ask the following questions: Why did Lieber make the particular changes that he did? What is the significance of these differences between the original and translated text? The chapter seeks to answer these questions through four arguments. In answer to the first question, we examine Lieber's motives for altering the text during translation by interpreting his statements within *On the Penitentiary System* itself. Lieber's motive was two-fold: he sought to highlight disagreements with Tocqueville and Beaumont, and he intended to promote his own independently written works. Lieber's motives give us a methodological framework by which we can properly interpret his changes to the text. Consequently, in answer to the second question, we next turn to elucidate three specific penal disagreements between Lieber, Tocqueville, and Beaumont, relying on both the text of *On the Penitentiary*

System and Lieber's later works. The three penal thinkers disagreed on the importance of administrative centralization, the relevance of history to penal progress, and the role of education and religion within penitentiaries. In sum, we see that whereas Tocqueville expresses a moderate and limited view of the potential for institutional reform of prisoners based on his notions of centralization, history, and religion, Lieber presents a relatively idealized hope for the potential reformation of individuals via penal institutions.

Questions of Motive: Why Make Changes to the Translation?

Although scholars have attempted to provide a reason for Lieber's changes to the original text during translation, they have not accounted for the textual indications of motive in *On the Penitentiary System*. Matthew Mancini suggests that in the multitude of textual alterations, "Lieber very nearly succeeded in changing the very focus of the study in his edition" since "Beaumont's and Tocqueville's objective had been to investigate America's system of criminal punishments as dispassionately as they could," while Lieber's purpose was to be "a passionate, loud, and inflexible supporter of one side."[10] Lieber was a stalwart partisan of the Philadelphia system. Whereas Tocqueville and Beaumont do not explicitly indicate their preference for either the Auburn or the Philadelphia penitentiary system in the original report, Lieber changed their argument to reflect support for the penal discipline of individual labor in a solitary cell. Pierson agrees with Mancini, arguing that Lieber's motive for correcting the original report stemmed from his strong belief "in the superiorities of the Pennsylvania system" (1938, p. 709). Frank Freidel also notes the extent of work Lieber accomplished in personally studying and evaluating penitentiaries, which put him "in no mood to subordinate himself to the anonymity of a mere translator" (1947, p. 98). All three scholars emphasize Lieber's involvement in the American penal debate and his desire to elevate the merits of the Pennsylvania penitentiary system over the Auburn system as the reasons for his translation alterations.

Certainly, Lieber intended to promote partisan support for the Philadelphia system because the translation would reach a different audience than the original report. In light of the political purpose of the report, Tocqueville and Beaumont might have refused to support one penal discipline over another as part of their strategy to convince the French public that penitentiary systems in general are a better option than either agricultural colonies or penal colonies. In contrast, Lieber was involved in a different type of public debate on the merits of solitude (represented by the Pennsylvania system) versus silence (represented by the Auburn system) as penitentiary disciplines. Thus, whereas Tocqueville and Beaumont primarily write to persuade the French public to consider penitentiary systems as a viable penal option to alternative institutions, Lieber uses the opportunity to translate the French work to persuade Americans to support a specific penitentiary discipline—Philadelphia's—since Americans already agreed on the merits of penitentiaries in general. The distinction in audiences explains, at least partially, why the focuses of the two texts are different.

Still, Lieber explicitly qualifies his support for the Pennsylvania penitentiary system twice in the translated text. Lieber argues that while the Philadelphia system is the best option, if communities cannot afford to establish a penitentiary modeled on the Philadelphia plan then they ought to proceed using the Auburn plan rather than risk having no penitentiary at all (Beaumont and Tocqueville 1833, p. xi, 52, 297). Thus, Lieber is not as inflexible in his support for the Pennsylvania system as Mancini and Pierson suggest. Like Tocqueville and Beaumont, Lieber's political philosophy ostensibly reflects a practice of moderation. Lieber complains that there is "a common fate of all questions of vital interest to society," that of running into extremes (Beaumont and Tocqueville 1833, p. xviii). Further on in his preface, Lieber states that "it is in respect to prison discipline, as in everything else, one of the wisest rules—guard against extremes, and do not allow the zeal with which you advocate certain means, to obscure the object sought to be obtained by them" (Beaumont and Tocqueville 1833, p. 301). Therefore, the question remains: what was Lieber's purpose in altering the translation? What did he think the object of prison discipline ought to be, and was it the same object that Tocqueville and Beaumont identified?

Indeed, it might be useful to ask whether Lieber *had* an ulterior purpose when making changes to the French text during translation, since he cautions readers not to interpret a systematized argument from his notes. According to the Translator's Preface, Lieber intended his footnotes to indicate his differing opinion with the authors and "to further elucidate their statements," but not to "form a regular series of comments" (Beaumont and Tocqueville 1833, p. vi). Nevertheless, the significance of the notes and appendices added by Lieber is further confirmed by the translator himself. Lieber takes the time in his Translator's Preface to draw attention to his additions:

> Notes and appendices are not infrequently treated with some neglect, and I would therefore take the liberty of suggesting to the reader disposed to dismiss the work after a perusal of the first half of it, containing the general account by the authors, that if the two great divisions of this publication differ at all in the degree of their importance, the higher will probably be assigned to the latter half [...] but both parts, though different in form, are not only closely connected with each other, but one is the necessary complement to the other. (Beaumont and Tocqueville 1833, p. vii)

Lieber's exhortation to readers to pay attention to the "latter half" of the work emphasizes the importance of the appendices, which constitute "half" the work in page length and which Lieber had the freest hand in altering (in addition to adding an appendix written entirely by himself, titled "On the Philadelphia Penitentiary"). Thus, although the writings do not by themselves constitute a systematic penal theory, they do contain penal arguments which can be analyzed. Lieber's warning against forming a cohesive argument from his notes or appendices is not intended to dissuade readers from interpreting his textual alterations.

Instead, Lieber's fragmented opinions scattered in his notes and additions to *On the Penitentiary System* point readers toward his larger publications.[11] This intention is confirmed when Lieber specifies his plans for future study in which he intends to treat "in a more connected form [...] the constitutional progress of the European nations, and their descendants, in all its branches."[12] As will be seen, Lieber considered the invention of penitentiaries as intimately connected to and reflective of progress in Western civilization. Additionally, Lieber often refers in his footnotes and appendices to the *Encyclopedia Americana*, a collection of essays that he was simultaneously editing at the time of translation.[13] Hence, the ideas contained in the notes and additions to *On the Penitentiary System* can be understood as forerunners to the developed thought later expressed in Lieber's more expansive works.[14] In sum, Lieber's changes during translation ought to be interpreted (a) as disagreements with Tocqueville and Beaumont (rather than simply expanding or correcting their insights), and (b) in light of his later, more systematic political writings.

Following Lieber's own indications of how to use and understand his translation alterations leads us to see that his contradictory footnotes and appendices reflect his fundamental theoretical disagreement with Tocqueville and Beaumont on the purpose of penitentiary systems. Lieber theoretically disagrees with Tocqueville and Beaumont on the merits of centralization when establishing penitentiaries, the role of institutions such as penitentiaries in the process of historical development, and the effectiveness of secular education to morally reform individuals within penitentiaries. These departures from the original argument of the French text are rooted in an assumption that the purpose of penitentiary systems is to aide in the historical, civilizational development of human beings. Lieber's departures from the original French text flow out of his differing theoretical premise, rather than result simply from a desire to promote a partisan political opinion.

Lieber's First Departure: Evaluating the Merits of Centralization

Tocqueville's criticism of Lieber's translation provides a starting point for discerning the differences between their penal thought. In a letter to Beaumont shortly after the American publication of *On the Penitentiary System*, Tocqueville complains: "…it happens that I have not been completely satisfied with his [Lieber's] translation. He has loaded it down with notes in which, in his capacity as a foreigner, he feels himself obliged to contradict the smallest truths that we utter about America. It's clear that he is singularly afraid of centralization."[15] As has been shown, throughout *On the Penitentiary System* Tocqueville and Beaumont acknowledge the benefits of administrative centralization, even while pointing out its disadvantages and the need to moderate centralization with a certain level of decentralization. Lieber, on the other hand, consistently characterizes centralization as a problematic form of structuring governmental and administrative power. By criticizing Lieber's fear of centralization, Tocqueville suggests that such a fear lies at the heart of the many changes Lieber made during translation.

Specifically, Lieber takes the time in one of his lengthy footnotes to indict France for its failure to realize the dangers of centralization. Early in the manuscript, Lieber characterizes the French penal system as vicious: "the French code is in general milder than the English, though much severer than the Prussian; but now it is very different, if we consider the whole machinery of the administration of French justice, civil and criminal […] Certainly, it is but simple truth if we call the administration of justice in France, barbarous in many instances" (Beaumont and Tocqueville 1833, p. 15). Lieber argues that such barbarism is characterized by a large number of convicted persons who are subsequently proved innocent, and by an increasing number of oppressive prosecution lawyers.

Later on, Lieber clarifies what he thinks is the source of the problematic barbarism in the French criminal justice system. Lieber writes:

> The tendency of the French government has been, for many centuries, towards the centralization of all power, and the annihilation of the individual life of communities [...] a French republic, indeed, has been decreed, but a republic never existed; there was always a central power at Paris, under whatever name it went, which absorbed the political life of the whole country, concentrated all power, and ruled without a check.... (Beaumont and Tocqueville 1833, p. 97)

Centralization, then, is the culprit behind the regressive condition of French prisons. Lieber defines "centralization" as the political power of a nation concentrated in one place and extending over "knowledge, commerce, industry, law, worship, roads, canals—everything" (Beaumont and Tocqueville 1833, p. 98). Centralization indicates a national government micromanaging the local political affairs of the people.

Moreover, centralization attains its height in "imperial government," exemplified by the French Republic. Lieber, in other words, is willing (where Tocqueville and Beaumont are not) to call the French government imperial. Lieber calls the French government "imperial" not because it seeks conquest over foreign peoples, but because it oppresses the local political activity of its own people. According to Lieber's definition, under an imperial government it is "of little use that those who rule are elected, or of little importance how they are elected, if they are checked merely by the letter of a written constitution, and not by the vigorous, healthy, free action of every part and limb of the great body politic" (Beaumont and Tocqueville 1833, p. 97). For Lieber, rule of law is only as strong as the political activity which supports and extends it. Lieber effectually calls constitutional government a parchment barrier to tyranny if not paired with rigorous local political activity. Because imperial government represents unchecked national political power that has administrative control over all levels of government in a country, it suppresses local political activity. Local government cannot politically innovate when the national government provides for all political exigencies because individuals do not feel the need to participate in their local governments.[16] Imperialism thus ultimately represents a centralized national government eating up the liberties of the people.

Lieber gives us three characteristics of liberty that help to clarify his understanding of the necessary relationship between liberty and local government: "liberty is positive," liberty is "a distinct system of politics and practical mode of government," and liberty is "developed in the history of a people" (Beaumont and Tocqueville 1833, p. 98). Unpacking the precise meanings of these three definitional understandings of liberty will help to further clarify Lieber's concern over centralization.

Positive liberty indicates the type of freedom is that is found through participation in government, rather than the natural freedom that is preserved by restricting the government's interference with the individual.[17] Lieber does not think that liberty is gained or preserved in a written constitution or institutional checks and balances. Rather, liberty is the ability of the individual to engage in independent political activity that consequently gives them "bracing consciousness of individual right" (Beaumont and Tocqueville 1833, p. 97). As will be explained in greater detail below, because Lieber conceives of human nature as fundamentally individualistic, and because individual rights stem from our existence as human beings, positive liberty satisfies each person's need to be recognized as an individual while also participating in the society that protects their rights. Thus, Lieber concludes: "Liberty cannot be *made*, cannot be guaranteed by a parchment, cannot be secured by an oath [...] liberty must be a national life, a *reality* which extends its ramifications to every part of society...." In calling liberty a "national life," Lieber indicates that the mores of the people are fundamentally inclined to value individual freedom and therefore to value participation in political activity that preserves and promotes such freedom.

The tyranny that results from centralization cannot therefore be characterized as simply power of the few over the many, but power that results from an abrogation of the right of association by the government. Lieber writes in a footnote to *On the Penitentiary System*:

> The question, so often made, why does history exhibit so many instances of whole nations allowing themselves to be tyrannized over by a few, to whom they sacrifice their dearest interests, and whom they serve with daily suffering, cannot be answered in a clearer way, than by the above statement because the rulers have the "power of association," and the oppressed are "isolated." Separate the interest of the officers of your government from that of the people, establish easy and rapid communications between the former, and destroy as much as possible free intercourse among the latter,

> deprive them of all opportunities of association, and you may rule with an iron scepter as long as you can maintain this order of things. (Beaumont and Tocqueville 1833, p. 26)

Lieber characterizes association as rightfully a power of the people in society; if rulers supersede the power of association, tyranny results. Notably, Tocqueville has similar ideas about the power of political associations in America, when he asserts that political associations are formed primarily by a minority to both "weaken the moral empire of the majority" and discover arguments which will "make an impression on the majority" (Tocqueville 2000, p. 185). Political associations thus assert the rights of the minority against the potentially tyrannical rule of the majority (Tocqueville 2000, p. 183).

The notion of positive liberty undergirds the second attribute of liberty as "a distinct system of politics and practical mode of government." Because positive liberty reinforces to the individual his understanding of rights and his sense of individualism, Lieber indicates that liberty best prospers in local governmental activity or nationalization, but not centralized national administration. Like local government, nationalization also satisfies and allows for the "general anxiety of man to be an individual and to individualize everything around him" by securing "those principles which are most favorable to a manly individual independence."[18] Because nationalization allows an individual to call a nation "my own," (i.e., it promotes a form of national pride connected to the individual's sense of self), it fulfills the requirements of liberty in the same way as decentralized local government.

Lieber's understanding of the difference between nationalization and centralization can be seen in his corrections to the original text of *On the Penitentiary System* on how to describe the federal relationship between the national and state governments in America. Lieber claims in a footnote that "our penitentiary system never would have risen and been carried through in a large country with a concentrated government."[19] The American political system contains a national, but not a centralized, government. Lieber goes on to say that characterizing American states as "provinces" is a common fault of foreign nations; instead, federalism closely unites, and somewhat blurs the distinction between, the operations of both state and federal government. Lieber argues that the states are "united by a federal tie into one family" and often substitutes "United States" in places where Tocqueville and Beaumont refer in the French to specific individual states.[20] For example, when Tocqueville and Beaumont write "the individual State administrations," Lieber translates the phrase as "the various branches of government in the United States" (Tocqueville 1984, p. 14). Hence, Lieber emphasizes the principle that the American government (conceived of as that of the whole nation) relies upon individual state action.

Most importantly, Lieber offers a third characteristic of liberty which allows us to better understand the precise problem Lieber sees in centralized government. Liberty is not only positive and a distinct political and governmental system. Liberty is also "developed in the history of a people." Political liberty exercised in local governments is intimately connected to Lieber's interpretation of history as a process of human progress. Centralization is problematic because it suppresses individual freedom expressed through political action, and thereby cuts off the process of civilization in human society. Lieber's fear of centralization is thus the product of his specific interpretation of history. By beginning with an analysis of Lieber's criticism of centralization and notion of human liberty, we are led to consider Lieber's use and interpretation of history.

Lieber's Second Departure: Imaginatively Interpreting History

Before examining the role of history in Lieber's political thought, we might note that while Lieber's political thought falls within the category of historicism, characterized by both the view that human history is working toward the final end of human freedom and the idea that each human society is defined by its history, Lieber ultimately disagrees with the Hegelian thread of historicism. While it is certain that Lieber took continental philosophy from both England and Germany and applied it within his American political context, Lieber's use of historicism is complicated (Freidel 1947, p. 149).

Scholars have generally rejected associating Lieber's political thought wholly with early historicism. Bernard Brown characterizes Lieber as primarily a "Kantian idealist," rather than a Hegelian (1951, p. 7). According to Brown, Lieber studied under Fries and Schleiermacher, who "were hostile to the new doctrines of Hegel, and Lieber absorbed this attitude after attending some of Hegel's lectures in Berlin" (1951, p. 16). Steven Alan Samson notes that Lieber "sought to distinguish his views from the dominant German schools of law and politics," namely the historical school stemming from Hegel's philosophy of history (1996, p. 45). On the other hand, C. B. Robson and Merle Curti argue that Lieber drew from the German historical school of thought but also tried to synthesize a historical viewpoint of political philosophy with a type of natural law theory (Robson 1942; Curti 1941). Frank Freidel similarly describes Lieber's political philosophy as follows: "He approached political theory as a German moralist awake to American practicalities; he based his system upon both historical and philosophical foundations..." (1947, p. 151). Freidel concludes that Lieber "drew upon the realism of the historical school, but also tried to preserve the idealism of the older philosophers," particularly in his reference to a theory of natural law.[21] Lieber thus falls only partially into the category of the "Historical School," those who argued against the social contractarians of the eighteenth century by positing that "the only legitimate approach to political matters is the "historical" approach, *i.e.*, the understanding of the institutions of a given country as a product of its past" (Strauss 1988, p. 61). Lieber's philosophy of history has roots in both Hegelianism and the Historical School.

Notably, Lieber developed his political thought amid a methodological debate between the Historical School and the philosophical school of Hegel.[22] Whereas the Historical School sought to critically interpret sources to determine their veracity as a guide to history, Hegel argued that historicist studies must be informed by philosophy. Thus, the debate centered on whether historical studies ought to be conducted on the grounds of particular facts and events or on an *a priori* idea that humanity is progressing steadily toward perfection. In Lieber's own words, he "endeavored to reconcile the historic development of the State with its philosophic ground."[23] Thus, Lieber tried to find a middling methodological ground between the two approaches to history.

Lieber's letters and public talks evidence his engagement with this debate. In 1834, Lieber severely criticized Hegel in a letter to a friend, claiming that Hegel was "full of arrogance and presumption" rather than "earnest, thoughtful investigation, and a discreet acknowledgement of previous experience."[24] Lieber paired personal attacks on Hegel with severe criticisms of Hegel's *Philosophy of History* throughout his lifetime. In his inaugural address to Columbia College in 1858, entitled "History and Political Science: Necessary Studies in Free Countries," Lieber rejects "those historians who seek the highest work of history in finding out a predetermined type of social development in each state and nation and in every race..." (Lieber 1881a, p. 340). In his lecture "The Ancient and the

Modern Teacher of Politics," given in 1859 at Columbia College, Lieber criticizes Hegel's dismissal of pragmatic history (falling under Hegel's class of Reflective History) as inconsistent, "suicidal to the philosopher" by breaking the continuity between historical periods, "unhistorical" since history itself demonstrates its ability to teach moral lessons, "unreal," "destructive," and "un-psychological" (Lieber 1881a, pp. 376–377). Lieber also rejected Hegel's idea of a "Spirit" working through History, any idea of inevitability in the process of civilization, and the Hegelian understanding that the Teutonic race is responsible for "civilizing" other races that cannot begin to progress on their own.[25] At the same time, Lieber criticizes the "historical school" that attempted to argue that "nothing can be right but what has been," relying on precedent and facts to replace political ideals. Lieber's use of history in his political philosophy must therefore be considered as distinct from both the Historical School and Hegelianism.

A study of history has two purposes for Lieber. First, it "favors the growth of strong men and is cherished in turn by them" (Perry 1882, p. 342). Historians usually write their works during times of great action and revolution in order to remember the good in the past and prepare the future generation to preserve such good. Second, "history shows us the great connection of things, that there is nothing stable but the progressive, and [...] that there is a microcosm of the whole past in each of us" (Perry 1882, p. 343). History is therefore "that science which treats of men in their social relations in the past, and of that which has successively affected their society, for weal or woe" (Lieber 1881a, p. 337). Lieber uses history as the standard of progress by which to critically analyze contemporary society. History shows us that human beings are progressive beings, and it demonstrates how to continue to progress toward the good.

Lieber's view of history leads him to contradict Tocqueville and Beaumont on the true cause of social unrest in his first lengthy footnote in *On the Penitentiary System*. Although Lieber admits that "we live [...] in an agitated period," as Tocqueville and Beaumont claim, he redefines the cause of such unrest.[26] Remember that Tocqueville and Beaumont argued there was both a spiritual cause (an unmoderated intellectual appetite for theory) and a material cause (the misery of the poor, which led to increased crime) for social unrest over recidivism.[27] In contrast, Lieber characterizes what he considers the true "restless disposition" that "existed during the last century in almost all the governments of the European continent" as the disposition to centralize administrative government. Centralization is particularly harmful to humanity because it creates a divergence from history's progressive trajectory toward civilization (Beaumont and Tocqueville 1833, p. 98).

Unlike Tocqueville and Beaumont, Lieber asserts that social unrest is a historical phenomenon. The present social disquietude is historical in that it lessens in magnitude when compared with the past. Lieber writes in his footnote:

> We live, everyone will admit, in an agitated period—one of those epochs (in the opinion of the translator) which are characterized in history by the conflict of new principles with old, and whose agitation can cease only when the former acquire a decided ascendancy over the latter. We must be careful, however, that the Present does not appear to us in those magnified dimensions, with which it never fails to impress itself on our minds, if we do not view the Past and the Present with conscientious impartiality, and examine both with unprejudiced scrutiny—in many cases the most difficult task of the historian. The present evil always appears the greatest; but if we allow ourselves to be thus biased, we shall be liable to mistake the real aim after which we ought to strive, and the means by which we endeavor to arrive at it, and unconsciously will lend assistance to those who, more than any others, raise in our age the cry at our disturbed times—the advocates of crumbling institutions. (Beaumont and Tocqueville 1833, p. xlv)

Lieber views history as a continuum of human progress: the past is always worse than the present, the present is always worse than the future. While Lieber does not specify a final end toward which humanity is moving in his brief discussion in *On the Penitentiary System*, history demonstrates where human beings have come from and proves that they will continue to progress into the future. Importantly, without such a historical viewpoint there is a danger of mistaking "the real aim after which we ought to strive, and the means by which we endeavor to arrive at it." The "real aim" and "means" are the new social and political principles progressively revealed through history. Lieber's perspective on history characterizes the present social problem not simply as unrest, but as unrest caused by a love of past enlightenment that distracts from changes that ought to be made or embraced in the present.

Unrest in society specifically stems from a dialectical clash in the present between old and new institutions brought about by the progression of history. Whereas Tocqueville and Beaumont argue that progress, particularly intellectual progress, has the potential to create new social unrest via the immoderate use of the imagination, Lieber qualifies that understanding of the "source of evil." According to Lieber, progress creates restlessness only when new social and political principles clash with old principles. In the absence of such conflict, progress does not by itself create unrest. Thus, social unrest will be resolved only when new principles introduced by progress overcome the old.

What are the new principles and what are the old principles that Lieber sees in conflict with each other because of historical progress? Lieber argues that "the interests which determine the condition of society have become more and more expanded; are of a general and national, not of a limited, individual, and therefore, arbitrary character" (Beaumont and Tocqueville 1833, p. xlv). Whereas older liberal political principles (such as those evidenced in the theory of the social contract) defended ideas of natural and sacred rights of the individual, new liberal principles recognize expanded, general, and national social interests.[28] Nationalism has replaced the tenants of the social contract theory and raised the level of rights and liberties above the individual. To attempt to preserve former ideas of the inalienable natural rights of individuals leads one to oppose "salutary and necessary reforms" and mistakenly praise "former times as those of happy ease."

Hence, the process of civilization has already occurred within humanity.[29] Human beings have learned that greater safety is achieved by living together rather than independently relying upon "mere physical security;" that free labor is more productive than forced labor; that "governments, supported by moral power, stand firmer than states founded on brutal strength;" and finally that "nations achieve their own interests by acting liberally rather than forcefully or fraudulently among other nations" (Beaumont and Tocqueville 1833, p. xxv). Each of these revelations added to man's knowledge of how to rightly organize societies in order to preserve individualism. Indeed, the present time reaps the good results of history, since "the study of a diseased or disordered state of our body, of the mind, or of political society, has led to the most important knowledge respecting their healthy state, and the nature of their organization" (Beaumont and Tocqueville 1833, p. x). Those persons living in the present have better knowledge of how a healthy political society can be organized than those who lived in past centuries.

In particular, a healthy political society promotes the greater rationality of individuals. Lieber's later writings flesh out the human end toward which history is moving. Progress, ultimately, represents a change in the rational "dispositions" of human beings. Lieber regards reason as the "noblest object in the scale of our terrestrial creation" (Lieber 1911, p. 97). History reveals humanity's increasing disposition to use reason, rather than revelation or passions, as the guide to organizing social life.[30]

Indeed, lack of reason results in disorganized social life, namely an increase in crime. Human beings are naturally good but frail, and therefore weak in the use of their reason (Beaumont and Tocqueville 1833, p. xxxv). Lieber's use of the word "vitiated" sums up the problem he sees with human nature: human beings act morally or immorally according to the free or impaired use of their reason. The individual's weak use of reason accounts for their criminal activity.[31] Instead of reason, criminals are impelled to action by "vitiated appetites and perverted desires" (Beaumont and Tocqueville 1833, p. viii). Most crimes result from "degenerate appetites or want of principles," rather than long-confirmed corruption (Beaumont and Tocqueville 1833, p. xxii). For example, poverty is often the cause of crime because of the limitations of the individual to rationally withstand physical or material difficulty (Beaumont and Tocqueville 1833, p. xxxv). Lieber adds that the common principles of human nature which induce us to act badly are "desires, temptations, and opportunities" (Beaumont and Tocqueville 1833, p. xxii, 292). Lieber thus asserts in a later footnote: "Few of those committed to prisons are accustomed to think: it is for want of thought that they become guilty" (Beaumont and Tocqueville 1833, p. 292). To avoid engaging in crime, the individual needs to learn to place reason above their material desires as the guide of life.

Specifically, human beings face two temptations that require the use of reason to avoid. Lieber explains that "generally, the causes which make a wicked person prefer the path of crime to an honorable life, are two-fold—idleness [i.e. reluctance to regular labor], and the love of excitement" (Beaumont and Tocqueville 1833, p. 297). Lieber terms these temptations "dispositions" and argues that they must be overcome by inverting them: instill a love of labor, and create reluctance toward excitement. Both dispositions tempt the individual to anti-social behavior, since labor enables a person to be a productive member of society, whereas love of excitement leads them to act on behalf of their own good. Lieber says that the common character of man rarely allows for a person to resist temptation "with the calm conviction of duty" (Beaumont and Tocqueville 1833, p. xxxi). Resistance to such temptation is the activity of a moral man who can rightly use his reason to balance the two components of his nature, his individualism and his need for society.

Although he allows that human beings are weak in their use of reason, Lieber also states that human beings are not completely depraved.[32] Lieber insists that there is a "code, written in every man's heart" that acknowledges certain crimes "as grave offences."[33] Therefore, human beings are fundamentally good and can be disposed to either good or bad actions. Lieber argues "that a convict is neither a brute nor a saint, and to treat him as either, is equally injurious to himself and to society" (Beaumont and Tocqueville 1833, p. xviii). Instead, "we always ought to consider criminals as redeemable beings" (Beaumont and Tocqueville 1833, p. 57). Human nature constantly has the potential to become more rational, and therefore more moral. Lieber says at one point that "mankind may not grow better, but a more correct knowledge of their true interest may become diffused among them, and may by degrees largely influence their general feeling…" (Beaumont and Tocqueville 1833, p. xxv). In other words, human beings will never progress to the point where they do not have to consider how to correctly use reason to facilitate their social interactions. The potential for the development of reason cannot be diminished by an individual's past history of crime or immoral activity.

Because reason is the highest faculty of human beings, the "great and constant task of man" is to gain victory "of mind over matter."[34] Lieber calls this task "civilization," which represents "the cultivation of all our powers and endowments, and whatever results from this cultivation, as well as the cultivation of all those ideas which have any connection with man's existence, as a member of civil society, or as a social being in general, and the adorning of his mind" (Lieber 1835, p. 4). Lieber does think that human beings have an established nature, given by God; yet this nature must undergo a process for the individual to reach his "truly natural state." Accordingly, Lieber understands human nature by looking at it from its most developed state of being, rather than from an early or primitive stage (as social contractarians proposed).

Civilization is not only the means to a greater use of reason; it is also the final telos of humankind. Lieber repeats his definition of civilization in *Political Ethics*, where he argues that civilization results from the character of human nature: "Civilization develops man, and if he is, according to his whole character and destiny, made for development, civilization is his truly natural state, because adapted to and effected by his nature" (Lieber 1911, p. 128).[35] Fundamentally, the nature of human beings includes a tension between an unending anxiety to be recognized as an individual and an inability to break free from all social relations. Human nature is simultaneously individualistic and social.[36] These primary impulsions within human beings require the use of reason to balance preserving the individual's own identity with the requirements that society makes for each individual to give up a part of that identity for social cohesion and to attain the common good. The telos of civilization, or of our nature as human beings, thus represents a state of reconciliation rather than tension between our innate individualism and sociability. An expanding use of reason gives humanity the tools to reconcile our dispositions toward individuality with our social responsibilities.

The notion of the process of civilization as an increased use of reason over passion which allows for a reconciliation of individualism and sociability accords with one of Lieber's added footnotes in the text of *On the Penitentiary System*, where he argues that it is consistent with the "common law" of humankind that the most depraved prisoners have a negative effect on the least depraved prisoners. The common law is defined as: "when a number of individuals having received a common impulse, are applying their activity toward a common aim, he who distinguishes himself most in this direction, exercises the greatest influence: the most learned among scholars, the most daring among soldiers, the most resigned among martyrs, the most virtuous among the virtuous, the most inspired among artists, the most wicked among criminals. Each propels his society further and quicker on its chosen path" (Beaumont and Tocqueville 1833, p. 21). Individuals pull society along the path of historical progress not by denying their individualism, but by reconciling it to the social demands of their circumstances. Hence, the circumstances determine whether progress is good or bad—the prisoner's reconciliation of their individualism within a community of criminals produces more crime, rather than positive moral progress. The first purpose of history, to favor the growth of strong men, promotes the second purpose of history, which is to show us the progress that has occurred from past to present.

Accordingly, Lieber's emphasis on the need for the development of human reason and the two-fold nature of human beings as fundamentally individualistic and social also explains his preferred choice of penal discipline as solitary confinement. Solitary confinement provides the right circumstances for the reconciliation of individualism to the moral norms of society outside the prison walls. The Philadelphia penitentiary system accomplishes this goal by prompting self-reflection through solitary confinement. In order to rightly use reason, human beings must be calm rather than agitated.[37] Lieber assumes that once a human being is put into a reflective state, "he must come to the conclusion that virtue is preferable to vice."[38] The discipline also prevents prisoners from conforming to the social norms of the criminal population by removing the inmate from any association with other prisoners.

More specifically, the state of reflection produced by solitary confinement calms pride within the individual. Pride is the source of discontent and thoughtlessness that centers the individual's mind on self, rather than society. Pride promotes a radical individualism that imbalances the relationship between each human being's individualism and need for society. Further, shame results from hurt pride and produces a deeper tear between the person's natural individualism and sociability. Notably, Lieber defines the correct use of shame, and conversely of human pride, by the individual's position relative to society. Lieber says: "The feeling usually produced in any man, by any punishment, is that of offended pride, of irritated self-love. The prisoner, at the moment of conviction, does not reflect on the justice of his punishment, but places himself in opposition to the rest of mankind, as an injured man, or, if he be of a better nature, with the embittered feeling of an outcast" (Beaumont and Tocqueville 1833, p. 293). Shame obstructs the prisoner's path toward re-entering society after incarceration. The goal of punishment, however, is not to allow the prisoner to withdraw further into self but to see his proper role in society. Lieber says, "There are many criminals, indeed, who themselves must see as well as others, that a concurrence of fatal circumstances has led them to crime, which, after they have really reformed, will remain a cause of self-reproach, but we do not believe need always deprive them of self-esteem" (Beaumont and Tocqueville 1833, pp. 293–294). The prisoner can experience guilt for their actions, but ought to be spared from shame.

To counteract shame, it is necessary to understand each individual's actions in terms of society. The criminal acted badly because of "fatal circumstances" in their social context that prompted them to commit a crime. Conversely, reforming the prisoner begins with an education on his proper relationship to society. Self-esteem is found in the feeling that one "forms an integral part of the community" and that by fulfilling one's duties, the community's welfare is promoted (Beaumont and Tocqueville 1833, p. 91).[39] For this reason, solitary confinement is the preferable punishment since it does not test human weakness by making the convict "consider that he is an outcast and associate of outcasts" in society.[40]

To summarize the argument thus far, Lieber relies on a particular interpretation of history to explain the reason for social unrest. According to

Lieber, history demonstrates the process by which man's nature attains its progress, or more specifically, civilization.[41] Civilization results from three aspects of human nature: individualism, sociability, and reason as the highest faculty of human beings. In particular, history reveals the progressive development of reason, which in turn allows human beings to structure their societies and government to give the greatest freedom to their innate individualism. By participating in society, and especially in local government, each person gains consciousness of their individualism, rightly understands their social responsibilities, and develops the use of their reason. Thus, in light of Lieber's view of history, we can understand his condemnation of centralization in *On the Penitentiary System* more fully. Centralization is a deficient form of organizing political power because it does not allow individuals to act on their natural need for participation in society, and by extension does not foster the notion of rightly balanced individualism. Centralization thereby inhibits the progress of human reason through history.

Importantly, Tocqueville differs from Lieber in his understanding and use of history. As Jack Lively points out, Tocqueville "had no interest in an historicist philosophy [...] it was not History or Progress which rendered the emergence of some form of social democracy necessary, but certain concrete psychological, social and economic conditions of contemporary society."[42] Still, Tocqueville does frame his political insights between two "poles" of history, namely the historical movement from aristocracy to democracy.[43] Marvin Zetterbaum notes that there is a paradox between Tocqueville's apparent refusal to judge between aristocracy and democracy, seemingly out of deference to history, and Tocqueville's lack of a "fully articulated defense of the inevitability thesis."[44] Tocqueville does not see History as an active force in human progress (or, at least, an inevitable one) so much as the context in which the past development of human beings, as well as the present options for human choice, can be understood. In other words, history is read to understand human possibilities for individual choice, not to understand the ultimate character of humanity's future, and predetermined, condition.[45]

To demonstrate Tocqueville's emphasis on choice rather than progress as the purpose of history, we can turn to Part I, Chap. 1 of *On the Penitentiary System*. It is significant that Tocqueville and Beaumont begin their report on the application of theory to practical public policy with a history (*historique*, rather than a *histoire*) of the development of such theory. Within their history, Tocqueville and Beaumont focus on the emerging differences between the Auburn and Philadelphia penal systems as alternatives to choose from. They aim to present facts in their order and circumstances, rather than give a narrative of actions and events with civilizational or progressive significance. History gives us knowledge of past experience so as to make an informed decision on the future. In the case of their first chapter, the historical development of two different penal disciplines gives readers the necessary knowledge to make a choice between the Auburn and Philadelphia penal discipline systems. The structure of *On the Penitentiary System* therefore mirrors Tocqueville's methodological use of history: a study of history gives us the options to choose from, rather than the choice that must be made.

Similarly, although Tocqueville and Beaumont deny the inescapability of the historical progress of civilization, they simultaneously seem to credit history with shaping the character of social conditions.[46] Throughout *On the Penitentiary System* the authors point out that the history of America and France renders them incomparable in terms of potential success in penal reform. Whereas America has a young society, exempt from public embarrassment and rich in soil and industry, France has a former history of crises that birth political divisions over its land and augment the people's poverty. America has maintained a separation of church and state from its birth, a social condition that France cannot claim (Tocqueville 1984, p. 234). America is industrious, while France is impoverished. The different social conditions resulting from different historical trajectories of both nations seem to account for the differences in crime each nation faces.

Still, while asserting that history can pose a problem in comparing the social conditions of two nations, the authors also suggest that history's consequences can be overcome. Thus, America only *seems* to furnish fewer criminals in comparison to France because of their differing social conditions. Tocqueville and Beaumont conclude that there is no evidence of America's lower crime rate. Americans simply lack the statistical documents necessary to prove crimes in proportion to the population of the entire Union. Indeed, the authors argue that America has the larger number of offenses, while France has more serious crimes committed (Tocqueville 1984, pp. 214–215).

More importantly, Tocqueville's and Beaumont's concern with the contradiction between progress and poverty, or between increasing civilization and simultaneously increasing crime, causes them to question the benefits of a theory of constant progress. We have seen throughout our discussion that Tocqueville and Beaumont are critical of overly imaginative penal theories that assume individual reform is entirely possible through institutional means. In their *Mémoire* to the French government requesting permission to journey to America, they are also critical of the assumption that an increase in civilization will bring an end to crime (Tocqueville 1984, p. 49). Civilizational progress apparently created a new set of social problems, including vagabondage, laziness, and theft as responses to economic fluctuations (Tocqueville 1984, p. 51). Later, in Appendix No. 17, No. 1 of *On the Penitentiary System*, Tocqueville and Beaumont present statistics proving that the number of crimes against persons and forgery does not decrease in proportion to increased civilization, at least in America (Tocqueville 1984, p. 387). The authors assert that the augmentation of both crime and civilization "takes place in an equal and uniform manner; it is difficult to attribute it to chance." Instead of relying on a historical assumption of (possibly inevitable) progress, Tocqueville wants us to understand the various choices we can make within historical, experiential, and human limits. Lieber, on the other hand, is willing to dismiss the contradiction between civilization and crime and between progress and poverty as temporary problems in the process of history. In other words, Lieber puts more faith in the eventual triumph of civilization and progress over crime and poverty because he assumes an unassailable trajectory to human history. Tocqueville and Beaumont claim that society is restless in part because increasing civilization has not yet ridded humanity of certain evils such as poverty or crime, thus revealing its potential deficiency to provide what it promised; Lieber claims that society is restless because of increasing governmental centralization that acts contrary to the needs of human nature and thereby inhibits the success of civilization. Lieber does not take the parallel increase of civilization and crime as symptomatic of a deeper problem with the theory of historical progress, as do Tocqueville and Beaumont.

Lieber's Third Departure: Public Education Versus Religion as the Means of Progress

Finally, Lieber's analysis of the penitentiary system as a social institution differs from Tocqueville's and Beaumont's because Lieber has a different understanding of the role of institutions in reforming human beings. Lieber not only insists on the study of the history of humanity as foundational to his penal theory, but more particularly, "institutions must be studied, their history as well as their operation cannot be understood by a superficial glance."[47] Political institutions, per Lieber, are how human reason is developed through history.

The turn to institutions as a primary means of furthering the process of civilization results from Lieber's assumption that an increase in human reason corresponds to an increase in political knowledge. Lieber says that "as it is in general one of the noblest tasks of man to make reason triumph over chance, it is peculiarly so in the province of law and justice" (Beaumont and Tocqueville 1833, p. xxxi). The direction of progress in terms of human collectivity therefore occurs "from physical force to the substitution of moral power in the art and science of government in general" (Beaumont and Tocqueville 1833, p. viii). Hence, as we have seen throughout the work, whereas Tocqueville and Beaumont rely on the need to direct or limit the human imagination as the ultimate cause for moral change, Lieber's interpretation of history causes him to turn to political institutions to explain possibilities for individual reformation.

Lieber especially turns to political institutions as the means of extending civilization. For Lieber, the state exists not only to protect the individual's primordial rights, such as by preventing some individuals from interfering with the rights of others. The state also has both a right and duty to attain the ends of human nature "by the combined energy of society for each individual" (Lieber 1911, pp. 156–157). Fundamentally, the state is a society based on individual rights which it secures via social means. Lieber defines a "right" as a "regulation and fixation of the use of individual moral freedom, which each man possesses as man, as rational and moral beings placed in society [...] it originates out of the just demand each one makes to enjoy this freedom" (Lieber 1911, p. 24). Rights can only exist between moral beings within society (Lieber 1838, pp. 25–26, 34). Further, all rights stem from Lieber's fundamental axiom of natural law: "I exist as a human being, *therefore* I have a right to exist as a human being" (Lieber 1911, p. 68). Rights result from the fact that human beings are naturally rational and moral.

Hence, the state is involved in maintaining the natural rationality and morality of human beings because it is a society based on rights. In his later essay on penal systems, Lieber specifies that "the state is an institution founded on justice, for protection *and the attainment of the highest objects of man*, who can attain them only in society, in which alone he can, according to his nature, ***unfold his entire humanity...*** " (Lieber 1838, p. 19; emphasis added). In his *Political Ethics*, Lieber similarly claims that it is the state that "very materially influences the moral well-being of every individual" (Lieber 1911, p. 79, 147). Lieber concludes that the process of civilization in history occurs through the activity of the state because human beings are naturally intended for society and because the state is the highest form of society which protects and promotes the individuality of human beings.

Governmental institutions are the tool used by the state to develop human reason. We see an example of this idea in terms of the case study on penitentiary systems. The invention of penitentiaries reflects the over-arching historical development of civilization as taking place in political and social institutions.[48] Lieber says, "…that community, which first conceived the idea of abandoning the principle of mere physical force even in respect to prisons, and of treating their inmates as redeemable beings […] must occupy an elevated place in the scale of political or social civilization" (Beaumont and Tocqueville 1833, p. viii). The societal transition from reliance upon corporal punishment to the use of psychological or instructional punishment in the penitentiary reflects an increased use of reason on the part of humanity.

In particular, the use of solitary confinement in the penitentiary represents the ascendancy of mind over matter in human society. Indeed, Lieber often omits translating "materielle" when it occurs within the French text, as though the word were redundant or unnecessary. Lieber further elides the distinction between material and moral causality in a footnote where he refutes Tocqueville's and Beaumont's criticism of the Philadelphia prison system. Tocqueville and Beaumont criticized the discipline of absolute solitude because it deprived the prisoner of an ability to resist temptation and do good; a prisoner can only act morally in absolute solitude because there is no opportunity to do otherwise. Lieber argues instead:

> To attribute a moral character to a submission which is produced only by the threat of instant corporal punishment in the moment of infraction, seems to me a solecism. The prisoner's moral exertion certainly is not more proved by submitting to silence because he would be severely punished, were he to break it, than by the material impossibility of breaking it; and whilst the former means to irritate, the latter leads to contemplation. (Beaumont and Tocqueville 1833, p. 40)

Prisoners do not have to be tempted with the opportunity to disobey in order to be credited with a choice to obey. Lieber removes the necessity for the individual to rationally exercise free will in crediting them with morality; instead, Lieber suggests that it is the environment of the individual which contributes to their moral character. In other words, for Lieber there is no substantive distinction between material opportunity and moral ability. Morality does not necessarily depend on volition. Whereas silence isolates a prisoner in a "moral respect," the whip "is a physical means" to enforce that morality since "it is not so much the actual pain inflicted upon the convict [...] as the knowledge of an inevitable and immediate punishment" (Beaumont and Tocqueville 1833, p. ix). Therefore, Lieber does not view the Philadelphia system of complete solitary confinement as simply a pragmatic or philanthropic penal policy; it is rather a social institution proving history's trajectory by representing the gradual ascendancy of reason over material circumstances through human institutions.

Because Lieber argues that institutions are one means of promoting the progress of civilization in a society, he consequently affords society different "rights" in relation to the prisoner than those Tocqueville and Beaumont are willing to allow. According to Tocqueville and Beaumont, society has the right to execute the death penalty only if indispensable to maintaining social order (Beaumont and Tocqueville 1833, p. 17). Society also has the right "to find in the work of the inmate the indemnity that it is due" (Beaumont and Tocqueville 1833, p. 37). To that end, Tocqueville and Beaumont say that society has the right "to punish with corporal punishments the convict who neither submits to the obligation of labor nor to other demands of the penitentiary discipline" (Beaumont and Tocqueville 1833, p. 44). In sum, Tocqueville and Beaumont believe:

> ...that society has the right to do whatever is necessary to its conservation and that of the order established in its midst: and we understand very well that an assemblage of criminals who have all broken the laws of the country, in whom every inclination is corrupt and every instinct vicious, cannot be governed in prison according to the same principles and with the same means as [one governs] free men whose inspirations are honest and whose every action conforms to the laws. We further hypothesize that the convict who wishes to do nothing would be violently obliged to work, and that severity is employed to reduce to silence those who do not observe it; the right of society in this regard does not appear questionable to us, at least if it cannot with the aid of milder means arrive at the same results. (Tocqueville 1984, p. 193, 292)

In other words, society has the right to demand and enforce obedience to its laws (Beaumont and Tocqueville 1833, p. 58). Lieber, on the other hand, affords society the right to create morally upright citizens via its various institutions. Specifically, Lieber argues that institutions should seek to affect the prisoner's mind through his emphasis on education within the penitentiary, whereas Tocqueville suggests that institutions would better seek to influence the heart through his emphasis on religion.

Based on his understanding of the importance of political and social institutions in the progress of history, Lieber particularly departs from Tocqueville's and Beaumont's articulation of the role of education in criminal reform. The initial disagreement between Lieber and the French authors surfaces in a lengthy footnote in Part I, Chap. 3. Tocqueville and Beaumont argue that "instruction spreads [...] a few seeds of corruption among men" by creating a host of new needs and multiplying social relations, yet education also "makes peoples richer and stronger" (Beaumont and Tocqueville 1833, p. 63). Education develops human intelligence, supports industries, protects the moral strength and material well-being of peoples, and incites passions that "become fertile in advantages when they can attain the goal they pursue." Hence, education has both benefits and disadvantages for human society.

Lieber gives a broader role to education than Tocqueville and Beaumont because of the importance of the growth in knowledge (and by extension reason) as part of the process of civilization. Lieber argues that Tocqueville and Beaumont have a faulty understanding of knowledge as "merely that information which exercises and enriches the understanding alone" and is therefore "neither good nor bad; it has no moral character of its own."[49] For Lieber, knowledge is "that light which is cast on the whole human soul; which reaches the heart as well as the head" (Beaumont and Tocqueville 1833, p. 64). Education provides progressive reasoning abilities to human beings, which in turn allow them to collectively traverse the historical path of civilization. The importance of education to historical progress thus might be one reason Lieber translates *l'instruction* as *knowledge*, rather than *education*, and wherever possible pairs both words together (even if not paired in the French).[50]

Lieber therefore objects to Tocqueville's and Beaumont's criticism that education spreads corruption among humanity. According to Lieber, Tocqueville and Beaumont can only assume that education is the cause of crime if they think that education makes "productive industry almost the sole national object" and promotes the short-sighted pursuit of "merely physical well-being" (Beaumont and Tocqueville 1833, p. 65). In Lieber's view, Tocqueville and Beaumont too narrowly connect the benefits of education to commercial well-being. On the other hand, because knowledge as a "light" is part of, but not the sum of, the broader development of civilization, Lieber accuses Tocqueville and Beaumont of confusing "knowledge" with "civilization."[51] The effects that Tocqueville and Beaumont ascribe to knowledge in reality ought to be attributed to the historical process of civilization. Moreover, knowledge promotes civilization just as civilization results in greater knowledge. Tocqueville and Beaumont appear to hold only a one-way view of the relationship between civilization and knowledge, rather than understanding the interplay between the two values.

Nevertheless, Lieber must still address the primary criticism lodged by Tocqueville and Beaumont against education: increased knowledge produces increased crime. In terms of penal reform, Lieber specifies that civilization "increases" the number of recognized crimes and offenses because it increases (1) "the variety of pursuits and mutual relations between men," (2) the "means and opportunities for prosecutions of crime," and (3) "our wants and our ambition" (Beaumont and Tocqueville 1833, pp. xxiv–xxv). In other words, the progress of human civilization *appears* to increase crime because it gives men new knowledge of their relationships to each other, of the scope of their activities, and of their desires. That knowledge is neither neutral nor negative in its "moral character" because it is part of the process of civilization. Knowledge of social relations alone does not make men sinful or criminal.

Furthermore, once human beings gain knowledge they cannot return to an ignorant state nor prevent further knowledge from being gained. Lieber suggests that there is no way to avoid the process of acquiring, discovering, and adding experience to human life when he says: "Man must either be inactive or once the impetus is given, he must move on from one change to another. His destiny is civilization…"[52] Lieber ultimately argues that, whether or not human beings are happier as a result of civilization, "the only alternative is between ignorant innocence and civilization" (Beaumont and Tocqueville 1833, p. 65). Because human beings cannot regress from a state of civilization, the process of civilization must be extended over all persons equally.

Lieber thus wholeheartedly supports public education as the means to reform prisoners and provide correct knowledge to citizens. The "practical art of government" is necessary "for the well-being of society, and the prevention of crime among civilized nations, who, in order to avoid the dangers of imperfect knowledge, have but one resource, that of diffusing knowledge, intellectual, moral, and religious, as far and wide, and in as high a degree as possible" (Beaumont and Tocqueville 1833, p. 65). Such diffusion of knowledge occurs in part through penitentiaries as social institutions. In terms of the prisoner, Lieber argues: "it ought always to be borne in mind, that the elements of knowledge are of the greatest importance to a prisoner. They have acquired so universal an influence in our society, that he who is deprived of them, stands in a very disadvantageous position to the rest of his fellow men—a position which will increase the difficulty of returning to the path of honesty" (Beaumont and Tocqueville 1833, p. 300). Thus, one of the primary goals of the penitentiary system is to impart the knowledge that will be necessary for the prisoner to become morally reformed and thereby re-enter society to fulfill his sociable nature. Additionally, Lieber argues in one of his footnotes to *On the Penitentiary System* that a prisoner should not keep any wages earned in prison; instead, "the best application of a surplus arising from prison labor, would be, perhaps, to the support of schools, if ever it should amount to a considerable sum" (Beaumont and Tocqueville 1833, p. 37). Lieber's support for public education remains unqualified throughout *On the Penitentiary System.*

For Lieber, the type of education that participates in the historical progress of civilization is always and necessarily public.[53] In contrast to public education, domestic education instructs human beings in religious morals but not necessarily social morals. The type of education that participates in the development of reason and the process of civilization is an institution of the government and therefore an extension of the state. In other words, the state participates in the process of civilization partially by engineering public education. Public education is the tool of the state used to civilize the individual, "and thus, by raising true men, to raise true citizens for the state and prepare man for his final destiny" (Lieber 1911, p. 364). In order to reach this "final destiny," public education cultivates within the individual "the feeling of our being linked to a society of moral beings and to a nation;" it clarifies our duties to society and thereby prevents "the various acts of selfishness, of absorbing egotism—of crime" (Lieber 1835, p. 8). Public education teaches men how to use their reason to mediate their two fundamental instincts, individualism and sociability.

Instead of public education, Tocqueville and Beaumont turn to religion as the social factor that links democrats to each other and teaches citizens their duties to society as moral beings.[54] The differences in views on education between Lieber, Tocqueville, and Beaumont stem from a different estimation of the role and potency of religion in human social life. As will be shown, Lieber understands the Christian religion as a historical fact, whereas Tocqueville thinks of religion as a permanent passion in the human heart and a crucial institution in democratic society.[55]

Lieber defines the role of religion as filling a personal need of the individual, rather than as simultaneously filling a public or institutional need in society. Lieber says explicitly in a letter: "I hope to show that it is the duty of the state to reform the criminal; at all events, it must be her aim not to make him any worse [...] on the other hand, I am far from taking the sickly religious and sentimental view. I have seldom seen any good result from exciting a prisoner's feelings in religious matters, but a great deal of good has been done by bringing him to a proper knowledge of his relation to the Creator" (Perry 1882, p. 112). Lieber thus allows only for the usefulness of a personal experience of the divine, rather than any formal or systematized religion. Lieber legitimizes the value of a personal experience of religion because "man is, among other things, a religious being, and religion will always shape and frame the whole course of his thinking, and tincture his feelings for better or worse" (Lieber 1881b, p. 526). The religious nature of each individual coincides with their "political," "exchanging," and "communicating" traits (Lieber 1881b, p. 527). In other words, religion is a passion that can be used for either good or evil in each individual's life, in the same way that political activity, commercial trade, or language can be used.

Still, the religious passion can only affect men if they are willing to allow formal religion a place in their life. Human beings must be taught how "to appear before their Creator" in a state of reflection, which subsequently "changes the thoughtless to the thoughtful" (Beaumont and Tocqueville 1833, p. 300). Yet there are multiple methods that human beings use to exclude formal religion from their life even when directly confronted with religious teaching. For example, Lieber notes that prisoners can sleep through sermons or "accustom themselves to very protracted slumbers" in their beds, rather than using their leisure time for religious study (Beaumont and Tocqueville 1833, p. 300). Lieber argues that the convict "would be liable to very great misunderstandings of some parts" of the Bible, "and sometimes, even, would select those from which his uncultivated and corrupted soul would derive no profit" because his mind is weak in its use of reason (Beaumont and Tocqueville 1833, p. 300). For Lieber, then, religion is part of a domestic education that does not act as a tool but as a product of civilization, an education that the individual can choose to make use of or ignore.[56]

Lieber's reliance on the personal aspect of one's relation to God, as opposed to the formal aspect of one's relation to the Church, again relates to his view of history and progress. Behind Lieber's understanding of human progress lies a definite theology, an understanding of the character of God and His relationship to human beings. Lieber argues that "the human mind was destined by its creator to expand, morally and intellectually; not for stagnation, but for life" (Beaumont and Tocqueville 1833, p. 65). God has orchestrated the development of reason through the progression of history. God is also the "Maker of History" who imposes His will on nations and gives to them a necessary patriotic spirit for social cohesion (Lieber 1881b, p. 98). Lieber thus appears to characterize the progress of civilization as the realization of God's plan for mankind.

Lieber nevertheless separates God's role in history from the processes of history, which are:

> Gradual agglomeration and union, conquest, and a certain uniformity imposed by the conqueror, successive and slow systematizing, social assimilation, or a great revolution with a sudden and entire reorganization according to some distinct plan (as was the case with France in her revolution of the last century), evolution and revolution, force, freedom, and accident.... (Lieber 1881b, p. 98)

Notably, formal religion does not have a central part to play in the process of civilization. Lieber instead reduces religion to the status of a sentiment of humanity and a "spirit of decency." Religion is concerned for the potentially innocent or those who could easily be restored to innocence if their "bad seeds" of poor education, weakness, rashness, or oppressive want are uprooted. Religion also requires society to concern itself with all criminals, those guilty of grave crimes and those guilty of first offenses due to undirected passions. Accordingly, Lieber sees the Bible as the source of "principles which must guide us—in our case, that of honoring man even in the criminal, and of shunning no labor to reclaim him" (Lieber 1838, p. 71). Yet religion itself does not play a part in restoring the criminal to his social "innocence." Although the Bible gives us moral principles such as the obligation to be charitable to the poor, political economy applies such principles to human life. Just as religion does not play a significant role in the processes of civilization, religion also does not play the primary role in reforming a criminal to become a moral human being.

An indication of Lieber's prioritization of education over the role of religion in society can be seen in Lieber's choice to not translate Tocqueville's and Beaumont's argument on the benefits of a religious society to the individual's moral reform. The translation choice is most evident in comparing specific sentences from the text. Lieber's translation reads: "The prisoner in the United States, therefore, breathes in the penitentiary a religious atmosphere, and is more accessible to this influence, because *his primary education* has disposed him to it" (Beaumont and Tocqueville 1833, p. 94; emphasis added). But compare Lieber's sentence to the original French: "The prisoner in the United States then breathes in the penitentiary a religious atmosphere that comes to him from all sides, and he is more accessible to this influence, because his primary education has disposed him to it *and he has always lived in a society where great respect for religion is professed*" (Tocqueville 1984, p. 235; emphasis added). Lieber thus omits translating the latter half of the sentence, which emphasizes the importance of a religious society in addition to one's primary education. Lieber ultimately subordinates the role of religion in human life to the pre-eminence of the state and its tool of public education. Religious beliefs alone cannot lead individuals to live a good human life.

Consequently, both authors provide different answers to the question of whether or not human beings can be reformed and by what means. Tocqueville allows for a greater influence of religion within society to positively affect the rates of crime and to morally reform prisoners within the walls of the penitentiary, whereas Lieber places more emphasis on the role of education. Lieber understands education as a tool of the state to continue to propel human beings along the rational path history has planned for them. Lieber considers religion to be a form of private education, a consequence of rather than a key tool in the process of history. On the other hand, we saw in Chap. 2 that Tocqueville consistently refers to the power of religion to affect the minds of prisoners in ways that penal discipline cannot, especially in religion's ability to moderate criminal imaginations by directing them to desire appropriate forms of honor.

Lieber's Idealistic Penal Theory as the Foil to Tocqueville's Moderate Penal Thought

Each of Lieber's additions and omissions to the text of *On the Penitentiary System* directed him to take opposite theoretical positions from Tocqueville and Beaumont, and thereby led him to find different penal solutions to the problem of crime. Lieber's objections to Tocqueville's and Beaumont's arguments regarding the reason for crime, education, and the state's relationship to individual prisoners reveal that there is sometimes more than one answer to these questions. Importantly, through the differences in translation between the original French and American editions of *On the Penitentiary System* we see two ideas of liberalism in relation to reform of both penal institutions and individuals emerge. Tocqueville assumes that human freedom results from individual choice and is sustained by moderate political and social activity. Human beings are given choices hedged in historical context. Further, our choices are also limited by an innate religious sense ingrained into our human nature and dependent on supra-institutional relationships. In terms of reforming the criminal, our knowledge of the historical circumstances out of which choice emerges and the limited power of institutions over individual choice leads us to moderated expectations of what the prison can and should accomplish.

Alternatively, Lieber assumes that human freedom results from a rational balance between our innate sociability and individualism. Freedom can be sustained by the individual's proper interaction with society, an interaction which must be protected from overcentralized government. Paradoxically, Lieber also assumes a far greater role for the state and its governmental institutions, such as penitentiaries and public education, in morally reforming individuals. Whereas Tocqueville has an ability to criticize the Philadelphia system of discipline for its error in supposing that a penitentiary as a political institution can alone change the hearts of men, Lieber wholeheartedly supports the Philadelphia system as crucial to reforming individuals morally. Both Lieber's condemnation of centralization and his emphasis on education are grounded in a comparatively idealistic vision of civilizational progress that is occurring through history.

Hence, Lieber's penal thought, revealed through subtle translation additions and alterations, gives us the appropriate foil by which to better understand how Tocqueville's penal reform can be considered "moderate." Tocqueville's penal thought balances the idealism assumed by Lieber in his views of the potential for reform and the means of reform. While Tocqueville does not entirely negate the power of the state or political institutions to positively impact individual prisoners, particularly by teaching habits of labor that will be useful to society, he seeks other social institutions (such as religion) to provide an alternative means for morally reforming criminals. Tocqueville also moderately calls for a balance between centralization and decentralization because he does not see local political activity alone as essential for protection of individual liberties. Indeed, Tocqueville argues later in *Democracy in America* that majoritarianism at the local level can be more tyrannical than a certain amount of centralization at the national level (Tocqueville 2000, pp. 235–239).

Moderation in penal reform thus requires an ability to hold a balanced conversation between two partisan views, such as centralization versus decentralization or religious versus civic education, rather than negating one or the other. Tocqueville's moderate penal work evidences a willingness to participate in a healthy partisan debate that seeks the best possible outcome for a public problem. Indeed, after evaluating whether France can appropriately implement the principles of American penitentiaries Tocqueville calls for such a partisan debate to further explicate the usefulness of the penal theory: "A controversy, even, would be desirable between the diverse organs of opinion, in order to state what are the disciplinary punishments that can be allowed without injuring public sentiment and those that are incompatible with our civilization and our mores" (Tocqueville 1984, p. 247). The task of policy crafting involves taking account of different answers to the same question and discerning which ought to guide our political action.

Lieber's emendations of the original French text of *On the Penitentiary System* also give us an understanding of the interpretive path needed to comprehend the meaning behind Tocqueville's and Beaumont's arguments. Lieber tells us what questions are at stake in a discussion of penitentiaries. Penitentiaries depend on knowledge of what is essential to human nature. Are human beings depraved beyond the possibility of reform? Is there hope of reforming criminals, and if so, what parts of the human being need to be affected? Does society have the potential to effect this reform, and if so, how? Through Lieber's objections to the original text we are shown these questions underlying Tocqueville's and Beaumont's advocacy for a specific policy measure in a particular country. Lieber broadens the import of the discussion on penal methods to depend on answers to universal, as opposed to particular, human problems. Thus, while Lieber's translation fundamentally diverges from the original notions of human nature and its moral reformation present in the French text, his translation also leads us to consider the underlying questions that must be answered to support one penal system over another.

Notes

1. See Pierson 1938, p. 377, 439; Perry 1882, p. 91. For some of their letters, see: Perry 1882, p. 140, 191–193; Tocqueville 2009, pp. 60–62, 65, 67–82, 84, 87, 99, 132, 145, 154, 161, 183, 231, 260.
2. According to Perry, Lieber witnessed the French invasion of Germany in his hometown of Jena and "conceived a bitter hatred of the French and their emperor..." (1882, p. 2).
3. Perry 1882, p. 104, 295. Lieber later accepted the position of Professor of Modern History, Political Science and International, Civil, and Common Law at Columbia College in New York, in 1857 (Hartigan 1983, p. 6).
4. See Letter from Lieber to Tocqueville, May 30, 1957, in Tocqueville 2009, p. 232. See also Freidel 1947, p. 237.
5. This chapter focuses on detailing and analyzing Lieber's penal thought in order to establish a basis for comparison between Tocqueville and Lieber. Since Tocqueville's penal thought has been elucidated in the previous two chapters, only a few focused discussions of Tocqueville's thought will be given here.
6. There is a tradition of scholarly comparison between Lieber's and Tocqueville's political thought; the earliest comparison occurred in 1858, when both authors were still living. See, for example, Tyler 1858, pp. 621–645; Clinton 2003; Dzur 2010.
7. The appendices Lieber explicitly notes that he altered are: No. 5 On Public Instruction; No. 6 Pauperism in America; No. 7 Imprisonment for Debt; No. 8 Imprisonment of Witnesses; No. 9 Temperance Societies.
8. For example, Lieber consistently glosses the medical analogies used in the text, translates "state" as "United States," "le pays" as "state," "l'instruction" as "knowledge," "l'administration" as "government," and avoids translating "l'âme."
9. It is important to distinguish between Lieber's translation and the original text because Lieber's translation has been the primary text used by American scholars and penal reformers to access Tocqueville's first published book. Lieber's translation was partially reprinted in the "Eighth Annual Report of the Board of Managers of the Prison Discipline Society of Boston," a large and influential organization founded by Louis Dwight to promote the Auburn prison system (1833, p. 219). Lieber's first edition was re-published in America in 1868 without any revisions. Two additional reprints of Lieber's translation were published by Augustus Kelley (1970) and Patterson Smith (1981). An abridged edition of Lieber's translation was also published by Southern Illinois University Press, edited by Thorsten Sellin (1979). In terms of American scholarship, Avramenko and Gingerich

(2014), Drescher (1968), and Boesche (1980) cite Sellin's reprinted and abridged edition of Lieber's translation; Schwartz (1985) cites the first French edition published by H. Fournier Jeune in 1833, while Wolin (2001) cites the French text reprinted in J. P. Mayer's definitive edition of Tocqueville's *Oeuvres Complétes, Écrits sur le système pénitentiaire en France et a l'étranger*, Tome IV, Vol. 1 (1984).

10. Mancini 2005, pp. 35–36. For instances where Lieber argues in favor of the Philadelphia Penitentiary System, see Beaumont and Tocqueville 1833, pp. xi, 9, 11, 13, 18, 25, 52–53, 55, 68, 85, 93, 153, 252, 287, 298.
11. Notably, Lieber published his translation of *On the Penitentiary System* in 1833, at least five years before the publication of the first of his systematic political works, *A Manual of Political Ethics* (1838). Regarding penitentiary reform, Lieber also later published *A Popular Essay on Subjects of Penal Law, and on Uninterrupted Solitary Confinement at Labor, as Contradistinguished to Solitary Confinement at Night and Joint Labor by Day, in a Letter to John Bacon, Esquire* (Boston: E.G. Dorsey, 1838) and *Remarks on the Relation Between Education and Crime: In a Letter to the Right Rev. William White, D.D., President of the Philadelphia Society for Alleviating the Miseries of Public Prisons* (Philadelphia: 1835).
12. Beaumont and Tocqueville 1833, p. vi. Lieber's intention seems to have come to full fruition in the publication of *On Civil Liberty and Self-Government* in 1853, a work that contrasts the "constitution" of England with the national character of France.
13. See Beaumont and Tocqueville 1833, pp. vii, xxxiv–xxxv, 20, 104, 144, 165, 167, 169, 249, 287.
14. An interpretive difficulty remains depending on whether Lieber's penal thought changed because of time and effort in later years, and if so, what are those specific changes. The "whole" of Lieber's penal thought cannot be said to stand in the shadows of the ideas in *On the Penitentiary System*. While acknowledging this limitation on my interpretive work, I will show how Lieber's criticisms of Tocqueville and Beaumont "open the door" to view his larger political philosophy, and how such a philosophy influences his approach to penal reform.
15. Quoted in Pierson 1938, p. 708. Tocqueville and Beaumont defend, in part, the merits of administrative centralization in *On the Penitentiary System* (Tocqueville 1984, pp. 178–189), which should be compared to Tocqueville's remarks regarding administrative centralization in *Democracy in America* I.1.5 (Tocqueville 2000, pp. 56–92).
16. As will be argued later, Lieber suggests that we progressively came to understand the importance of local government through enlightenment. Importantly, Tocqueville also emphasizes the need for townships, or local communities, to have as much administrative power as possible because

participation in local government educates citizens in their duties and liberties. Yet Tocqueville presents this education as a preservation, rather than progression, of freedom. Moreover, Tocqueville describes the most local government in America, townships, as natural to man and therefore antithetical to enlightenment. See Tocqueville 2000, pp. 57–58, 63–65, 76.

17. In emphasizing the importance of political activity in local communities to create liberty, Lieber expands on Tocqueville's and Beaumont's argument that theory must be moderated by practical action, and vice-versa. In this issue, Lieber argues similarly to Tocqueville and Beaumont: "In political economy we know nothing in the abstract. That which is not true in practice is not true at all. The theory is necessarily false that is not verified in practice, or derived from reality and actuality. In one word, nothing can be true in theory without being true in practice" (Lieber 1881b, p. 408). See also: Brown 1951, pp. 26–27. Lieber expresses the relationship between theory, action, and human progress concisely in *Political Ethics* when he says: "Think and act, and you will influence" (1911, p. 98).
18. See: Perry 1882, p. 121; Lieber 2001, p. 56.
19. Beaumont and Tocqueville 1833, p. 12. See also Lieber's addition to a footnote on p. 14, where he claims that the worst American prisons are better than many prisons in Europe, and Lieber's footnote on p. 33, where he recommends Mr. Vidocq's *Memoirs* as a source of descriptions of the French *bagnes* and the "most revolting abuses in French prisons."
20. See, for example, Tocqueville 1984, p. 1, 11, 12, 30.
21. See: Curti 1941; Robson 1942, 1946.
22. For a more developed explanation of the historical development and interaction of these two branches of historicism, see Adcock 2014, pp. 49–53.
23. Perry 1882, p. 132. Of course, this project sounds remarkably similar to Hegel's own desire to make philosophy the bedrock on which historicism rested.
24. Letter to Mittermaier, September 13, 1834; quoted in Freidel 1947, p. 112.
25. Brown 1951, p. 48. See also Lieber's letter to Bluntschill, where he says: "I consider Hegel's 'spirit of history,' as an independent, separate entity, to be nonsense…" (Perry 1882, p. 412).
26. Beaumont and Tocqueville 1833, p. xlv. Later, *On Civil Liberty* opens by defining the restlessness: "Our age, marked by restless activity in almost all departments of knowledge, and by struggles and aspirations before unknown, is stamped by no characteristic more deeply than by a desire to establish or extend freedom in the political societies of mankind" (Lieber 2001, p. 2).
27. For a deeper analysis of Tocqueville's and Beaumont's opening lines, see Chap. 2 above, where the authors are shown to have critiqued French reformers for an immoderate love of theory.

28. According to Lieber, "Inalienable rights are very excellent things if rightly understood, but great bugbears if handled by superficial minds, who feel rather than reason, and whose feeling again is the result of early, sometimes accidental impressions rather than the effect of a well-schooled heart; but the human heart requires as much schooling as the head" (Lieber 1838, p. 73; see also p. 15, 21). Brown argues that "Lieber objected to the contract theory, because it overlooks the fact that *society* exists beyond the forms of government, and that society has always existed, together with the controls and authority which later become institutionalized in the government" (1951, p. 42). Lieber seems to reject the social contract notion of inalienable rights on the basis of his understanding of human nature as simultaneously individual *and* social (Brown 1951, pp. 58–59). Individual rights can be protected from government, which is the tool of the state, but not from society itself. For example, while property rights are natural because they stem directly from the basic assumption of natural right, which is the right to obtain the material things necessary to exist, property rights can be abridged if the needs of society demand it.
29. Notably, Lieber does not specify any countries that are more or less civilized, although he consistently points out that Prussia or Britain have previously made reforms which Americans later claim to have been the first to enact.
30. Man's "original" state has little bearing on how "social" Lieber believes man will ultimately be. Lieber thinks that human beings are naturally social creatures. Still, unlike Hegel's understanding that there are groups of human beings who continue to exist in an undeveloped condition and who are therefore radically individualistic, Lieber emphasizes the importance of individualism to the social human being even after he enters society. See also Lieber 1911, p. 116.
31. See: Lieber 1838, p. 20; 1911, p. 37. The conscience, according to Lieber, gives human beings an original idea that there is a difference between right and wrong, but does not naturally have the capacity to apply the principle of a distinction between right and wrong to specific circumstances and decisions. The conscience must therefore be exercised with reason.
32. In *Education and Crime* Lieber says that it would be bold "to assert that man's nature is so thoroughly bad, that in whatever way it be cultivated, if cultivated at all, it shoots forth the germs of its seeds of corruption—a view which would be repugnant to our most sacred conceptions of the goodness as well as the wisdom of our creator" (1835, p. 7).
33. Beaumont and Tocqueville 1833, pp. 300–301. Those offenses are theft, bankruptcy, and robbing.
34. Beaumont and Tocqueville 1833, p. viii. See also Lieber 1911, pp. 127–128.

35. While Lieber never identifies a time when individuals did not live in society, such as the existence of a "savage man" who relies wholly on his senses rather than his reason, he does argue that the individual is moved to civilization through the acquisition of private property and the formation of the family. The individual attains both property and family "not because of any rational realization of possible advantages," but because each individual must carry "out the dictates of his physical make-up…" (Brown 1951, p. 41). According to Lieber, "civilization, for which man is destined […] begins with private property" because "civilization creates wants" (Beaumont and Tocqueville 1833, p. 65). Man has desires that lead him to acquire property, ease, leisure, and the pursuit of knowledge, all of which culminates in civilization. Both property and the family also best express each person's individuality. Lieber says later in his life, "Man yearns to see his individuality represented and reflected in the effects of his exertions—in property" yet property gained and disposed of "for the benefit of his individual family" (Perry 1882, pp. 120–121). Both the family and property rights originate from the physical and psychological nature of human beings and thus exist prior to the formation of any government. It is the movement beyond the acquisition of property and the formation of the family that represents the general movement from relying on material causes to becoming a moral being.
36. According to Freidel, Lieber "envisaged man's life as revolving around the twin poles of individuality and sociality" (1947, p. 159). See also Brown 1951, p. 39.
37. Lieber's consistent appeal that punishment "calm" rather than "agitate" the individual mirrors his understanding of social unrest.
38. See: Beaumont and Tocqueville 1833, p. 40, 45, 293.
39. Here Lieber disagrees with Tocqueville's and Beaumont's solution to the problem of shame, which was to turn the criminal toward religion. See the discussion above in Chap. 2.
40. Beaumont and Tocqueville 1833, p. x. In *Political Ethics*, Lieber teaches that man's individuality is indispensably connected to his morality: yet, at the same time, man links to man in a society and society moves from stage to stage in progress (1911, pp. 58–59, 111–112). Compare: Beaumont and Tocqueville 1833, p. v; Lieber 1839, pp. 16–17; 1911, pp. 106–107.
41. Brown argues on the contrary: "Lieber's theory of method is illuminated by his approach to the study of history. He dismissed the suggestion that history might reveal to us the operation of social laws or patterns of change. The real value of history is rather to remind us of the depth of our social and national traditions, and thus to help us appreciate the context in which ethical claims develop. A wise study of the past (i.e., history) will be social analysis, so that men will be made aware of their ties to past generations and of the stability of their institutions" (1951, p. 29).

42. Lively 1962, p. 33. According to Lively, Tocqueville thought that history "should be used to give some guidance as to the future trends of society and government, but it should not be erected into a Leviathan before which petty human wishes and ideals stood impotent" (1962, p. 41). Ceasar argues that Tocqueville rejected rationalism's paradox of asserting boundless human choice and the limitations of such choice in history (1985, p. 660). See also Rahe 2012. Pitts argues that "although Tocqueville occasionally used the notion of social stages to account for indigenous practice or to justify European conquest, neither here nor in his later works did Tocqueville develop a thoroughgoing theory of progress, and he remained critical of such theories and justifications of empire when he encountered them among his English acquaintances" (Tocqueville 2001, p. xvii). For scholars who see a similarity between Tocqueville's and Hegel's arguments, see Beem 1999; Villa 2005; West 1991. Mitchell calls Tocqueville a "moral historian" who sees history as "less than an objective record of the past than a profound disclosure of the very trajectory of the human spirit" (1995, p. ix). Salomon argues that Tocqueville had a "historical consciousness" or "knowledge of the definitive character of a constellation of political and social forces, conditioned by the past and directed toward the future" (1935, p. 406). Finally, Ossewaarde argues that Tocqueville sees that "the relationship between civilization and barbarism is always a power relationship" (2004, p. 164).
43. See Mitchell 2008, pp. 543–564. Adcock suggests that Lieber shares the "conception of a grand social transformation from aristocracy (which they equated with feudalism) to democracy" (2014, p. 70).
44. Zetterbaum 1964, p. 612. Zetterbaum concludes by arguing that "Tocqueville's understanding of history is inseparable from his neutrality concerning aristocracy and democracy" (1964, p. 613). Sara Henary suggests, on the other hand, that Tocqueville's "historical narrative" of the shift from aristocracy to democracy is intended to highlight the incompleteness of both inequality and equality as principles that guide human life (2014).
45. Compare to Gargan 1963.
46. Gillespie 2009, p. 284; Gargan 1963, p. 342.
47. Beaumont and Tocqueville 1833, p. vi. See also Thayer 1881, p. 32; Farr 2005.
48. Benson perhaps overstates the significance of Lieber's penitentiary thought to his political philosophy broadly speaking in her idea that Lieber "developed political science as a science of punishment" and "put the prison at the center of his theory of the state" (2015, p. 382).
49. Beaumont and Tocqueville 1833, p. 64. The disagreement on education carries over into the appendices, where Lieber explicitly declines to trans-

late "the general remarks of the authors on public instruction in the United States" (Beaumont and Tocqueville 1833, p. 169).

50. See, for example, Part 1 Chap. 3 of *On the Penitentiary System*.
51. However, it could be argued that Tocqueville and Beaumont make this inversion knowingly: they see the fundamental principle in Lieber's argument as *reason* developing, and draw out a critique of both reasoners (philosophers and philanthropists) and the reasoning behind a historicist framework. In other words, it is possible that Tocqueville and Beaumont are not confusing education and civilization, but are criticizing Lieber's view of civilization in their use of the term "education," since it clarifies the root assumption that enlightenment always promotes human progress.
52. See: Lieber 1835, p. 5; 1911, pp. 127–128.
53. See: Lieber 1835, p. 7. Notably, Lieber says in *On the Penitentiary System* that knowledge as a skill, rather than a light, "is, in itself, in most cases, neither good nor bad" (Beaumont and Tocqueville 1833, p. 63). Thus, his thought developed between the translation of *On the Penitentiary System* and *Education and Crime*, by adding the distinction between knowledge and instruction. Lieber begins *Education and Crime* by stating that while instruction designates the imparting of knowledge, the more comprehensive meaning of education "designates the cultivation of the moral, mental, and physical faculties of the young; it includes, therefore, instruction" (1835, p. 4).
54. One question that might clarify Tocqueville's understanding of human progress is whether Tocqueville draws any connection between human religiosity, which is supposedly inherent in man and has the ability to elevate human activity, and human perfectibility. Is the inherent longing for immortal things which religion provides the same, confused with, or a contributor to the human desire for perfectibility? While a discussion of the answer to this question lies outside the scope of this book, it is important to keep in mind.
55. Lawler argues that "Tocqueville follows Pascal in showing that the need for faith is at the core of man's true greatness" based on man's hope for resolution to the contradictions of human existence (1993, p. 145). Mitchell provides an excellent analysis of why democracy in particular acutely needs an orientation toward the eternal, according to Tocqueville (1995, pp. 183–187). For similar arguments on Tocqueville's understanding of the natural inclination to belief in human immortality, see Mansfield 2010, p. 53; Yenor 2004, pp. 10–17.
56. In *Political Ethics*, Lieber describes religion thus: "Nothing can bridle man's passions, and the undue action of the necessary primary agents of the human soul, but civilization, society, and that which can be cultivated in it alone in any high degree, knowledge and religion. Religion belongs to civilization" (1911, p. 134).

References

Adcock, Robert. 2014. *Liberalism and the Emergence of Political Science*. Oxford: Oxford University Press.

Avramenko, Richard, and Robert Gingerich. 2014. Democratic Dystopia: Tocqueville and the American Penitentiary System. *Polity* 46: 56–80.

Beaumont, Gustave de, and Alexis de Tocqueville. 1833. *On the Penitentiary System in the United States and Its Application in France, with an Appendix on Penal Colonies and also Statistical Notes*, trans. Francis Lieber. Philadelphia: Carey, Lea & Blanchard.

Beem, Christopher. 1999. *The Necessity of Politics: Reclaiming American Public Life*. Chicago: University of Chicago Press.

Benson, Sara M. 2015. A Political Science of Punishment: Francis Lieber and the Discipline of American Prisons. *New Political Science* 37 (3): 382–400.

Boesche, Roger. 1980. The Prison: Tocqueville's Model for Despotism. *The Western Political Quarterly* 33: 550–563.

Brown, Bernard Edward. 1951. *American Conservatives: The Political Thought of Francis Lieber and John W. Burgess*. New York: Columbia University Press.

Ceasar, James. 1985. Alexis de Tocqueville on Political Science, Political Culture, and the Role of the Intellectual. *American Political Science Review* 79 (3): 656–672.

Clinton, David. 2003. *Liberalism Confronts the World: Tocqueville, Lieber, and Bagehot*. New York: Palgrave Macmillan.

Curti, Merle. 1941. Francis Lieber and Nationalism. *Huntington Library Quarterly* 4 (3): 263–292.

Drescher, Seymour. 1968. *Dilemmas of Democracy: Tocqueville and Modernization*. Pittsburgh, PA: University of Pittsburgh Press.

Dzur, Albert. 2010. Democracy's "Free School": Tocqueville and Lieber on the Value of the Jury. *Political Theory* 38 (5): 603–630.

Farr, James. 2005. From Moral Philosophy to Political Science: Lieber and the Innovations of Antebellum Political Thought. In *Francis Lieber and the Culture of the Mind*, ed. Charles R. Mack and Henry H. Lesesne, 113–129. Columbia: University of South Carolina Press.

Freidel, Frank. 1947. *Francis Lieber: Nineteenth-Century Liberal*. Baton Rouge: Louisiana State University Press.

Gargan, Edward. 1963. Tocqueville and the Problem of Historical Progress. *The American Historical Review* 68 (2): 332–345.

Gillespie, Michael Allen. 2009. *The Theological Origins of Modernity*. Chicago: University of Chicago Press.

Hartigan, Richard Shelly. 1983. *Lieber's Code and the Law of War*. Chicago: Precedent.

Henary, Sara. 2014. Tocqueville and the Challenge of Historicism. *The Review of Politics* 76 (3): 469–494.

Lawler, Peter Augustine. 1993. The Restless Mind. In *Tocqueville's Defense of Human Liberty: Current Essays*, ed. Peter Augustine Lawler and Joseph Alulis, 63–85. New York: Garland Publishing.

Lieber, Francis. 1835. *Remarks on the Relation Between Education and Crime: In a Letter to the Right Rev. William White, D.D., President of the Philadelphia Society for Alleviating the Miseries of Public Prisons*. Philadelphia: N.B.

———. 1838. *A Popular Essay on Subjects of Penal Law, and on Uninterrupted Solitary Confinement at Labor, as Contradistinguished to Solitary Confinement at Night and Joint Labor by Day, in a Letter to John Bacon, Esquire*. Boston: E.G. Dorsey.

———. 1839. *Legal and Political Hermeneutics, or, Principles of Interpretation and Construction in Law and Politics: With Remarks on Precedents and Authorities*. Boston: C.C. Little and J. Brown.

———. 1881a. *The Miscellaneous Writings of Francis Lieber, Volume I: Reminiscences, Addresses, and Essays*, ed. Daniel Coit Gilman. Philadelphia: J. B. Lippencott and Co.

———. 1881b. *The Miscellaneous Writings of Francis Lieber, Volume II: Contributions to Political Science*, ed. Daniel Coit Gilman. Philadelphia: J. B. Lippencott and Co.

———. 1911. *Manual of Political Ethics*, 2nd ed., ed. Theodore D. Woolsey. Philadelphia: J. B. Lippincott.

———. 2001. *On Civil Liberty and Self-Government*. Union, NJ: The Lawbook Exchange.

Lively, Jack. 1962. *The Social and Political Thought of Alexis de Tocqueville*. Oxford: Clarendon Press.

Mancini, Matthew. 2005. *Alexis de Tocqueville and American Intellectuals: From His Time to Ours*. Lanham: Rowman and Littlefield.

Mansfield, Harvey. 2010. *Tocqueville: A Very Short Introduction*. Oxford: Oxford University Press.

Mitchell, Joshua. 1995. *The Fragility of Freedom: Tocqueville on Religion, Democracy, and the American Future*. Chicago: University of Chicago Press.

———. 2008. Tocqueville for a Terrible Era: Honor, Religion, and the Persistence of Atavisms in the Modern Age. *Critical Review* 19 (4): 543–564.

Ossewaarde, M.R.R. 2004. *Tocqueville's Political and Moral Thought: New Liberalism*. New York: Routledge.

Perry, Thomas Sergeant. 1882. *The Life and Letters of Francis Lieber*. Boston: James R. Good and Company.

Pierson, George. 1938. *Tocqueville in America*. Baltimore: The Johns Hopkins University Press.

Prison Discipline Society. 1833. *Eighth Annual Report of the Board of Managers of the Prison Discipline Society*. Boston: Prison Discipline Society.

Rahe, Paul. 2012. Tocqueville on Christianity and the Natural Equality of Man. *The Catholic Social Science Review* 17: 7–20.

Robson, C.B. 1942. Francis Lieber's Theories of Society, Government, and Liberty. *The Journal of Politics* 4 (2): 227–249.

———. 1946. Francis Lieber's Nationalism. *The Journal of Politics* 8 (1): 57–73.

Salomon, Albert. 1935. Tocqueville, Moralist and Sociologist. *Social Research: An International Quarterly of Political and Social Science* 2 (4): 405–427.

Samson, Steven Alan. 1996. Lieber on the Sources of Civil Liberty. *Humanitas* IX (2): 40–62.

Schwartz, Joel. 1985. The Penitentiary and Perfectibility in Tocqueville. *The Western Political Quarterly* 38: 7–26.

Strauss, Leo. 1988. Political Philosophy and History. In *What Is Political Philosophy? And Other Studies*, 56–78. Chicago: University of Chicago Press.

Thayer, M.R. 1881. Biographical Discourse. In *The Miscellaneous Writings of Francis Lieber*, ed. Daniel Coit Gilman, vol. 1, 13–45. Philadelphia: J. B. Lippincott.

Tocqueville, Alexis de. 1984. *Œuvres Complètes: Écrits sur le système pénitentiaire en France et à l'étranger, Tome IV, Vol. 1*, ed. Michelle Perrot. Paris: Gallimard.

———. 2000. *Democracy in America*, trans. and ed. Harvey Mansfield and Delba Winthrop. Chicago, IL: University of Chicago Press.

———. 2001. *Writings on Empire and Slavery*, ed. and trans. Jennifer Pitts. Baltimore: Johns Hopkins University Press.

———. 2009. *Tocqueville on America After 1840: Letters and Other Writings*, ed. and trans. Aurelian Craiutu and Jeremy Jennings. Cambridge: Cambridge University Press.

Tyler, Samuel. 1858. De Tocqueville and De Lieber as Writers of Political Science. *The Princeton Review* 30 (4): 621–645.

Villa, Dana. 2005. Hegel, Tocqueville, and 'Individualism'. *The Review of Politics* 67 (4): 659–686.

West, Thomas. 1991. Misunderstanding the American Founding. In *Interpreting Tocqueville's Democracy in America*, ed. Ken Masugi, 155–177. Savage, MD: Rowman and Littlefield.

Wolin, Sheldon. 2001. *Tocqueville Between Two Worlds: The Making of a Political and Theoretical Life*. Princeton: Princeton University Press.

Yenor, Scott. 2004. Natural Religion and Human Perfectibility: Tocqueville's Account of Religion in Modern Democracy. *Perspectives on Political Science* 33 (1): 10–17.

Zetterbaum, Marvin. 1964. Tocqueville: Neutrality and the Use of History. *The American Political Science Review* 58 (3): 611–621.

CHAPTER 5

Tocqueville's Moderate Penal Reform Beyond 1832

Tocqueville's and Beaumont's tour of American penitentiary systems and subsequent publication of the first edition of *On the Penitentiary System* was the beginning of a lengthy political career in penal reform for both men. Tocqueville and Beaumont continued to work at reforming French penal laws from 1833 to 1845. Most of their work thus occurred in what has been called "the golden age for penology in France, from 1820 to 1840 … " (O'Brien 1982, p. 13). The friends' joint penal work was marked by two revised editions of *On the Penitentiary System*, published respectively in 1836 and 1845. To complete our study of the work, it will be worthwhile to briefly review Tocqueville's and Beaumont's continuing efforts in penal reform and thereby to understand the practical effect the work had on French public policy. The purpose of this chapter is to examine the French penal debates in which Tocqueville and Beaumont were participants, divided into eras marked by the republication of *On the Penitentiary System* in France (1833–1836, 1837–1845). We will specifically consider two major changes to the revised editions of *On the Penitentiary System*: the substantive introduction added to the second edition and Tocqueville's speech to the Chamber of Deputies in 1843 added to the third edition.[1] By analyzing these documents, this study is intended to answer the questions: What are the significant differences between all three published editions of *On the Penitentiary System*? Through these differences, can we see Tocqueville's ideas on penal reform change or develop over time and, if so,

E. K. Ferkaluk, *Tocqueville's Moderate Penal Reform*,
Recovering Political Philosophy,
https://doi.org/10.1007/978-3-319-75577-9_5

how? What impact, if any, did the publication of *On the Penitentiary System* have on penal reform in France? The answers to these questions will help us to further understand the practical effects of the moderate liberalism that Tocqueville utilized throughout his political career, especially as it applied to his work in public policy.

The Policy Debate from 1833 to 1836

To a great extent, the penal debate that occurred in France during the five years following Tocqueville's and Beaumont's publication of *On the Penitentiary System* involved the authors in the same arguments they addressed in their initial report. Debates centered on whether France should establish penal colonies, the merits of corporal punishment, the fiscal costs of establishing penitentiaries, and above all how to best reduce recidivism. After returning from France in 1832, and while drafting *On the Penitentiary System*, Tocqueville and Beaumont took the time to visit several French prisons so as to draw appropriate comparisons between French and American penal systems.[2] Tocqueville visited the *bagne* at Toulon in the latter half of May 1832; afterwards, he inspected the prisons of Marseille (Geneva) and Lausanne (Switzerland). Beaumont joined Tocqueville at the prison at Roquette on August 7; around August 10, Tocqueville visited the House of Refuge of l'Oursine; on August 11, he went to the hospital-prison at Saint Lazare, which was dedicated to female criminals.[3] Finally, he visited the Hotel of Bazancourt, a type of juvenile detention center, in mid-August 1832. The friends completed writing *On the Penitentiary System* the very next month and submitted the report on October 15 to the Minister of Commerce and Public Works. H. Fournier Jeune agreed to publish the work for the general populace, and the first notice of its publication appeared in December 1832.

Tocqueville's notes on his visit to the prisons at Toulon and Geneva reveal the pre-eminence of the Auburn system over that of Philadelphia in his initial penal opinions.[4] The *bagne* at Toulon, operating on the basis of common labor, failed to reform prisoners and instead allowed for increased corruption because prisoners worked without organized workshops (Tocqueville 1984b, pp. 45–61). Nevertheless, a *bagne* was cheaper than the central prison in both erection and maintenance (one of the advantages of the Auburn system over Philadelphia's). In his criticism of Geneva, we find that Tocqueville complained of the cells being too large, the existence of common recreation times (prisoners congregated together without either silence or solitude), all forms of luxuries for the prisoners (such as libraries, cafeterias, and the generous distribution of a *pécule*), the excessive price of construction for the prison, numerous recidivists, and the equal application of the discipline on all prisoners regardless of differences among them (Tocqueville 1984b, p. 67). In short, Tocqueville concluded that the prison system "had nothing in common with the American system," indicating his new standard of judgment (Tocqueville 1984b, p. 65). Furthermore, Tocqueville recommends as the first (but not only) remedy to the problems at Geneva that efforts be taken to establish silence through a rigorous discipline. His recommendation reflects the principle of the Auburn system, which used silence rather than absolute solitude as the primary means of disciplining prisoners.

The initial response of the French and European public to the publication of *On the Penitentiary System* was glowing, as the appendix of collected reviews added to the second edition demonstrates (Tocqueville 1984a, pp. 441–450). Indeed, the work earned the Prix Monthyon from the Académie des Sciences Morales et Politiques shortly after its publication. However, it did not take long for initial applause to turn into skepticism of Tocqueville's and Beaumont's penal suggestions. Most notably, Pierson suggests that the revised Introduction to the second edition was specifically created to respond to the criticisms of the Inspector General of the *Maisons de Détention*, M. de La Ville de Mirmont, which he published in his book *Observations sur les maisons centrales de detention, à l'occasion de l'ouvrage de MM. de Beaumont et de Tocqueville*, 1833 (1938, pp. 710–711).

Subsequently, in 1836, the French government commissioned new representatives (architect Guillaume Blouet and judge Frédéric-Auguste Demetz) to conduct a second study of American penitentiaries, particularly those modeled on the Philadelphia system. The commissioning of the Blouet and Demetz report reflected a newly formed agreement in France on the need to use penitentiaries (at least in part) to reform the criminal justice system (Drescher 1968, p. 136). Blouet's and Demetz's report focused on the psychological and bodily effects of solitary punishment upon prisoners and architectural layouts for complete solitary confinement (Perrot 1984). The report also revealed an emerging disagreement over which penitentiary system was superior; whereas Tocqueville's and Beaumont's first edition of *On the Penitentiary System* remained relatively non-partisan in its analysis of the Auburn and Philadelphia systems, Blouet and Demetz strongly supported the Philadelphia system.

In light of these historical developments, the introduction to the second edition shows us the first policy impact of the initial publication of *On the Penitentiary System*. Support for penal colonies as a legitimate alternative to penitentiary systems shifted from prominence to a small minority during the debates of the early 1830s. There was, in Tocqueville's and Beaumont's words, a "happy revolution" which occurred in the spirit of the general councils. In 1825, 42 general councils favored establishing a penal colony, whereas in 1833 (about one year after the first publication of *On the Penitentiary System* in France), only 3 remained in favor of that penal method (Tocqueville 1984a, p. 115). Part of the shift can be attributed to Tocqueville's work in articulating the fiscal difficulties of such a policy. Tocqueville continued to critique supporters of penal colonization in the early days of the penal debate, evidenced by a note in the Tocqueville archives which criticizes Blosseville's book promoting the establishment of penal colonies, *Histoire des colonies pénales de l'Angleterre dans l'Australie* (1831), for its over-saturation with minutiae details which obscure the expense and risk of penal colonies (Tocqueville 1984b, p. 63). Support for penal colonies remained throughout French penal debates into 1845, but from 1833 onward it was a minority opinion.

Instead, by the time Tocqueville and Beaumont published their second edition of *On the Penitentiary System*, public opinion consistently called for penitentiaries as the solution to reforming the French criminal justice system. Tocqueville and Beaumont note in their introduction to the second edition that because the issue of penal reform via incarceration is social, it did not garner any political passions. The absence of political agendas produced a "perfect homogeneity of sentiments" among the public that penitentiaries were the solution to rising recidivism (Tocqueville 1984a, p. 113). The authors argue that public agreement over such an important public policy issue, in a period when agreement was rare, signified the strength of penitentiary systems as modes of penal reform. Still, the penal debate in France had shifted from a debate about which penal *method* was best to reduce recidivism, to a debate about which penitentiary *discipline* was best to reform prisoners.

Thus began a decade-long debate in France surrounding the cellular penitentiary system, most commonly referred to as the Philadelphia system. The debate was shaped by two partisan camps. On the one hand, men such as Marquet-Vasselot, Faucher, La Rochefoucauld-Liancourt, and Charles Lucas opposed absolute solitude, instead favoring the Auburn method of silent work in common areas during the day and solitude by night. Toward the beginning of the debate, Tocqueville joined this side by supporting the Auburn system as more practical, both financially and because it appeared to cohere best with the social character of the French people. On the other side stood those who supported the cellular, and especially the Philadelphia, model of absolute solitude: Brétignères de Courteilles, Demetz, Blouet, Bérenger, Allier, and Moreau-Christophe (Perrot 1984, p. 27). These men argued that reformation of the prisoner can best take place in complete isolation.

The introduction to the second edition of *On the Penitentiary System* (1836) begins by noting the points of agreement among these partisans. All agreed (1) that the object of the prison was to either reform the prisoners whom society had momentarily rejected, or to prevent them from becoming more corrupt while in the prison; (2) that the primary cause of corruption in prison stems from the relationships and communication between prisoners (occurring both day and night); (3) that there are two means to both make criminals better and remove the cause of corruption: silence and isolation (Tocqueville 1984a, p. 87). Thus, there was ostensible agreement on both the goals of the penal system, the challenges facing pursuit of those goals, and the alternative ways to resolve such difficulties. As will be shown, Tocqueville navigates French penal debates by balancing assumptions regarding the purpose of prisons (as either reformation or prevention of corruption) and the means of reformation.

What were the points of disagreement in the penal debate that would take place over the next few decades? As noted above, partisans debated the issue of how much solitude to give a prisoner—whether such solitude should be complete (exemplified by the Philadelphia system), or whether it should be broken by work in common rooms during the day (represented by the Auburn system). By the time the second edition of *On the Penitentiary System* was published, Tocqueville and Beaumont note that seven new American states had joined the penal reform movement, but only one adopted the Philadelphia system (Tocqueville 1984a, p. 89). Their note points toward their own inclination to favor the Auburn system over the Philadelphia one. Additionally, after publishing the second edition, Tocqueville wrote to a friend that the Auburn system of solitude by night, common work during the day should be considered "as the first principle of science" (Perrot 1984, p. 30). Tocqueville admitted that the Philadelphia system lauded by Demetz was simpler, more efficacious, and produced more frequent reformations among prisoners, but he steadfastly maintained until late in his career that the system was too costly for France to consider (Drescher 1968, p. 136).

The second edition's expanded introduction also includes a new consideration of causes behind the commonly understood problem of increasing crime, a second point of disagreement among penal partisans during that time. The list of hypothesized causes for the increase in crime in Britain, and especially the increase in crime among those under 21 years of age, is varied. Some blamed the immoderate use of strong alcohol for breaking down the preventative effects of education, civil rule, and penal laws. Others attributed the increase of crime to education itself, which gives common people new needs and passions that cannot be satisfied; still others blamed industrialization's increased reliance on machines, which reduced the need for laborers and increased the unemployed population. Finally, there were those who argued that society's knowledge of crime, rather than the amount of crime, had increased: thus, because there are better police agents, they discover more offenses, and because there are milder criminal laws, more persons are being sent to jail. A perceived increase in crime can be attributed to a more efficient police force and less severe legal penalties rather than to the presence of more criminals (Tocqueville 1984a, p. 97). Tocqueville and Beaumont argue that in addition to these potential causes, England's penal experience demonstrates that crime has increased as a logical consequence of the ineffectual use of penal colonies as a punishment.

Significantly, Tocqueville and Beaumont do not attempt to claim that any one cause is the primary source of increased crime in France. Instead, they are willing to take a moderate view that crime is caused by a variety of complicated, inter-related factors. It is the task of the policy analyst to consider all potential causes of crime. Tocqueville and Beaumont thus dismiss outright the debate on ultimate causality, instead arguing that partisans should focus on solutions to recidivism which address a host of social and political causes.[5]

Partisans also continued to debate the means of establishing penitentiary systems, whether through a centralized governmental plan or through decentralized local initiatives. Tocqueville and Beaumont consequently turn again to evaluate the problems that administrative centralization and decentralization pose to prison management, problems that they addressed in their first edition of *On the Penitentiary System*. This time, the authors make their arguments through a case study on penal reform in Great Britain. After explaining the many "great anomalies" that pervaded English prisons, due to each individual prison being run by local municipalities, Tocqueville and Beaumont argue that it is difficult not to see increased centralized political authority over prisons as favorable to the penitentiary cause. Centralization allows for systematization of discipline within prisons, as demonstrated when the British Parliament seized control over establishing new prisons and enacted laws that would ensure their uniformity of discipline and maintenance. The government left only the right to inspect prisons to the municipal governments (Tocqueville 1984a, p. 92). Despite their acknowledgement of the difficulties that arise in decentralized penal systems, Tocqueville and Beaumont are still hesitant to pronounce Britain's centralized penal efforts successful, arguing that more time is needed to prove whether centralized penal reform is beneficial in the long term.[6]

Moreover, Tocqueville and Beaumont proceed to point out new problems with centralized administration of prisons which they did not address in the first edition of *On the Penitentiary System*. Specifically, a centralized government tends to accomplish tasks that are either ignored or rejected by public opinion. Thus, when the government resolves upon a policy, "centralization gives it great facilities to carry it out," even when public opinion does not ask for such a change. On the other hand, when public opinion *does* request a change (such as using imprisonment rather than deportation to punish convicted persons) from a centralized administration, even an obscure governmental agent can block its implementation. Centralization, in other words, holds greater advantages for the government than for public opinion (Tocqueville 1984a, pp. 94–95). While the example of English penal reform proves the original argument in the first edition of *On the Penitentiary System*, that centralization lends greater stability and uniformity to a government's executive powers than decentralization provides, it also reveals a new source of conflict between the people and the government. Centralization partially insulates the government from the whims of the majority. That insulation, however, can be problematic if the government is unwilling to act when the public calls for reasonable policy changes (Pierson 1938, p. 711).

Similarly, France's marginal penal reform activity from 1833–1836 supports Tocqueville's and Beaumont's original argument in *On the Penitentiary System* that centralization problematically reduces the speed of innovation in a nation. Despite consensus among the French public on the need for penal reform, and the new government's incentive to prove its concern for the poor via revised penal laws, problems with administrative centralization over the penal system in France continued to emerge as obstacles to finding any kind of partisan agreement via experimentation.

Since the publication of the first edition of *On the Penitentiary System*, the administration of the Ministry of the Interior had done virtually nothing to support establishing American-styled penitentiary systems in France.

Yet Tocqueville and Beaumont argue in their second edition that only small emendations to existing laws needed to be made. French penal laws already indicated that solitary confinement, one of the touchstone disciplines of American penitentiaries, was to be used as a punishment for rebellious behavior in prisons.[7] The same law also prescribed silence at night and while prisoners worked in the common rooms (a second discipline central to American penitentiary systems), thus leaving prisoners free to communicate only during recreation hours in the courtyards. The law *effectively* established the fundamental principles of penal discipline found at the Auburn penitentiary (solitude and silence) (Tocqueville 1984a, p. 128). Thus, the law did not need to be fundamentally changed before the Ministry could establish the penitentiary regime. France simply needed to generalize the laws that already existed and were applied to a portion of its prison population.

Despite its recalcitrant attitude toward promoting reform called for by the public, the Ministry was ostensibly willing to establish a trial penitentiary in Limoges. The penitentiary would contain 200 of the most dangerous prisoners in solitary cells based on the Auburn system. However, Tocqueville and Beaumont accuse the Ministry of killing the movement to establish penitentiaries based on the American model before it even began (Tocqueville 1984a, p. 133). They argue that Limoges ought to contain newly convicted prisoners, rather than long-confirmed convicts, so as to best highlight the advantages of the American penitentiary system (Tocqueville 1984a, p. 133). It is a false hope to believe that the penitentiary will be able to morally reform the most perverse criminals and keep prisoners in silence when they are already accustomed to communicating freely with each other. Tocqueville and Beaumont therefore argue that the administration chose to test run a single penitentiary institution because its severe discipline is a last-ditch measure to keep the worst criminals under control, not because it effectively utilizes a religious influence, supports the moral regeneration of criminals, or instills the powerful impression of good social habits (Tocqueville 1984a, p. 134). By populating Limoges with prisoners convicted for life, the Ministry will falsely discredit the merits of the penitentiary system by ignoring the limits of human nature which Tocqueville and Beaumont clarified in their first edition. The administration would also evade establishing a national penitentiary system by re-directing public opinion. The failure of Limoges will tempt "the crowd, which too often sees only the surface of things [...] to attribute a failure to the principle whose mode of execution alone has been the cause" (Tocqueville 1984a, p. 134). Centralized administrative government not only ignores policy changes requested by the public, it also attempts to manipulate public opinion by conducting experiments destined for failure.

Subsequently, Tocqueville and Beaumont address several excuses used by the Ministry of the Interior to postpone establishing penitentiaries. The administration of the Ministry of the Interior claims to oppose penitentiaries because they rely on the use of whips to maintain silence when prisoners work in common. To this objection, Tocqueville and Beaumont argue that the American penitentiary at Wethersfield presents an example of a penitentiary established on the Auburn plan that succeeds without recourse to bodily punishments (Tocqueville 1984a, p. 120). To the objection that the penitentiary system creates difficulties in keeping prisoners silent while walking between their cells and the common workshop, Tocqueville and Beaumont respond that maintaining complete silence is already successfully accomplished at Sing Sing, Wethersfield, and Charlestown, albeit on a smaller scale than 1500 prisoners (Tocqueville 1984a, pp. 121–122). To the objection that the penitentiary system does not allow prisoners any recreation, Tocqueville and Beaumont respond that honest free workers only rest from their work at meals, just as the inmates in a penitentiary system (Tocqueville 1984a, p. 122). Additionally, statistics prove that prisoners who live in penitentiaries without recreation have fewer deaths than those who are allowed to physically exercise but live within prisons that do not maintain either silence or solitude (Tocqueville 1984a, p. 123). Even if one insisted on a form of physical exercise for prisoners, it could be done militantly, as in the Milbank penitentiary in England. Tocqueville and Beaumont conclude from examining these many excuses that the centralized administration of prisons stemming from the Ministry of the Interior incorrectly applies the sacred principles of nature and humanity which they invoke (Tocqueville 1984a, p. 124). While the Ministry claims to desire to pursue penal reform, they have avoided making small changes in penal law and discipline within existing French prisons which would greatly improve the lives of prisoners. There is a special form of hypocrisy stemming from bureaucratic fear of innovation in public policy making.

In the end, Tocqueville and Beaumont argue that establishing penitentiaries in France depends first upon the willingness and initiative of the central government. However, if the central government refuses to act, the movement for reform can come from the different departments in France. The departments can, without the support of the central government, erect their own houses of justice for the accused and houses of arrest for defendants and correctionally convicted. These institutions can then serve as the proper models for improving the central houses of correction (Tocqueville 1984a, pp. 135–136).

Hence, the introduction to the second edition indicates not only a policy issue at stake (a question of which penal discipline was best), but also a governmental issue to be addressed. The majority of Tocqueville's and Beaumont's arguments in their introduction to the second edition of *On the Penitentiary System* evidence the continued problems with centralized administration over French prisons, indicating that their original examination of decentralized American penitentiaries did not have much success in altering either the opinions or actions of French penal administration. At the same time, the difficulty with the centralized French criminal justice administration confirms the legitimacy of many of their original warnings against too much centralization. Notably, Tocqueville and Beaumont do not advocate explicitly for either the Philadelphia or Auburn system in their introduction to the second edition. Instead of attempting to resolve the policy problem of how much solitude prisoners ought to have in French prisons, they shift the focus of the argument onto the reasons why penal reform has not yet begun in earnest within France. The centralized administration stemming from the Ministry was the primary policy roadblock to overcome, and Tocqueville and Beaumont direct all their newly added arguments in the second edition to challenging the excuses of the Ministry.

The Policy Debate from 1837 to 1845

If Tocqueville and Beaumont were still hesitant to argue strongly on behalf of either the Auburn or Philadelphia system in the decade containing the first and second publications of *On the Penitentiary System*, the third edition demonstrates their ostensible policy change in favor of the Philadelphia system (Drescher 1968, p. 137). In 1837, Tocqueville was made the reporter for a commission responsible for investigating and reforming department prisons. The commission gathered statistical documents and interviews not only from French prisons, but also on prisons in Italy, Switzerland, Prussia, and England (Perrot 1984, p. 31). During this time, Tocqueville corresponded with the most notable penal experts from around the world; Michelle Perrot notes letters in the Tocqueville Archives with "Julius, Varrentrap, Arnim in Prussia; Crawford, Sir. J. Russell, Sir James Graham in England; the Marquis Carlo Torrigiani of Florence..." (1984, p. 31). Beaumont joined the parliamentary commission from 1838–1840. The government made small reforms to its prisons on May 10, 1839, when an order was issued to stop all use of wine and tobacco in prison, make work obligatory for prisoners, establish a rule of silence in the central prisons, increase surveillance, begin to conduct primary schools for prisoners, and allow prisoners to begin sending their earnings from prison labor to their families (Tocqueville 1984a, p. 2, 123–125). Yet these reforms only slowed the increasing number of recidivists, rather than reducing that statistic.

On June 20, 1840 Tocqueville wrote and presented the committee's report to the Chamber. The report recommended using the punishment of solitary confinement for those accused of crimes (*les inculpés, les prévenus, les accuses*), and for those convicted of petty crimes. Both types of criminal were considered to be generally innocent, whether in fact or intention, and not yet corrupted as older, more experienced criminals were. Thus, keeping such persons in solitary confinement would ensure their relative preservation from the influences of other criminals, and perhaps their reformation. The subsequent parliamentary debate focused on whether solitary confinement was harmful to body and mind or whether it was a form of moral treatment for the souls of prisoners. In the end, the Guizot government withdrew the bill for revisions.

On July 5, 1843, Tocqueville submitted a second report to the Chamber, which was subsequently printed in the third edition of *On the Penitentiary System* (published in 1845).[8] The report exemplified a moderate approach to avoiding the extremes of both the Auburn and Philadelphia systems, against which serious objections had arisen in partisan camps in the Chamber of Deputies. Beaumont praises the report in an published in *Le Siècle*, saying, "It did not adopt either [system] [...] but, while rejecting both modes of imprisonment, it has borrowed from them all those principles which are essential to the reform of prisons" (Tocqueville 1984a, pp. 476–477). Although the report begins by claiming that there were no fundamental revisions to the original proposal of 1840, Tocqueville now changes partisanship and writes wholly in favor of a revised form of the Philadelphia system of solitary confinement, to be applied to all levels of prisons in France.[9] There are four primary reasons why Tocqueville now argues in favor of solitary confinement, whereas before he was reticent to fully support one discipline over the other.

In part, Tocqueville's new support for the Philadelphia system was a calculated political move to overcome the political challenges posed by the Auburn system. The Auburn system of prison discipline simply drummed up too much opposition for any hope of its use in France. Tocqueville argues that while the Auburn discipline of common work in silence was the more popular system worldwide, prevented "the largest disorders of mores," made prisoners more productive, and was easier to establish than the Philadelphia system, it nevertheless relied too heavily on the use of the whip to maintain silence. Tocqueville notes an increase of mortality in all prisons where collective silence "had been energetically and most completely maintained" (Tocqueville 1984b, p. 130). In his 1843 speech to the Chamber in defense of the report, Tocqueville goes further in his denunciation of the corporal punishment necessary to support the Auburn system: "it [the system of silence] is effective only on condition of being revoltingly harsh [...] Sometimes it happens, as in France, that it is simultaneously harsh and ineffective, and this is the reason: in France we have not generally been able to make use of the Americans' energetic method—which consists of mercilessly beating the criminal. Happily our mores are opposed to it" (Tocqueville 1968, p. 75). As was the case is 1832, French mores still did not support the effective use of the whip in prisons. In some of their prisons, the French had attempted to replace the use of the whip with increased surveillance, but this method increased the cost of hiring guards and was less effective.

Further, Tocqueville argues that the multiplicity of punishments which are needed to enforce silence are, in fact, contrary to the reform of the criminal. Excessive corporal punishment fosters indifference, exasperation, and discouragement to those prisoners who desire to live a good life after fulfilling their sentence. Even if it is possible to maintain absolute silence during all hours of the day, the Auburn system still allows prisoners to see and know each other, and thus when prisoners leave the prison they are in danger of being recognized by a former inmate. Tocqueville says that once returned to a free society, "they [former prisoners] reciprocally prevent each other from returning to the good; they do evil to each other, and they form these criminal associations which, in recent times especially, compromised the public security and the life of citizens" (Tocqueville 1984b, p. 132).[10] Thus, Auburn presents too many difficulties in its proper execution without ensuring the promised result of reforming criminals.

Given the many political and social problems with the Auburn system, Tocqueville instead proposes the gradual but total incorporation of solitary confinement in every kind of national prison (departmental prisons, central prisons, and "maisons de travaux forces" which eventually replaced the *bagnes*) (Perrot 1984, p. 33). He asks the Ministry to begin such a conversion of French prison discipline by isolating those accused of crimes and those who were sentenced to spend one to six months in prison; these persons were not hardened criminals, and would be more susceptible to corruption by fellow prisoners if not isolated.

Second, Tocqueville now supports establishing the Philadelphia system as a concession to the inevitability of enacting penal reform via a centralized, rather than decentralized, system. Tocqueville comes to recognize the near impossibility of decentralizing prison administration in France. Although initially reticent to embrace centralized administration of French prisons, Tocqueville later argues that centralized administration of prisons is necessary to enact the measures of penal reform proposed by his committee. He gives two reasons: first, public morality and the common good require that equal punishments are applied to the same crimes. Uniformity in execution can be obtained only by allowing the central power to direct all prisons. Yet because centralization does not allow a government to "direct and monitor at each instant all its agents in the exercise of complicated and detailed rules," utilizing the relatively simplistic discipline of solitary confinement benefits the nation's attempt at uniformity (Tocqueville 1984b, p. 134). The Auburn discipline system would be too complicated to properly enforce under a centralized administration. In contrast, solitary confinement is easier to administer and relies upon simple and uniform rules which can best succeed in a nation with a centralized government. Tocqueville thus recommends centralizing the executive power over prison administration, while keeping surveillance decentralized and in the hands of local authorities. To enable localities to retain their right and responsibility of surveillance, Tocqueville suggests creating commissions staffed by the most eminent citizens in the locality.

Tocqueville has also become convinced that solitary confinement is most suitable to effecting the moral reform of certain prisoners. The argument over whether solitary confinement was a moral prison discipline was heavily debated in the years leading up to his report of 1843; Tocqueville's arguments connecting the Philadelphia discipline to prisoner morality reflect his acknowledgement of the need to resolve such a debate. Tocqueville qualifies his argument in support of solitary confinement's moral effects by recognizing that changing a great criminal into a virtuous man is both difficult and rare. Yet solitary confinement prevents prisoners from becoming more corrupt, which is "the only result perhaps that is prudent for a government to propose" (Tocqueville 1984b, p. 134). Here Tocqueville reverts to his principle evident in the first edition of *On the Penitentiary System*, that a prudent statesman will account for the limits in human nature when seeking to reform individuals. Tocqueville goes on to praise a third aspect of solitary confinement: "of all systems of imprisonment, it is the most proper to vividly strike the imagination of citizens, and to leave deep traces in the mind of prisoners. In other words, there is none which, by the fear that it inspires, is more proper to stop first crimes and to prevent recidivism" (Tocqueville 1984b, p. 135). Although Tocqueville does not explain how solitary confinement can be a preventative measure to the wider society, he does argue that solitary confinement reduces recidivism because it breaks apart the "society of criminals" that exists within the larger society.[11]

Fourth, Tocqueville argues that the Philadelphia system will be more economical than the present state of French prisons. Tocqueville still asserts that prisons utilizing the discipline of solitary confinement cost more to build than those that employ silence and common labor, due to the large number of cells necessary to construct. However, he argues that in the long term the prisons cost less to maintain since fewer guards are needed to enforce the discipline. Thus, Tocqueville is willing to concede the initial financial cost of establishing solitary confinement as the primary discipline in French prisons because he takes a long-term perspective on the benefits of the discipline. Above all, he argues that "individual imprisonment, making crimes rarer, will make criminals less numerous" (Tocqueville 1984b, p. 139). The question for Tocqueville at this point was not whether the Auburn or Philadelphia system would be costlier by comparison, but whether the Philadelphia system would successfully repress crime, reduce recidivism, and thereby best safeguard the lives and wealth of citizens. Tocqueville thus declares that, whatever the cost of solitary confinement, "an intelligent society will always believe to regain in peace and even in riches whatever it spends usefully on its prisons." A social investment in prisons was worth every penny to honest citizens.

Tocqueville nevertheless squarely addresses the possible financial problems with a prison built on the principle of solitary confinement in contrast to the Auburn system. He specifically answers two concerns regarding the type of labor that solitary confinement allows prisoners to engage in. There were concerns that the industries which could be performed in solitary confinement would not be useful to the prisoners after their release from prison. Many of the prisoners worked in an agricultural trade before entering the prison, which would be impossible to continue within four walls. Thus, prisoners would be expected to learn an entirely new trade, and a trade that would not necessarily benefit them after returning to society. Tocqueville also addresses the corresponding problem that the types of industries performed in solitary confinement produce less goods than those that can be accomplished in a common workroom, which increases the overall costliness of the prison by reducing its profits. He suggests that this latter point is too cloudy to determine with any certainty, and gives examples of prisons built on the Auburn system which also do not cover expenses with profits (Tocqueville 1984b, p. 138). Additionally, in comparison to existing European prisons, the labor of prisoners in solitary confinement produces more favorable results.

In his defense of the Philadelphia system, Tocqueville must also answer two large objections to the discipline. First, opponents raised the objection that solitary confinement does not allow for enough variation to proportionally punish all crimes. Opponents to solitary confinement argue that the punishment can only be varied in its duration, and thus does not "strike the imagination of the public" effectively enough to act as a preventative measure. Tocqueville responds by noting that imprisonment has only recently emerged as a new form of punishment, leaving the death penalty and forms of disgrace as viable punishments in the French penal code. Additionally, prisons can adjust the rigor of solitary confinement for individual prisoners by altering food allotments, workloads, and remuneration for such work, depending on the classification of the crime or prisoner behavior.

Most importantly, Tocqueville must respond to concerns that solitary confinement does not civilize prisoners, and instead leads prisoners to a host of mental illnesses. On this issue, Tocqueville articulates his opposition's argument in detail, working through four specific criticisms. The criticisms are as follows: first, because the prisoner is entirely deprived of his free will in solitary confinement, he cannot make either a bad or good use of it. Hence, "he is not taught to conquer himself, since he is incapable of failing." There is no opportunity for moral choice in solitary confinement. Second, because the prisoner is alone, he is not sensitive to the opinions of his fellow men. He cannot emulate good citizens, and thus cannot positively progress in civic morality. Rather, "it is to be feared that he will become worse." Third, critics argue that solitude is an unnatural state of being, and thus either destroys or irritates the human spirit. Many prisoners who undergo solitary confinement consider "society as an implacable tyrant." While in prison, the incarcerated only wait to avenge themselves on society, rather than seek to become good citizens. Finally, "solitude has the effect of disturbing reason," and often leads to suicide (Tocqueville 1984b, p. 140).

Tocqueville does not dismiss any of the above four criticisms of the mental and social effects of solitary confinement upon prisoners. Instead, he first uses the American experience in solitary confinement to argue against the assumption of critics that these results will especially be felt among the French because of their increased cultural need for sociability. Tocqueville's objection here reflects his research for the first edition of *On the Penitentiary System*, particularly his interview with prison director Elam Lynds (of the Sing Sing penitentiary), who claimed that "the easiest to govern were the French; they were those who submitted most readily and with the best grace to their fate when they judged it inevitable" (Tocqueville 1984a, p. 343). On their tour through American prisons, Tocqueville and Beaumont asked similar questions of penal directors and inspectors regarding their estimation of the suitability of the penitentiary discipline system for the French people, and relied heavily on the experience of such persons to draw their judgments. Tocqueville therefore argues that the French character is indeed suitable for punishments such as enforced silence or solitary confinement, regardless of the cultural differences between America and France.

Tocqueville then proceeds to give answers to each of the four points made above, engaging in a nuanced dialogue with the objections. Responding to the first objection that solitary confinement does not adequately direct the prisoner's free will, Tocqueville answers that the Auburn system of directing the free will by fear of whipping or hunger was not a good alternative. Those who comply with prison rules enforced by corporal punishment tend to be the worst criminals who can calculate their long-term advantage by their short-term obedience. Thus, any prison discipline is faced with the difficult choice of attempting to positively engage the free will of the prisoner to desire obedience by either corporal punishment or solitude. Neither solitude nor enforced silence are persuasive measures, instead relying upon different forms of coercion.

To the second objection, that prisoners kept in solitary confinement are not exposed to the healthy pressures society can place upon their behavior, Tocqueville questions the assumption that social pressure always exercises a good influence upon individuals. He argues, "as to the action men can have upon each other, it can only be pernicious [...] public opinion pushes towards vice, not virtue, and ambition can scarcely ever do good" (Tocqueville 1984b, p. 141). Not only should prison reformers be aware of the negative moral effects that a community of criminals can have upon each other, but they also need to be aware of the limited moral effects that society in general can have upon criminals. There is not a clear choice between the "goodness" of society and the "evil" of inmates when seeking to influence the moral nature of prisoners. Instead, a moderate evaluation of the problems and advantages with all types of human society is the best approach to understanding the possibilities and limitations of reforming prisoners. Thus, Tocqueville recommends only allowing prisoners to have contact with those who are considered to be the most honest persons in society—most notably, chaplains, doctors, and prison directors. Such strict control over the relational influences in a prisoner's life can be best implemented using solitary confinement.

Tocqueville spends the most time discussing concerns about the effects of solitary confinement upon the mental health of prisoners. Opponents to solitary confinement argue that the discipline aggravates the rebellious and vindictive part of the human spirit and causes severe depression leading to self-inflicted bodily harm or death. Again, Tocqueville does not deny these psychological consequences of the discipline he now defends. In his speech to the Chamber, Tocqueville admits that attempting "to change the point of view from which the inmate views human relations" will produce "rarely, very rarely [...] alarming symptoms" (Tocqueville 1968, p. 84). Instead of denying the problem of mental health issues, his argument is intended to persuade opponents that establishing solitary confinement is still the most moderate course of action to pursue and can itself be moderated to avoid the psychological problems it has the capacity to produce in prisoners.

Tocqueville begins to address his opponents' arguments by insisting that partisans agree on certain points before engaging in their discussion. First, partisans must agree that because imprisonment is an unnatural state of being for humans, it will inevitably deteriorate the functions of mind and body. Such consequences are inherent in punishment itself.[12] Second, partisans must also agree that “the object of prisons is not to restore the health of criminals or to prolong their lives, but to punish them and prevent their imitators” (Tocqueville 1984b, p. 142). Here Tocqueville weighs the rights of society to pursue retribution and deterrence against the rights of individuals. Even if the lifespan of prisoners is slightly shorter than that of free men, justice still prevails for humanity in general if society has achieved those goals of punishment. Further, after reviewing the statistics of four prisons (Glascow, Roquette, Philadelphia, and Auburn), Tocqueville argues that although the Philadelphia prison measures poorly in comparison to the other three prisons in terms of mortality rates, it measures better in comparison to the existing prisons in France. Additionally, the mortality rates of French soldiers, ostensibly free persons honorably serving their country, far exceed those of prisoners in the Philadelphia penitentiary. Only by agreeing on these fundamental realities can partisans hope to have a fruitful debate on the psychological problems posed by solitary confinement.

Even if prisoners do not experience greater mortality rates in solitary confinement, they do experience “hallucination” and “mental overstimulation,” two illnesses Tocqueville does not deny. He therefore argues that France should adopt the principle of solitary confinement while rejecting the discipline of absolute solitude which causes such mental difficulties. As will be shown, Tocqueville moderates the discipline of solitary confinement by intentionally advocating for certain institutional limits upon the solitude of the prisoner. Further, he argues that the construction of the building itself will help to alleviate mental stress caused by solitary confinement: engaging prisoners in the work of building the prison, ensuring adequate air flow between cells by creating larger halls, and avoiding excessive monuments or ornaments, will all help prisoners to avoid mental illness (Tocqueville 1984b, p. 146).

In his support for a moderated solitary confinement, Tocqueville returns to the principle of the need to rely upon religion within penitentiaries to effect moral reform, an idea originally evident in the first edition of *On the Penitentiary System*. One of the greatest advantages of the discipline of solitary confinement lies in its ability to affect the heart of the prisoner through religious penal disciplines. Tocqueville claims that “individual imprisonment is assuredly, of all systems, that which leaves the most chances for religious reformation” (Tocqueville 1984b, p. 148). Contradictorily, Tocqueville’s praise of the religious aspect of solitary confinement comes on the heels of his criticism that it is because “the

Philadelphia prison was created for a religious purpose even more than for social interest" that it produces mental issues among prisoners in solitary confinement. The principle of absolute solitude resulted from religious ideals that, if left completely alone, the prisoner would turn to God for comfort. Religious reformers did not consider the less extreme goal of separating prisoners from each other while still encouraging healthy relationships with other members of society. In other words, religion in America led penal reformers to the extreme principle of isolation, rather than to the moderated principle of separation.

Importantly, although Tocqueville now recommends the Philadelphia system of solitary confinement, he draws a careful distinction between isolation and separation. The French ought to separate prisoners from fellow criminals who could have a corrupting influence on them, but not isolate prisoners altogether from society. As Beaumont claims in his article published in *Le Siècle* in support of the 1843 bill, "Isolation was the fundamental character of the Philadelphia system. Separation is the essential trait of the new French system" (Tocqueville 1984a, p. 477). Tocqueville's newly drawn distinction between isolation and separation allows him to justify solitary confinement as separation from evil (namely, criminal) influences, but not isolation from any good social influences. Tocqueville therefore recommends that, while keeping the religious purpose of solitary confinement, one temper its extremes by purposefully hiring several chaplains of different religious backgrounds who can visit with the prisoners frequently. Doctors, teachers, and chaplains would all be key personnel in French prisons to avoid the mental problems associated with absolute solitude. Although the prisoner would not be isolated completely, they would successfully be isolated from corrupting influences and maintain communication with healthy influences.

Tocqueville's distinction between isolation and separation reveals that although Tocqueville was willing to embrace the Philadelphia system as a means of reform, he still maintains his initial concerns with the system and seeks to moderate its extremes. Tocqueville concludes: "The chamber sees clearly what has been the general goal of the commission [...] the point of departure for the founders of the Philadelphia penitentiary system was to render solitude as complete as one can imagine. The system of the bill tried to diminish it as much as possible, to reduce it to only the separation of criminals from each other" (Tocqueville 1984b, p. 149). Tocqueville's modification to the Philadelphia system represents the work of a statesman who can evaluate the rigor of a mode of punishment in consideration of the needs of individuals.

Tocqueville also recommends a limitation to be placed on the duration of solitary confinement, as it was to be practiced in French prisons. His proposed law recommended a limit of 12 consecutive years in a solitary cell, after which the prisoner would be allowed to labor in common workrooms in silence. Tocqueville acknowledges that this limit was heatedly debated among committee members; foremost among criticisms was the argument that by limiting the years of solitary confinement, "one defeats the good so laboriously produced" by the discipline (Tocqueville 1984b, p. 165). Moreover, the limit would apply only to prisoners who committed the most dangerous crimes and who thus received the longest punishments, sentences stretching beyond 12 years. The state had a greater interest in keeping such criminals in solitary confinement, rather than putting them in contact with other prisoners. Critics further argue that because cellular imprisonment is not isolation, only separation, it is an obligation and privilege to live apart from criminal society.

Yet Tocqueville defends the limitation on the same principle of balancing the evidence of theory and practice which he used to evaluate the penal disciplines in his first edition: solitary confinement has been shown by both theory and practice to be severe on the mind.[13] In particular, even if you allow visits from family and friends, these visits inevitably become more and more rare over the duration of the punishment, thus further isolating the prisoner from outside society. Such social isolation inflicts a special toll on the prisoner's mind; it deprives them of hope, convinces them of their abandonment by fellow citizens, and often leads them to violence. Limits upon solitary confinement are thus beneficial both for the mental health of the prisoner and for the society which will eventually receive prisoners back.

In sum, Tocqueville's policy change evidenced in his speech to the Chamber in 1843, a shift from primarily supporting the Auburn system to advocating for the Philadelphia system, can be characterized as an effort in moderation. As noted above, Tocqueville takes the time to lay out the arguments debated in the committee on most of the articles in the proposed law. Many of the votes in the committee were passed with a narrow margin of 5–4, indicating heightened partisanship for certain measures. Yet Tocqueville is able to balance the arguments of both sides, acknowledging where an opposing argument's strengths lay, but also relying heavily on historical, practical, and sometimes comparative experience to ground the committee's reasoning and final decisions.

Additionally, although Tocqueville now advocates rigorously in favor of establishing the Philadelphia system of solitary confinement in prisons, a policy measure he previously opposed, he takes steps to place institutional and legal limitations upon the severity of solitary confinement and to engage in debate toward that end. Tocqueville recommended the following limits upon solitary confinement: (1) the punishment could not exceed 12 years, (2) a part of the prisoner's salary, which belonged to the state, would be given back to him when he left the prison, and (3) some flexibility in the right of visitation, which had been rigorously denied in 1836 (Perrot 1984, p. 33). Specifically, prisoners ought to be able to receive visits from family, friends, and their lawyer (Tocqueville 1984b, p. 122, 149). Each of these limits was a hard-fought win from within the committee. While Tocqueville does not wholeheartedly endorse the system of solitary confinement, he is willing to recommend the punishment under limited terms. The limitations on solitary confinement, especially the time limit which allows prisoners to return to an Auburn system of silent work in common, indicates that Tocqueville allowed for a change in means to gain the end in mind, which was to reform French prisons to cohere with the principles of moral reformation that the American penitentiary system reflects.

Furthermore, Tocqueville is now willing (where before he was hesitant) to allow for greater centralized administration over prisons. Tocqueville carefully parses what kind of increased centralization the committee calls for; centralized administration in execution of the penal reform, yet retention of local surveillance over the prison itself. Both of these policy "switches" evidence Tocqueville's moderate ability to accept the terms of an opposing view while still modifying the application of that opinion to cohere with his principles.

In his speech to the Chamber of Deputies in 1843, Tocqueville also attempts to moderate or balance the excuses of the Ministry and Chamber, which slowed down any kind of reform, and the demand from the public for reform. Tocqueville's frustration with the slow reform in France is most evident in his report of 1843. At one point, he implies that even if the Chamber did not see its responsibility to care for public security and morals as compelling enough to provoke action, the rules of good administration ought to provoke them to decide which penal system would guide the creation of new prisons and reform of the old (Tocqueville 1984b, p. 126). At this point, too, public opinion called for the complete dismantling of the *bagnes*, a request that the Ministry had also ignored.

According to Tocqueville's account, only a small number of persons argued in favor of keeping the *bagnes* for their preventative effect in society. Such arguments contended that persons tempted to commit great crimes are dissuaded by fear of the punishment enforced in the *bagnes*. On the other hand, partisans for solitary confinement claimed that life in the *bagnes* was freer, less monotonous, and healthier than in prisons. While the *bagnes* are hard on the body, solitary confinement is hard on the soul. Thus, even the most hardened criminals prefer the *bagnes* to solitary confinement. Tocqueville's specific pleas to the Chamber to begin implementing the Philadelphia system in central prisons as an alternative to the *bagnes* is thus a political move to push the government to accomplish the public's will, even while he concedes that the administration over prisons will continue to be centralized in France.

Wins and Losses from Tocqueville's and Beaumont's Penal Debates

Over the course of their lifetime, Tocqueville's and Beaumont's efforts in penal reform were largely unsuccessful. By the admission of the authors themselves, the printing of the third edition proved the inability of the French government to act to reform prisons. In their "note from the editor," the authors acknowledge that even as late as 1844 it was still true to say that the controversial questions of prison reform were still timely, and still of both theoretical and practical interest (Tocqueville 1984a, p. 86). Although the law proposed in 1833 was favorably received in the Chamber of Deputies during debate in 1844, passing a vote on May 18 by 231 to 128, it was questioned in the Chamber of Peers.[14] Tocqueville acknowledged that the report of 1843 would not effect an immediate solution. In his preface to the third edition of *On the Penitentiary System* Tocqueville writes: "Everyone knows that the bill intended to realize the reform of the prisons, and adopted by the Chamber of Deputies, will not be voted on this year, nor even discussed by the Chamber of Peers…" (Tocqueville 1984a, p. 86). At best, Tocqueville hoped the Chamber of Peers would appoint a Committee to consider the bill and prepare a report for the next discussion, which is precisely what happened. The Chamber especially asked whether the proposed reforms were compatible with the penal code and the code of criminal instruction, although Tocqueville had pointed out such points of compatibility wherever possible in his report. Debates in the Chamber of Peers further slowed any practical implementation of penal reform in France.

France ultimately failed to establish a uniform system of penitentiaries that utilized any form of solitary confinement (absolute or partial), mostly due to the interruptions brought by political instability. Louis Napoleon Bonaparte's *coup d'état* on December 2, 1851 ended any progress on cellular prisons (Drescher 1968, p. 144). France instead began a system of penal colonization on Guiana in 1851, which included sending convicts bi-annually to three islands: Royal, St. Joseph, and *Île du Diable* (Devil's Island). Penal colonization continued, despite growing opposition, until 1938; the facility at Devil's Island was completely shut down in 1946 (Roth 2006, pp. 82–83).

Despite the largely stagnant movement in penal reform, there were a host of small changes to the French penal system in the years 1836–1837, including directives that limited the right of outside persons to visit the central prisons, restrictions on the ability of prisoners to correspond with those outside the prison, maintaining the absolute rule of silence, increased regulations reducing the use of the *pécule* and alcohol in prisons, and establishing work as a means of punishment (Tocqueville 1984a, pp. 26–27). The French passed legislation authorizing the transition from older prisons to penitentiaries in 1836, and in 1839 a directive from the Ministry of the Interior outlawed all communication between prisoners. Despite these small movements toward implementing the principles of the American penitentiary system, the French government did not start openly debating the merits of transitioning prisons to cellular construction until 1838, when Montalivet asked local prefects to consult the general councils on the matter (Tocqueville 1984a, p. 27). As has been discussed, that debate lasted for almost a decade, with no significant practical results.

Nevertheless, *On the Penitentiary System* sparked a necessary national conversation in France on three key penal issues. First, *On the Penitentiary System* elucidated the distinct differences between the Auburn and Philadelphia forms of solitary confinement which became the primary point of debate in the decades to follow. The work provided an opportunity for the public and government to openly and rigorously debate the merits and implementation of penitentiaries by setting aside the distraction of the potential for penal colonies. Although penal colonies were established at the end of the era of penal debate, they came only at the cost of increased centralization, a potential problem that Tocqueville and Beaumont warned of in *On the Penitentiary System*. Additionally, Pierson rightly notes that the conversation begun by Tocqueville and Beaumont on the penitentiary idea, albeit unsuccessful during both authors' lives, proved helpful in 1870 after the fall of the Second Empire when renewed interest in penitentiaries spurred the implementation of the Compromise of 1840 (1938, pp. 715–717).

Second, the work encouraged the growth of houses of refuge for children in France. Mitchel Roth writes that several juvenile delinquent centers were founded between 1827 and 1840, “inspired by the Houses of Refuge in vogue in America” (2006, p. 102). In their second edition of *On the Penitentiary System*, Tocqueville and Beaumont proclaim their success in bringing to light a need for increased care for juvenile delinquents; the authors note the growth of juvenile delinquent centers in eastern France (Tocqueville 1984a, pp. 82–83, 116). Additionally, a new appendix appeared in the second edition, titled “Houses of Refuge in Germany and Prussia,” which attempted to directly address the lack of such institutions in France (Tocqueville 1984a, p. 428).

Further, in his speech to the Chamber in 1843, Tocqueville notes that the committee on penal reform unanimously approved the principle of establishing additional houses of refuge for young children. The committee focused on answering the question of who determines when juvenile delinquents could leave houses of refuge to be placed in apprenticeships. Arguing that judges were too unfamiliar with the youth’s character, behavior in the house of refuge, and readiness for an apprenticeship, the committee suggested that the decision be made jointly with the administration of the house of refuge and the judicial authority. Additionally, the committee argued that patronage societies were needed to make the apprenticeship programs successful.[15] The houses were to contain juvenile delinquents whose crimes were excusable given their age (according to both law and reason) and children who had been found innocent by a court, but who the judge was hesitant to return to their families. The goal of the system was, just as was described in the first edition of *On the Penitentiary System*, to reform through education rather than to reflect punishment or public vengeance for crime. Tocqueville and Beaumont thus sustained a relatively successful call to remedy crime and promote social rehabilitation among the youth throughout their political careers.

Principally, Tocqueville shows us through his two decades of legislative involvement in penal reform the means of compromise necessary to any moderate politician seeking effective policy change.[16] Despite Tocqueville’s ultimate “switch” in partisanship from subtly supporting the Auburn system to publicly advocating for the Philadelphia system, there is a notable consistency that expands our understanding of Tocqueville’s moderate liberalism. Tocqueville’s discussion of penal reform revolves tightly around the question posed by crime to the liberal order, which is, how to simultaneously secure liberty for individuals (even those who have broken the law) and security for society. Throughout his discussion in all three editions of *On the Penitentiary System*, Tocqueville carefully balances the right of society to punish and protect its citizens against the right of prisoners to safety and the possibility of reformation from the state's institutions. Tocqueville's priority throughout his work in penal reform is to insist on the ability of the prisoner to re-enter society as a functioning member, and to seek out the responsibilities of both prisoners and state to ensure that end. Yet the state also needed to consider the financial costs which prisons pose to free citizens, the possibility of deterrence (or preventing future crimes by setting the example of a heavy legal consequence), as well as the state's limitations in shaping the hearts and minds of individual prisoners (Tocqueville 1968, p. 82). This balancing act between the good of society and the good of the individual demanded an ability to moderate competing visions of freedom, such as the need for increased governmental centralization to accomplish the task of promoting individual prisoner's interests. In the end, Tocqueville shows us that the path toward a moderate penal policy demands a constant balance of both theory and practice, a willingness to act and allow experience to guide re-evaluation of theories, and an ability to see that the common good includes both rights for individuals and for society as a whole.

Notes

1. Other changes to each edition include the following: to the second edition, the authors added new explanatory footnotes throughout the text, an appendix entitled "Some notes from the English translator, Dr. Julius," as well as an appendix containing extracts from both French and foreign journal reviews praising *On the Penitentiary System*. Both appendices added to the second edition were excised from the third edition, which instead included the "Report made by M. de Tocqueville in the name of the committee responsible for examining the bill on prisons (meeting of July 5, 1843)." The third edition also lacked appendices Nos. 9, 12, and 13, statistical notes 5–9 in No. 14, statistical notes 6–12 in No. 17, all of which were included in the first and second editions. Finally, less than 75 minor changes were made to the wording between all three editions.
2. Before leaving for America, Tocqueville visited prisons at Versailles (August, 1830; a *maison d'arrêt*) and Poissy (September; a *centre nationale*). See: Brogan 2006, p. 143.

3. The visit to Roquette would prove immensely useful in the decade following, since Roquette came to be used as an example of solitary confinement which produces profits from the labor of prisoners. See Beaumont's second article in *Le Siècle*, re-published in Tocqueville 1984a, pp. 478–479.
4. Indeed, throughout *On the Penitentiary System* there are indications that Tocqueville and Beaumont preferred the Auburn system, given their special praise of the Wethersfield prison that utilized the Auburn discipline of separation at night and common labor during the day and their inclusion of appendices on the costs of erecting the prison. See: Tocqueville 1984a, p. 208, 243.
5. In the debate on Tocqueville's 1843 bill held on April 26, 1844, Tocqueville again asserts that he has not blamed prisons alone for increased rates of crime and recidivism. Instead, he has also looked to the mores, beliefs, laws, and particular needs of the people. However, he argues that prisons play a significant role in the increase of crime and recidivism because they do not inspire sufficient terror of punishment for crime in the general society, and because they corrupt rather than morally reform the inmates. Tocqueville 1984b, p. 219.
6. Whereas Drescher asserts that the issue of prison reform "first brought Tocqueville and Beaumont to an awareness of the insidious nature of the modern tendency toward centralization," he subsequently argues that "they readily agreed to centralized administration in order to accomplish reforms in this area" (1968, p. 145). Drescher argues that Tocqueville eventually supported a complete centralization of power within the penitentiary which was necessary to support the internal desocialization project of penitentiaries. Hence, Drescher sees Tocqueville and Beaumont as performing a reversal on the issue of centralization. My argument here and in Chap. 3 deepens Drescher's vision of Tocqueville's shift on the issue of centralization. Tocqueville and Beaumont continued to support decentralization of the penal system within political society (outside of the penitentiary), while simultaneously acknowledging the need for centralized power within the penitentiary. Understanding that Tocqueville and Beaumont see a need for balance between modes of power in different social and political spheres helps us to understand that the "shift" does not occur on a level plane. In other words, the shift does not represent a reversal but a consistent appeal for moderate balance of centralization in one area and decentralization in another. Notably, the highly centralized internal authority structure of the penitentiary depended on a decentralized authority over penal reform in general; only by having an engaged local public would prisoners in solitary confinement have access to visiting ministers, Sunday School teachers, and so forth which was crucial to the project of reforming individuals. Thus, Drescher is only partially correct when he asserts a

"reversal" of thought in terms of centralization. Finally, as I show here, Tocqueville and Beaumont did echo some of their fears of centralization in their work during the 1840s, contrary to Drescher's claim (Drescher 1968, p. 149).

7. Tocqueville 1984a, p. 127. Tocqueville and Beaumont specifically analyze Article 614 of the Code of Criminal Procedure.
8. In September and October 1843, Beaumont published a series of articles in *Le Siècle* in defense of Tocqueville's report and the legislative bill, albeit he did so anonymously. The articles were fiercely criticized by Léon Faucher, to whom Tocqueville wrote a detailed refutation. See: Tocqueville 1984a, p. 29.
9. In his speech defending the bill of 1843 to the Chamber of Deputies on April 26, 1844, Tocqueville asserts that "there is only one system. This single system consists in separating convicts from one another" (Tocqueville 1968, p. 74). Yet such separation can occur by either silence or walls.
10. For a striking example of this problem, see Tocqueville's interview with a prisoner in the Philadelphia penitentiary from October 1831 (Tocqueville 1984a, pp. 336–338).
11. Tocqueville's revised argument that solitary confinement promotes moral behavior also helps him to shift support toward deportation of criminals. Tocqueville later allowed for the prudence of deporting criminals after they spent 10–12 years in solitary confinement because such imprisonment would decrease the risk of creating an immoral colonial society (Forster 1991, pp. 143–144).
12. Tocqueville emphasizes this point in his speech to the Chamber: "imprisonment of any kind creates susceptibility to insanity" (Tocqueville 1968, p. 86).
13. Experience still confirms this fact, as Christopher Epps (Commissioner of Corrections for the State of Mississippi) testified before the Senate Judicial Committee's hearing *Reassessing Solitary Confinement: The Human Rights, Fiscal, and Public Safety Consequences* (2012). Epps described a slow degeneration in the use of solitary confinement in the Mississippi Department of Corrections; whereas the punishment was intended to be used "for the most incorrigible and dangerous offenders" and only until they demonstrated good behavior, in practice it came to be used as a permanent holding place for gang members, the mentally ill, and disruptive prisoners.
14. Notably, the bill was passed with the following revisions: the length of solitary confinement was reduced from 12 to 10 years, and rather than moving prisoners to the Auburn system following solitary confinement, they were to be transported outside of France (Pierson 1938, p. 713).

15. However, note Tocqueville's personal criticism of patronage in his review to the Academy of Moral and Political Sciences of M. R. Allier's book *Etudes sur le système pénitentiaire et les sociétés de patronage* (1842) (Tocqueville 1968, pp. 90–97). Tocqueville argues that a system of governmental patronage (or, welfare) would "add very heavy and even unbearable obligations to those that already burden our citizens," as well as erase efficacy by negating the principle of voluntarism in charity (1968, p. 95).
16. Here I depart from Pierson's criticism that Tocqueville and Beaumont were "narrow partisans" (1938, p. 716).

References

Beaumont, Gustave de, and Alexis de Tocqueville. 1833. *On the Penitentiary System in the United States and Its Application in France, with an Appendix on Penal Colonies and also Statistical Notes*, trans. Francis Lieber. Philadelphia: Carey, Lea & Blanchard.

Brogan, Hugh. 2006. *Alexis de Tocqueville: A Life*. New Haven: Yale University Press.

Drescher, Seymour. 1968. *Dilemmas of Democracy: Tocqueville and Modernization*. Pittsburgh: University of Pittsburgh Press.

Forster, Colin. 1991. French Penal Policy and the Origins of the French Presence in New Caledonia. *The Journal of Pacific History* 26 (2): 135–150.

O'Brien, Patricia. 1982. *The Promise of Punishment: Prisons in Nineteenth-Century France*. Princeton: Princeton University Press.

Perrot, Michelle. 1984. Tocqueville Méconnu. In *Œuvres Complètes: Écrits sur le système pénitentiaire en France et à l'étranger, Tome IV, Vol. 1*, 7–44. Paris: Gallimard.

Pierson, George. 1938. *Tocqueville in America*. Baltimore: The Johns Hopkins University Press.

Roth, Mitchel P. 2006. *Prisons and Prison Systems: A Global Encyclopedia*. Westport, CT: Greenwood Press.

Tocqueville, Alexis de. 1968. *Tocqueville and Beaumont on Social Reform*, ed. and trans. Seymour Drescher. New York: Harper Torch Books.

———. 1984a. *Œuvres Complètes: Écrits sur le système pénitentiaire en France et à l'étranger, Tome IV, Vol. 1*, ed. Michelle Perrot. Paris: Gallimard.

———. 1984b. *Œuvres Complètes: Écrits sur le système pénitentiaire en France et à l'étranger, Tome IV, Vol. 2*, ed. Michelle Perrot. Paris: Gallimard.

United States Senate Committee on the Judiciary. 2012. *Reassessing Solitary Confinement: The Human Rights, Fiscal, and Public Safety Consequences*. U.S. Government Printing Office. https://www.judiciary.senate.gov/imo/media/doc/CHRG-112shrg87630.pdf. Accessed 14 November 2017.

CHAPTER 6

Conclusion: Tocqueville's Penal Reform and Today's Penal Problems

The preceding chapters have briefly outlined the philosophical and political purposes of *On the Penitentiary System*, distinguished some differences between the penal thought of Lieber and Tocqueville as liberal thinkers, and evaluated the evolving impact that Tocqueville's ideas on penal reform had upon French penal debates in the mid-nineteenth century. To conclude this work on Tocqueville's penal thought, I want to note some of the important questions that remain and briefly reflect on the implications that a study of *On the Penitentiary System* has for the present.

Two Remaining Questions

Although the work has clarified Tocqueville's arguments on penal colonization, it only briefly addressed how Tocqueville's initial rejection of penal colonies in *On the Penitentiary System* squares with his later support for the French Algerian colonization project. It would be especially interesting to know if there is any theoretical relationship between Tocqueville's work and interest in penitentiary systems and his later work examining the Algerian colonies. We have already provided a basis for understanding these two political concerns as related in our argument that Tocqueville originally conceived of penitentiary systems as an alternative policy to the establishment of penal colonies. Nevertheless, there are other associations between the policy endeavors Tocqueville chose to define his political

E. K. Ferkaluk, *Tocqueville's Moderate Penal Reform*,
Recovering Political Philosophy,
https://doi.org/10.1007/978-3-319-75577-9_6

career. Both policies reflect a concern for the lowest classes of society as those most prone to criminal activity. Further, the execution and maintenance of both penal colonies and Algerian colonization challenged the powers and political capability of the centralized French government. These, and other similarities, are waiting to be fleshed out in the future and will help to lend a clearer and more consistent view of Tocqueville as a statesman.

A second important, but largely unanswered, question that remains from this study is how do the themes of *On the Penitentiary System* compare to Tocqueville's larger works, especially *Democracy in America*, which followed so closely in publication? It is possible that the themes within *On the Penitentiary System* can be seen as a precursor to the more developed ideas in *Democracy in America*. Although the work has, as often as possible, footnoted or incorporated explanations of the links between ideas in both works, no systematic comparison has been drawn between the two. I sought to understand *On the Penitentiary System* on its own terms, rather than through the lens of Tocqueville's later writings.

Still, it might be helpful to briefly sketch a comparison between one shared theme of *On the Penitentiary System* and *Democracy in America*, in order to provide the basis for a future study. As has been shown, at the root of both the theoretical and practical arguments in *On the Penitentiary System* stands Tocqueville's and Beaumont's assumption that the public imagination is at least partially responsible for penal policies that are either beneficial or harmful to both the individual (as in the case of their philosophical purpose) and the nation (as in the case of their political purpose). In the first case, the authors argue that the idea of penitentiaries succeeds by establishing a moderated ideal for reform and by rightly directing the inmate's imagination to desire honor afforded through an honest life of self-sufficiency in society. In the second case, the authors politically temper the desire for penal colonies in France and instead guide the French public to embrace a moderate penal system that is possible given their resources and circumstances. Tocqueville and Beaumont argue that the dangerous desire to establish penal colonies depends on a two-fold improper use of the imagination (by both penal reformers and the poorest classes), and thus they attempt to persuade the public to reject Britain's example and embrace American penitentiaries. Hence, the argument of *On the Penitentiary System* might be summarized as rightly directing the public's imagination to achieve effective penal reform in France.

Tocqueville's later work also includes a discussion of what a statesman ought to consider when attempting to moderate the democratic public's political imagination. For example, in I.2.9 of *Democracy in America*, Tocqueville presents the argument that religion "confines the imagination of Americans within certain limits and moderates their passion for innovation" (Tocqueville 2000, p. 278). Because Christianity prevails without obstacle in American society, it makes "everything [...] certain and fixed in the moral world [...] so the human spirit never perceives an unlimited field before itself." Christianity forces even revolutionaries to avoid the idea that "everything is permitted in the interest of society" by bolstering both the morality and equality of human beings (Tocqueville 2000, p. 280; emphasis added). Democratic peoples may want equality at any price, but religion teaches them that they have moral obligations which limit how they attain greater equality. Religion therefore particularly supports the mores of equality that are coveted within a democracy by limiting the extent of the democratic imagination.

By arguing that religion limits the political imaginations of citizens, Tocqueville implicitly shows us that it is the religious imagination that lies at the basis of the proper use of freedom. Religion "prevents [democratic citizens] from conceiving everything and forbids them to dare everything" (Tocqueville 2000, p. 280). Religion therefore gives democratic citizens the moral limits by which to properly use their freedom. Indeed, Tocqueville goes further in his argument: without religion, democracy offers the world the complete legitimization of all future tyrants under the ruse of claiming that despotism is permitted in the interest of society. Thus, tyranny can be understood in its most basic form as the ability to imagine and dare beyond limits; tyranny results from the abuse of the imagination.

The warnings of the need to moderate public imagination in a democracy, made explicit in *Democracy in America*, are implicit throughout the text of *On the Penitentiary System*. The discussion of *On the Penitentiary System* in this work thus forms the basis from which we can, in the future, explore the potential for preventing democratic tyranny in its case study on the development and execution of public penal policy.[1] Furthermore, the arguments on the imagination in both works confirm the positive connection between civic religion and moderate imaginations. *On the Penitentiary System* shows us the impact of religion upon the individual prisoner's moral imagination; *Democracy in America* shows us the impact of religion upon the nation's political imagination. Religion limits the potential tyranny over inmates in a penitentiary by revealing the incapacity of the state to effect moral reformation through purely material means. Religion also limits the potential tyranny of a majority in a democratic society by insisting on moral limits to our political actions.

The interpretation in this book is merely a beginning of the work that needs to be done to understand *On the Penitentiary System* and its place in Tocqueville's corpus. It is the hope of the author that this analysis of *On the Penitentiary System* clears the pathway for further studies of Tocqueville's political work in French penal reform and penal thought. While the work explicates the main themes of *On the Penitentiary System* that are fundamentally necessary to grasp the meaning and purpose of the text, more work needs to be done to systematically compare the ideas in *On the Penitentiary System* with those of Tocqueville's major works, *Democracy in America* and *The Old Regime and The Revolution*. This future work is part of an ongoing project to understand Tocqueville's political thought as a philosophy that asks questions of and appeals to universal truths, as well as undergirds the prudent decision making of the legislator. As intonated in Chap. 1, Tocqueville was not simply a politician, nor was he thoroughly a philosopher. Tocqueville's political thought instead demonstrates a blend of understanding policy alternatives to particular problems in light of potentially absolute answers to universal questions.

Moreover, while Tocqueville's larger works present his deeper insights into political philosophy, the ideas are sometimes obtusely presented in his major works' length and organization. *On the Penitentiary System* presents scholars of Tocqueville's writings the unique opportunity to read a concise work that demonstrates Tocqueville's philosophical method applied to a particular political problem facing his nation during a specific time. Future comparisons of the case study on penitentiaries in *On the Penitentiary System* to the themes of Tocqueville's larger works will therefore help us to see his philosophical ideas more clearly.

Lessons from *On the Penitentiary System* for the Modern Incarceration State

Not only does *On the Penitentiary System* have the potential to give us a deeper understanding of Tocqueville's political thought, but Tocqueville's penal lessons in *On the Penitentiary System* are also fruitful in helping us to understand the problems attending our current democracy. Some veins of modern thought are especially tempted to imagine a future devoid of peculiarly human problems, a future that lacks poverty or that sees the complete and universal use of reason come to fruition. These material goals reflect the implicit desire that mind fully conquer matter, or more concretely that human beings overcome, through technological and political advancements, the problems that nature presents to us. Tocqueville and Beaumont remind us that hope in such theories must be grounded in experience. Experience is the moderating test of whether society can ever truly eradicate homelessness, or end hunger, or regulate Wall Street to the point where no corruption exists. Human experience grounds the imagination in realistic limits.

Nevertheless, because Tocqueville's and Beaumont's evaluation of the American democratic experiment is rooted fundamentally in an *a priori* understanding of universal human nature, we also need to ask ourselves whether experience can be a guide to political ideals if such a view of human beings is no longer held, at least not by the larger society. More generally, if a political society does not think that human beings have a universal, unchanging nature, or if such a society thinks that human nature is malleable, then the limit to the democratic imagination disappears. Tocqueville and Beaumont show us in *On the Penitentiary System* how a theoretical view of the human life and person holds immanent consequences for political policies.

In concluding this work on Tocqueville's penal reform, it would be useful to note a few specific areas where Tocqueville's penal thoughts have the potential to aide us in our own pursuit of penal reform in twenty-first-century America.[2] We have, as much as possible, attempted to draw such conclusions throughout the work, but it would also be helpful to note contemporary implications that emerge more broadly from the work as a whole. To that end, I will address three main areas of contemporary penal concern which Tocqueville's *On the Penitentiary System* enables us to address in a moderate way: navigating the relationship between crime and social mores, how to address multiple causes of crime, and the objects of any penal system as proportionality, rehabilitation, and reintegration.

First, Tocqueville gives us a heightened awareness that the health of a society determines the success of a penal system. Tocqueville himself was keenly aware of the need to study his own society to understand the unique sources of crime and the potential solutions available to reformers. Hence, at the outset of *On the Penitentiary System*, Tocqueville and Beaumont reject drawing a strict parallel comparison between France and America, despite their ostensible purpose to study American penitentiaries in order to improve the French penal system. While extensive comparisons of France and America takes place in four different places in the main text, as well as in Appendix No. 18, entitled "Some Comparisons Between France and America," each of these portions of the text center on a general theme: a strict comparison between America and France would be imperfect because the two nations have different social conditions.[3]

A strict comparison is rejected first of all because France's penal problems are unique, since the two nations have different conditions of existence (Beaumont and Tocqueville 1833, p. 131). The conditions of existence in any nation are laws, mores, and resources. All three conditions must overlap with each other precisely; otherwise, it is impossible to draw a comparison between two nations. For example, the United States has penal laws that punish activities which French laws do not consider to be an offense, such as crimes against religion and mores. America, conversely, does not punish bankruptcy, whereas French laws do consider bankruptcy a crime. These are examples of a potential difference in the way each individual country links mores to law.

Even if the laws in two different states uphold the same types of mores, there are differences in how a state prosecutes breaches of those laws. At the time of Tocqueville's and Beaumont's journey, some of the most religious states of the Union were most rigorous in convicting citizens for deviating from established mores. The question thus arises: does the law define a nation's mores, or do mores condition the efficacy and character of the law?

Tocqueville and Beaumont answer the implicit question by arguing that if the mores targeted by laws are different, it is almost impossible to know whether one nation's citizens are more ethical or law-abiding than another. For example, political mores reflect the citizen's habitual inclinations to either obey or resist the law (Tocqueville 1984a, pp. 236–7). The majority in the United States possess "a spirit of obedience to the law" or a "spirit of submission to the established order" while France has "in the spirit of the masses [...] an unfortunate tendency to break the law" or a "penchant for insubordination" (Tocqueville 1984a, pp. 234–235). These differences in mores affect how the law is crafted, publicly supported, and governmentally administered in both countries. Further, the more scrupulous a nation's laws, the more moral deviancy is revealed. Thus, even if the definition of "corrupt" were universally acknowledged, the mores of a people can pose "moral obstacles" to the rule of law.[4]

Even if the laws and mores align correctly, the nations might not have equivalent resources to execute the law. Legislation in two different countries can identify the same crime but supply different punishments. Tocqueville and Beaumont argue that it would be necessary to abolish the diversity of punishments from the French penal code, since variety in punishment leads to multiplication of the number of prisons. Differing resources extends to current penal structures built on different theories; for example, in America prisons are built with individual cells based on the principle of separating prisoners from each other, whereas French prisons are built to combine prisoners. In his report to the Chamber in 1843, Tocqueville emphasizes the need to choose the regime of the prison before beginning to build the prison: "If the State is forced to build a rather considerable number of new prisons, it is evident that it is necessary to fix the regime which will be in these prisons in advance; for the plan of a prison and the regime that it chooses to apply to the prisoners that it contains are two correlative things and should not be envisioned separately" (Tocqueville 1984b, p. 127). Architectural layouts of prisons reflect the mode of discipline it employs.

Furthermore, economic factors could differ between both countries. The cost of building new prisons based on the cellular system would be less in France than in America because raw materials are less expensive, and the price of the workforce is lower. Although building new prisons on the cellular system would cost less in France than in America, the success of a new penal law necessitates an initial expenditure to update the buildings and legal authorization of a new penal theory before being implemented (Tocqueville 1984a, p. 222).

Finally, the problem of comparing two country's penal systems results from differing structures of government. Even if laws, mores, and resources are all comparable, to prove the relative merit of prison systems in two countries there needs to be a comparison of the number of criminal re-committals. Yet centralization in France allows for more data to be found on the individual convicts and indicted persons, giving greater "means of investigation" than in America (Tocqueville 1984a, p. 137). Without an equivalent data set, it is impossible to evaluate the success of American penitentiaries in reducing recidivism or to draw a firm conclusion of causality between prison discipline and crime rates.

What is the reason for making so many distinctions between France and America? Tocqueville and Beaumont ultimately declare that "America can be compared only with herself" because any penal reform needs to take account of the unique social, historical, and institutional habits of the people. Because penitentiaries are intended to reform individuals, to some extent the cultural and civic habits of those individuals dictate the method and means of reforming a penal system. By distinguishing the social, historical, and institutional characteristics of France and America, Tocqueville and Beaumont thereby distance themselves from committing the French public wholly to the American system of penal reform. Instead, the authors indicate the successes of America and point out the problems necessary for France to address within its own borders. We might therefore begin to think how a study of penal reform in the twenty-first century dictates first a detailed sociological study of the culture, government, and persons involved such reform. The need to understand our mores dictates taking account not only of studies within prisons but also of studies on the general population.

If we understand that social factors ought to be considered in the pursuit of penal reform, the next question to ask is this: which social causes contribute the most to increased crime and imprisonment? Most commentators on prison reform in the last decade have agreed that the rate of American imprisonment has unprecedentedly skyrocketed in inverse proportion nation. Scholars and politicians thus agree that the criminal justice system needs reform, particularly to reduce the prison population, provide opportunity for better fiscal penal spending by states and the federal government, and enhance rehabilitative (as opposed to retributive) efforts for prisoners. Such an agreement is the first step toward a moderate mode of penal policy. Yet however urgent the need for reform may appear, we still do not agree on the means of reform. We are consequently in the same position as nineteenth-century France, where there was general agreement that prisons needed reformed, but disagreement on whether to implement the Auburn or Philadelphia modes of prison discipline.

Part of the contemporary disagreement about means results from a confusion of causes behind the growth of the prison state. As has been shown, in the first edition of *On the Penitentiary System* Tocqueville and Beaumont give a sustained argument that there are both material and moral causes for the increase of crime. The second edition's introduction lists alcohol, education, and industrialization as additional potential causes. In his report to the Chamber of 1843 (included in the third edition), Tocqueville answers the question of what is the cause of increasing crime by arguing that it would be foolish to pin the cause of crime on the poor condition of prisons alone. Instead, one must consider "the more or less rapid development of industry and movable wealth, penal laws, the state of mores, and especially the strengthening or decadence of religious beliefs" (Tocqueville 1984b, p. 119). That is not to say that prisons can be excluded from such a list; Tocqueville says that prisons augment the number of crimes by first hiding the fear of punishment from the eyes of citizens, and by secondly not correcting or preventing the corruption of prisoners.

Nevertheless, Tocqueville's willingness to see a multiplicity of social causes behind crime, and thus a complex combination of solutions to crime, teaches us a valuable lesson in penal reform policy. Recognizing a variety of causes allows us to agree to disagree on the "number one" cause of increased crime or imprisonment. By setting aside disagreements about which cause is primary, we can approach the problem from a variety of perspectives and find a host of solutions. For example, we can discuss solutions such as making legal and social efforts to reduce increasing drug usage in American society, revising or avoiding new mandatory sentencing laws that over-penalize such usage, and giving individual judges an increased ability to determine sentencing that fits the crime.

A final conclusion we can draw for modern penal reform from a study of *On the Penitentiary System* can be understood as a focus on what the aims of prison reform ought to be. At the end of the introduction to the second edition of *On the Penitentiary System*, Tocqueville and Beaumont helpfully articulate four standards for measuring punishment within prisons: (1) there should be no unnecessary rigor or deprivation, (2) the punishment must be measured fairly in relation to social expectation, (3) the punishment must be in harmony with the *moeurs* of the people, and (4) the punishment must be reconciled to the sacred laws (*les saintes lois*) of morality and humanity (Tocqueville 1984a, p. 136). Proportionality rightly encapsulates the object of the first two standards, while the proper relationship between the individual and society succinctly characterizes the third and fourth standards. We must be willing to balance rigor with fairness, the social mores of the people with theoretical consistency in policies, and secular institutional solutions with religious contributions.

Above all, Tocqueville emphasizes throughout his arguments in support of the penitentiary system that rehabilitation and reintegration of the prisoner should be the primary aims of the prison system, enforced through limited means. The distinction between moral reformation and prevention of corruption resurfaced throughout Tocqueville's discussions of penal reform in the 1830s and 1840s. By 1843, Tocqueville was willing to argue in support of establishing the Philadelphia system in France because it best prevented the corruption of prisoners, even if moral reform was still too difficult a goal to hope for in most prisoners. Since communication was perceived as the main form of corruption among prisoners, the separation from criminal society provided by solitary cells was the best way to prevent communication and thereby corruption.

Today, our political and legal spheres include questions over whether solitary confinement is the best means of promoting the type of rehabilitation that reduces recidivism and enables a prisoner to successfully reintegrate into society. President Obama said of solitary confinement in a speech to the NAACP on July 14, 2015:

> The social science shows that an environment like that is often more likely to make inmates more alienated, more hostile, potentially more violent. Do we really think it makes sense to lock so many people alone in tiny cells for 23 hours a day, sometimes for months or even years at a time? That is not going to make us safer. That's not going to make us stronger. And if those individuals are ultimately released, how are they ever going to adapt? It's not smart. (Obama 2015)

Obama echoed Justice Anthony Kennedy's argument on solitary confinement given in a concurring opinion to *Davis v. Ayala* (2015), where he drew upon scholarly research to argue that "years on end of near-total isolation exacts a terrible price."[5] Kennedy particularly criticizes solitary confinement for its effects on the minds of prisoners, such as inducing suicide and mental illness. Kennedy also argues that the relative merits of solitary confinement have not been properly re-evaluated because "the public may have assumed lawyers and judges were engaged in a careful assessment of correctional policies, while most lawyers and judges assumed these matters were for the policymakers and correctional experts." Additionally, the Senate Judiciary Committee held a hearing in 2012 which further questioned the legitimacy of solitary confinement as a mode of punishment due to the negative mental effects on prisoners.[6]

These are good questions to ask; because our culture has shifted in society, so too have the means by which we can effect change within persons who are citizens of that society. The invention of solitary confinement depended on an assumption that the prisoner's isolation from other human beings would bring them into closer relation with both self and God, particularly through the work of chaplains in the prison. In other words, "solitary" confinement or isolation did not leave the individual truly alone; it re-arranged the focal point of the inmate's source of companionship. Tocqueville saw these effects of solitary confinement in his tour through the Philadelphia prison, when he notes that almost every prisoner he interviewed mentioned their increased desire to read the Bible, their newly found inwardness, and their reflections on their families. Solitude thus heightened the prisoner's awareness of the potentially best relationships in life (to God and family) by distancing them from the worst relationships (to other criminals). However, the cultural understanding of relationships to both God and family has changed dramatically since the 1800s. While America has grown increasingly less religious, younger generations are staying at home longer with their parents and delaying establishing households of their own or getting married.[7] This shift has changed the effects of solitary confinement as a means of reform. It is still true that human beings are social creatures who need meaningful relationships and labor to thrive. The question, however, has become: what constitutes a meaningful relationship to modern American citizens? What relationships promote the healthiest social and political engagements? And how to teach prisoners the value of such relationships while in prison?

Additionally, Tocqueville teaches us how to balance of the goals of rehabilitation and restitution. Tocqueville's and Beaumont's emphasis on the merits of labor in giving dignity to prisoners and acting as a means of future reintegration into society help to support renewed attention to projects meant to incorporate rehabilitative job training programs in prison or as a substitute for incarceration. Yet the emphasis on rehabilitation for the prisoner must be balanced against the need for retribution for the state. In his evaluation of whether prisons should provide wages for prisoners, Tocqueville errs on the side of caution because he sees moral degeneracy in French prisons stemming from "luxuries" such as cafeterias and alcohol. Tocqueville argues against giving prisoners a large wage for their prison labor because he prioritizes the rights of the state over the rights of the incarcerated individual; the state ought to use the money earned by the prisoner to reduce prison maintenance costs for citizens and the government. Tocqueville's argument results partially from a guiding theory of restitution, which stipulates that not only is the criminal subject to penalty prescribed by law, but is also responsible for repaying a debt society incurs by enforcing such penalties. Although emphasizing the rights of the state when discussing labor wages in prison, Tocqueville still thinks that prisoners should collect part of their wage, since it enables them to support their families and leave prison with a modest sum to use when re-establishing themselves in society. Yet Tocqueville also found that, if given too large an amount of money when leaving prison, former prisoners were more likely to become recidivists because their moral natures were not steeled against the temptations denied to them in prison.

Above all, Tocqueville's penal involvement consistently demonstrates that penal goals and programs are evaluated and enforced best by moderation. Moderate penal reform demands an openness to partisan debate that takes account of multiple approaches to balancing the needs of individual prisoners and the rights of the state, an active attempt to mediate imaginative hopes against circumstantial possibilities, as well as a willingness to test theory with practice and continue to re-evaluate policies far into the future. Moderation also seeks justice for both the individual and society, and thus remains a particularly important political virtue to exercise when balancing the interests that individual prisoners and society have in the problem of punishment. *On the Penitentiary System* shows us how Tocqueville pursued such moderation in his involvement in French penal reform. The virtue is, perhaps, not only the best way to attain the multiple and inter-related goals of punishment but also the clearest lesson for the contemporary pursuit of penal reform.

Notes

1. In other words, the conclusions of the four studies conducted by Avramenko, Boesche, Gingerich, and Wolin need to be understood in light of the idea of human nature presented in *On the Penitentiary System*.
2. For an interesting discussion of how distinctively American attributes (such as love of democracy, Protestant religiosity, procedural fairness, and the ideal of equality) originally described by Tocqueville influence the current incarceration state's harshness, see Whitman 2007.
3. See, for example, Tocqueville 1984a, pp. 207–218, 227–247, 262–266.
4. Tocqueville 1984a, p. 237. Remember that for Tocqueville, "mores" comprises "the whole moral and intellectual state of a people," including their notions, opinions, and ideas that shape habits (Tocqueville 2000, p. 275). Maletz notes that Tocqueville does not think ancient customs contribute to *mores*; in that sense, Tocqueville draws more from Montesquieu's notion of a "spirit" behind the laws than from Cicero's understanding for his definition (2005, p. 4).
5. *Davis v. Ayala*, 576 US (2015) (Kennedy A. concurring opinion).
6. United States Senate Committee on the Judiciary 2012.
7. Fleming 2016; Fry 2017; Pew 2015.

References

Beaumont, Gustave de, and Alexis de Tocqueville. 1833. *On the Penitentiary System in the United States and Its Application in France, with an Appendix on Penal Colonies and also Statistical Notes*, trans. Francis Lieber. Philadelphia: Carey, Lea & Blanchard.

Fleming, John. 2016. *Gallup Analysis: Millennials, Marriage, and Family*. Gallup News. http://www.gallup.com/poll/191462/gallup-analysis-millennials-marriage-family.aspx. Accessed 14 November 2017.

Fry, Richard. 2017. *It's Becoming More Common for Young Adults to Live at Home—And for Longer Stretches*. Pew Research Center. http://www.pewresearch.org/fact-tank/2017/05/05/its-becoming-more-common-for-young-adults-to-live-at-home-and-for-longer-stretches/. Accessed 14 November 2017.

Maletz, Donald. 2005. Tocqueville on Mores and the Preservation of Republics. *American Journal of Political Science* 49 (1): 1–15.

Obama, Barack. 2015. *Remarks by the President at the NAACP Conference*. Philadelphia, PA: The White House Office of the Press Secretary. https://obamawhitehouse.archives.gov/the-press-office/2015/07/14/remarks-president-naacp-conference. Accessed 14 November 2017.

Pew Research Center. 2015. *America's Changing Religious Landscape*. http://www.pewforum.org/2015/05/12/americas-changing-religious-landscape/. Accessed 14 November 2017.

Tocqueville, Alexis de. 1984a. *Œuvres Complètes: Écrits sur le système pénitentiaire en France et à l'étranger, Tome IV, Vol. 1*, ed. Michelle Perrot. Paris: Gallimard.

———. 1984b. *Œuvres Complètes: Écrits sur le système pénitentiaire en France et à l'étranger, Tome IV, Vol. 2*, ed. Michelle Perrot. Paris: Gallimard.

———. 2000. *Democracy in America*, ed. and trans. Harvey Mansfield and Delba Winthrop. Chicago: University of Chicago.

United States Senate Committee on the Judiciary. 2012. *Reassessing Solitary Confinement: The Human Rights, Fiscal, and Public Safety Consequences*. U.S. Government Printing Office. https://www.judiciary.senate.gov/imo/media/doc/CHRG-112shrg87630.pdf. Accessed 14 November 2017.

Whitman, James Q. 2007. What Happened to Tocqueville's America? *Social Research* 74 (2): 251–268.

Index[1]

[1]Note: Page numbers followed by 'n' refer to notes.

E. K. Ferkaluk, *Tocqueville's Moderate Penal Reform*,
Recovering Political Philosophy,
https://doi.org/10.1007/978-3-319-75577-9

C

D